DAUGHTER OF THE KING

DAUGHTER
OF THE KING

SANDRA LANSKY
AND WILLIAM STADIEM

WEINSTEIN
BOOKS

Printed in the United States of America.

Cataloging-in-Publication data for this book is available from the Library of Congress.

ISBN: 978-1-60286-215-9 (print)
ISBN: 978-1-60286-216-6 (e-book)

Published by Weinstein Books
A member of the Perseus Books Group
www.weinsteinbooks.com

Weinstein Books are available at special discounts for bulk purchases in the U.S. by corporations, institutions and other organizations. For more information, please contact the Special Markets Department at the Perseus Books Group, 2300 Chestnut Street, Suite 200, Philadelphia, PA 19103, call (800) 810-4145, ext. 5000, or e-mail special.markets@perseusbooks.com.

First edition

10 9 8 7 6 5 4 3 2 1

To the memory of Daddy

CONTENTS

ACKNOWLEDGMENTS

I would like to acknowledge the wonderful support of the following people: Dick Cami and Nick Pileggi, who always believed that I had a story to tell. Vince Lombardo, Gary Rapoport, and Aaron and Kaley Lombardo, who have always encouraged me. And especially my Daddy, Meyer Lansky, who never gave up on me; without him I wouldn't have a story to tell. To Rusty Goodman and Micki Marlo, who have been there for me forever. To my brother Paul and my nephew Meyer Lansky II, for keeping the family name alive. Special thanks to Bill Stadiem for his skill, help, and patience in helping me tell my story; to Dan Strone for selling it; and to Weinstein Books for publishing it.

INTRODUCTION

BY NICK PILEGGI

I had known Sandi Lansky for about twenty years before I could get her to even think about writing a book. She was smart and charming and she and her husband of many years, Vincent Lombardo, were great company, but she had no interest in writing about growing up as Meyer Lansky's daughter. It was clear that she loved her father and enjoyed travelling the world with him and was clearly pained by what she saw as his harassment by the government, especially toward the end of his life when the Justice Department exerted extraordinary political pressure on Israel to extradite him on bogus charges that were quickly dismissed.

When I first laid eyes on Sandi, I saw her father. The slight build and dark piercing eyes were unmistakable. While I had never met Meyer Lansky, I had seen him on several occasions having dinner with his pal and partner, Vincent "Jimmy Blue Eyes" Alo, at Frankie and Johnny's Steakhouse, on West 45th street, in Manhattan's theater district. (It's still there and still good.) Lansky's and Alo's presence was not only fascinating to a young police reporter like me, but the restaurant's usually disagreeable waiters, long bored by Broadway's biggest stars, were suddenly transformed. "He's here." "Did you see him?" "Where?" "Table six?" Their excitement was palpable in the room. They were so in awe of him that the usually surly waiters were giddy with excitement.

The irony, of course, was that many of the waiters excited by Lansky's presence had also been his victims. Some of the older waiters, still hefting dishes on bad feet, often lamented they were only working because they were in hock to their bookmakers. These were the men who had lost their cars, lost their houses, even lost their wives because of the quiet unpretentious man at table six sawing away at his steak. Somehow, it did not seem to matter to them. They were simply in awe of the man who had turned their vice into a national pastime and made illegal betting routine. Because of Lansky, they could place their bets and collect their winnings as reliably as Wall Street—maybe more so. It was Lansky who created and presided over the *guys and dolls* America that did not exist until he started putting it together during the Prohibition years.

However, while I always knew that Meyer Lansky was one of the most intriguing of organized crime's founding fathers, he was probably the least known. Oh, there had been articles and books and television documentaries and movies about him, but somehow the "Little Man" was always missing. In *Godfather II*, Mario Puzo and Francis Coppola came close with their fictional "Hyman Roth," a part played by the great Lee Strasberg, but all it did was make me want to know more about the real man himself.

I wanted to know, for instance, how a slight, five-foot-five-inch, Lower East Side youngster, born in Grodno, in 1902, survived growing up on some of the most dangerous streets in America. How did an impoverished eighteen-year-old maneuver his way through the Roaring Twenties and murderous gang wars of Prohibition to emerge a multimillionaire and one of the key men responsible for organizing organized crime? And, of course, how could an elementary school dropout create a multibillion-dollar, nationwide illegal gambling empire without an office, a secretary, or even an untapped phone? Today, math whiz casino executives go to MIT, the Harvard Business School, and Wharton to try and master the gambling algorithms that Meyer Lansky carried around in his head.

We know, according to the Kefauver Senate Hearings in 1951, that Lansky prospered not only because he knew how to count, but because he was adept at bribing the sheriffs, judges, and county officials wherever he opened a speakeasy or an illegal casino. He even put the off-duty deputy sheriffs on the payroll as valet parkers to dampen any potential for whistleblowing in the ranks. In 1933, when Prohibition ended, Lansky was thirty-one years old and had earned the trust of some of the least trusting men in America. With the support of his boyhood pal, Charles "Lucky" Luciano, he convinced the syndicate bootleggers to convert their speakeasies into roadhouses and nightclub-casinos catering to illegal gambling just as they had catered to illegal booze. The local politicians and sheriffs were now happy to go along and continue to take bribes to "overlook" the new illegal casinos just as they had "overlooked" speakeasies.

For Lansky and company, the timing could not have been better. When Prohibition ended in 1933, the nation was in the middle of its worst depression. Banks were closed. CEOs were selling apples on the street. Stockbrokers were going out Wall Street windows, while Lansky and his bootlegger pals were one of the only sources of major capital in the country. They were sitting on suitcases of cash, and it was Lansky who began investing their money in the illegal casinos, sports books, and telegraph wires that have kept the bookmakers around the country busy until the present day.

With Lansky's death I had given up even getting the details of *his* life, but as my conversations with Sandi continued over the years, I realized that *her* life would make an incredible book. Here was the story of a willful adolescent daughter who could not be controlled by one of the most powerful and feared men in the country. In many ways, I came to realize, she was too much like him.

Sandi's was a rich life. She grew up in a vast apartment at the Beresford on 81st Street and Central Park West and later in a huge suite at the St. Moritz Hotel on Central Park South and Sixth Avenue. The Beresford apartment had a terrace so large she could ice skate on it all winter. There were piano, singing, and ballet lessons at which she was not very good, but she had a horse and she loved to ride. She rode and took lessons in Central Park and was good enough to show at Madison Square Garden. Her father was so proud he would follow her around from one horse show to the other when he wasn't out of town. He was her biggest fan.

When you grow up in her father's world, you rarely had any friends from the outside. Sandi had Joe Adonis' daughter, Benny Siegel's two daughters, Abner "Longy" Zwillman's son, among other mob princes and princesses down at the Jersey Shore, which was known as the Gangster Riviera. These children lived lives almost as insular as their parents. They weren't encouraged to bring strangers into the house. Looking back there's no question that Sandi and the other progeny of the men who created organized crime were terribly isolated.

As a twelve-year-old, Sandy walked around with far more money than she does today. She always had $20 bills stuffed in her pockets and she was always instructed to take taxis, which were considered a luxury back then. Sandy had been repeatedly told never to take a bus or public transportation because her mother was worried that she'd be kidnapped. The children of wealthy mobsters like Lansky were often the subject of kidnappings because it was impossible for men like her father to go to the FBI or police for protection. If their kids were kidnapped, Lansky and his cohort would be forced to pay the ransom and straighten things out later.

Because of Meyer's travel schedule, scholastically Sandi's schools changed with the racing seasons. She started her classes at the toney

Birch Wathen in New York and then she'd move her studies, such as they were, to Miami Beach during the winter. In the spring, the Lanskys would move back north and Sandi would be reenrolled in her New York school.

But then, when Sandi was ten, her mother got sick, and Sandi's tightly controlled life was shattered. Anne Lansky, buckling under the stress of being married to the Mob, had a nervous breakdown and was institutionalized. Over and over. Since her father was traveling most of the time, to Cuba, Las Vegas, Europe, setting up casinos and secreting millions, Sandi was alone, with the servants, in the vast Beresford apartment, with her brother Buddy, who suffered from a crippling variation of cerebral palsy. Her older brother, Paul, couldn't take the dark side of Lanskyism. He fled to military school, then graduated from West Point. He was the real version of the golden boy Al Pacino character in *The Godfather*, except Paul got out and stayed out, devoting his life to his country rather than to crime.

What a schizoid existence it was for poor Sandi, who, in order to escape the gloom of her broken family, married at sixteen to a seemingly dashing, rich playboy of twenty-three. Her father's daughter, Sandi knew how to drive a hard bargain. You can't look after me, Daddy. But my husband can. Meyer knew his own limitations. He gave in. Big mistake. After fathering a child, Meyer's new son-in-law quickly revealed himself to be a gay fortune hunter. After the marriage imploded, Sandi took to the nightclubs with a vengeance, cutting a swath on the New York–Miami circuit that included every kind of man, from Dean Martin and the Rat Pack, to Gary Crosby (Bing's son) and Hollywood royalty, to billionaires like Charles Revson, of Fire and Ice cosmetics fame.

Sandi, leaving her new baby, Gary, at home with maids, went out on the town, from dusk to dawn. She was, in effect, a "Mob Deb." She had her own tables at night clubs like the Harwyn, the Stork, El Morocco, and the Copacabana when she was barely old enough to enter such places. Of course she did. Her father and his friends literally owned the joints. Meyer had thought about having her barred, but then he was afraid she'd go to the kind of deadfalls that would be even more dangerous. In the end, he tolerated Sandi's wild life, because he always had some very tough guys keeping an eye on her.

Such were the tantalizations that Sandi danced before me. But that was it. She wouldn't talk about her father, and the more I saw that talking about herself might be even more illuminating, she pulled the plug on that as well. Hers was the era of "Sweet Smell of Success," of Walter Winchell and Damon Runyon and "Guys and Dolls." That was Sandi's world. Sandi's story could tell us more about Meyer Lansky and the universe he mastered than all the Senate hearings, grand juries, and FBI wiretaps combined. But she simply wouldn't talk.

When my wife, a screenwriter and Hollywood director, met Sandi, she was both charmed and intrigued. Nora wasn't as interested in the Meyer Lansky organized crime story as she was in a young woman's coming of age in her father's world. As the years passed, however, and after turning down countless offers from newspapers, magazines, book publishers, and movie producers looking for the story about her dad, Sandi began to change her mind. Just about every one of her father's friends was dead, and Sandi finally began to maybe feel free enough to tell her story.

It wasn't until Bill Stadiem came along, however, that things began to come together. Bill has an amazing gift for relaxing people and unlocking their great stories. He did it with Marilyn Monroe's maid, with Frank Sinatra's valet, with Strom Thurmond's secret black daughter. And now he has done it with Meyer Lansky's daughter.

Bill Stadiem has written a wonderful book I never thought would be written. But she told it, he wrote it, and we get an inside look into a world only Sandi Lansky could show us. I'm delighted.

CHAPTER ONE

THE UNCLEHOOD

I opened my big mouth, and I thought Daddy was going to kill me. We were at the Majestic Theatre on West 44th Street in April 1945. He had taken me to *Carousel,* which was the hottest ticket on Broadway. It was a huge treat. Daddy loved Broadway musicals, and so did I. Two years before, when I was just six, he had taken me to my first one, *Oklahoma!* I don't know why Mommy didn't come. She hadn't come to *On the Town* or *Mexican Hayride,* either. I know she loved the music, and I know she loved dressing up and dressing me up in the beautiful clothes she bought me in the children's department of Saks Fifth Avenue. Maybe she went to matinees with her girlfriends. Whatever, I was thrilled to be one of the youngest people at the show. I felt so grown up. I had Daddy all to myself. I adored being his little princess.

We had the best seats in the house, five rows back, right in the middle. What was really unusual was that, even though the house was packed—the show had sold out months in advance—no one was sitting in any of the seats in front of us. Had all of these people somehow gotten sick? I later learned that Daddy had bought all the seats so nothing would block our view. He seemed like a giant to me, but he wasn't very tall, maybe five foot four or five, in a stretch, so those empty seats were a real luxury. And no luxury was too much for my father. He had the nicest clothes, custom-made dark suits made of the softest cashmere, custom shirts, custom shoes, custom hats. My older brother Buddy told me Daddy got all his clothes made because he was too little to fit into ready-to-wear. Buddy was a wiseguy, a big tease. Daddy dressed this way because he *could*. He looked rich. He was rich.

People at the theatre seemed to know him. We got a lot of looks, not stares, because nobody seemed to dare look at us for too long, but people were definitely noticing us in a very respectful way. That made me feel important, and I liked it. One usher greeted us. "Good evening, Mr. Lansky." My father gave the usher a chilling look. When his eyes twinkled, Daddy was full of joy, but when those eyes turned dark, it was like a devastating gamma ray, some kind of secret weapon that had been used in the horrible war that had just ended. The usher shriveled. Then I saw why. When a couple near us heard his name, they cut quick glances to each other as if to say, we're in the presence of someone special. Special for what, I did not know, but maybe it wasn't good. The moral seemed to be that the Lanskys should be seen but not heard. Low-key was the rule.

And then I blew it. I was loving the play, the dance numbers, the great Rodgers and Hammerstein songs, like "June Is Bustin' Out All Over." But then, in the second act, things turned dark, as dark as Daddy's look when the usher dared speak his name. The romantic hero, Billy Bigelow, turns into a criminal. Apprehended by the police, Billy falls onto his knife and dies. Dies! I was devastated. I already loved him, and he was dead. "Daddy, they *killed* him!" I gasped at the stage. Suddenly, the silent theatre somehow became even more silent. All eyes were upon us. And Daddy gave me one of those "if looks could kill" terminal stares. It only lasted a moment, but it seemed like an eternity. And then he took my hand and gave it a loving squeeze. The twinkle came back to his eyes, and he stroked my hair. All was forgiven.

The show went on, though I cried my eight-year-old eyes out before it was over. My little outburst had given at least a few people in the theatre who knew who Daddy was the scary thrill of a lifetime. "They killed him." I had no idea, but Daddy had surely heard that accusation before, just as he would hear it again. As America's Gangster Number One, the architect of Murder Incorporated, and a million other deep and dark rumors, Meyer Lansky was one of the most feared men in a fearsome city. If I said "Daddy, they killed him," there were a lot of people who believed that my father had arranged it.

Daddy took me to Times Square a lot to have dinners with my "uncles." They weren't really uncles, but they certainly felt like family to me. Again, Mommy never seemed to come, just Daddy and me. The place we went to most was Dinty Moore's on West 46th Street. The actors may have gone to Sardi's, and the Damon Runyon "guys and dolls" may have gone to Lindy's, but everybody who was anybody went to Dinty Moore's—the big politicians, the big Broadway impresarios, the big newspapermen, and my uncles. It was a favorite of all the New York legends: Florenz Ziegfeld, Mayor Jimmy Walker, Irving Berlin, George Gershwin, and Meyer Lansky. With its gleaming white tiles and polished brass, white tablecloths, white starched napkins, you almost needed sunglasses to go into the place. It was as brightly lit as a Broadway stage, a place to see and be seen. Moore's was very masculine, with an endless mahogany bar. The tinkling of ice cubes in the ocean of scotch that the men drank could sound as loud as wind chimes. I was pretty much the only kid there. The only other girls were basically arm candy, beautiful actresses and models less than half the age of their big-shot consorts. It wasn't a wife place. Maybe that's why Mommy stayed home.

Daddy always had the seat of honor, the top table, the first one on the left as you entered the dining room. The waiters treated him like a pasha and made a great display of cutting up my food for me. At age eight I still had no clue how to cut up my food, particularly the steak or chicken that called for a knife. It would take me years to learn. I had no need. Maybe the idea was that knives were for hoodlums, not for little ladies like me. Maybe young royalty weren't supposed to cut their own food.

Whatever, nobody had bothered to teach me. I didn't think about it. I accepted being waited on as my way of life. I was that spoiled, way beyond mere princessdom.

The Irish ran Moore's, which had been around since before World War I, back in 1914, but the restaurant's menu was pure New York melting pot. Where else could you get the city's best corned beef and cabbage and gefilte fish under one roof? Back in 1931 the city's reigning food critic, Rian James, declared that it had "the best plain, foody food in all New York." James also noted that "Dinty Moore's charges more for its good, homey, foody food than any similar establishment in America." No problem. Daddy and the other bigwigs who made Moore's their home could afford it. It was what today might be called a "power" restaurant, a favorite of the men who ran New York and the world, catered to by old pro waiters in crisp black Eisenhower military jackets. It was the kind of place where General Eisenhower, or MacArthur, or Patton might come if they were in town. No other restaurant, except for maybe the 21 Club, had as illustrious a clientele. Still, even as a little girl, I got the sense that the generals, the politicians, the big bankers all lived in a different world from that of Daddy and my uncles. At least in public, it was a parallel universe, very close, but it did not intersect with ours. They didn't say "Hi" to us, and we didn't say "Hi" to them.

Whenever Daddy and an uncle seemed to want to talk about something serious, I didn't really need a cue to exit. That dark look on his face told me when to take off and go hang out with the pretty blonde hat-check girl, who would let me help her sort the ladies' mink stoles and the gents' vicuña topcoats.

Daddy was always having dinners with my uncles, not only at Moore's but at seemingly half the top restaurants in New

York—Longchamps, Gallagher's, Cavanagh's, L'Aiglon. My own favorite wasn't any of these grand white tablecloth places, but the Automat, where the food was delivered by magic from behind glass doors. That wasn't an uncles place, but Daddy knew I loved it, so he would take me there. Wherever he went, the restaurant owners all bowed down to him. He conducted so much of his business at meals because he believed the government had tapped our phones at home. I never saw a man more laconic on the telephone. While Mommy loved to chatter away forever with her girlfriends, Daddy's phone conversations were like Morse Code.

Who were these uncles of mine? To begin with, they were unique, in how they looked, in what they did. Like Daddy, they were great dressers. They dressed like Cary Grant, like Fred Astaire, like movie stars. But their voices echoed the mean streets where they had grown up. They often sounded like the Brooklyn, Bronx, and Harlem first-generation immigrants that they were. But how they had risen, proof that America was truly the land of opportunity, open to any and all. Daddy was born on the Fourth of July, in Russia, but he took the date as a sign, a good omen, of an all-American future.

There was "Uncle Frank" Costello, who was the king of New York, and there was "Uncle Abe" Zwillman, who was the king of New Jersey. Uncle Frank may have taken an Irish name and dressed in bespoke English pinstripes, but he was straight out of the boot of Italy, with a deep raspy voice that he blamed on a botched throat surgery. He had a huge Italian nose that made me want to call him Pinocchio, but I didn't dare.

Uncle Abe was taller than most basketball players, a real giant. Unlike most of the other uncles, Uncle Abe sounded as good as he looked, maybe because he was born in New Jersey and English was his first language. His real name was Abner, but his nickname was

"Longy," both in honor of his height and his "length." When I was old enough to hear such things, my brother Buddy told me about the legendary endowment of Uncle Abe. He must have had something, because he stole away movie star Jean Harlow from Howard Hughes.

If Uncle Abe was the king of New Jersey, Uncle Joe and Uncle Willie were his crown princes in this presuburban realm of green hills and horse farms that was considered the Camelot of gangland. Uncle Joe was Joe Doto, but the world knew him as Joe Adonis. The name fit him perfectly. He was the handsomest man I ever saw, a rugged Clark Gable type but more put together, slicked back hair, and oh, what clothes. There were lots of mirrors at Dinty Moore's, and sometimes I could catch Uncle Joe stealing an admiring glimpse at himself. Why not? He was worth looking at.

Uncle Willie wouldn't have won any beauty contest or fashion show, but he would have taken the charm sweepstakes. He was also a natty dresser and had everything custom-made in Italy. His trademark was a priceless diamond stickpin in his ties. He was Willie Moretti to us, sometimes Willie Moore to others, and he was even shorter than Daddy, which, at first, I thought was why Daddy liked him—he was a man he could look down on. When the two rulers of New Jersey, Zwillman and Moretti, stood together, they looked, not like kings, but like the cartoon Mutt and Jeff. Unlike Daddy, who was as quiet and controlled as a Supreme Court justice, a man who never showed his hand, Uncle Willie was a storyteller and the court jester of our extended family. That was not to say he wasn't powerful; he just played it light. He was our link to the other Broadway, not of power, but of flash. He knew all the stars at Sardi's and all the operators at Lindy's.

Our other main connection to the stars was Uncle George Wood, the all-powerful William Morris Agency executive who arranged for talent to be booked into the grand nightclubs all around the country that were controlled by Daddy and my uncles. If I thought about it, and I did not, I probably would have said that my father, as straight and low-key as he was, was in the entertainment business. Which I guess was the truth. But Daddy didn't seem very entertaining. Uncle Willie was, and Uncle Georgie even more so. He was Mister Showbiz, incredibly dapper, fast talking, name dropping, with the filthiest mouth I had ever heard. And no number of baleful disapproving stares from Daddy could force Uncle Georgie to censor himself. Today they might call it Tourette's Syndrome. Back then, Buddy called it "fuck-ese."

"Fucking, cocksucking, motherfucking, kike, sheenie, guinea wop bastard son of a bitch" was the kind of stream-of-consciousness profanity that Uncle Georgie's mouth might unleash. Yet all of Hollywood, and all of Broadway, was crazy about him. They were also mortally afraid of him, not just because of his booking power, but because of his closeness to my father and his circle. If George Wood told an actor or actress "You're dead in this town," they would take it literally. Because I knew how incorrigible he was, whenever Uncle Georgie dropped by our table, at Dinty Moore's or wherever we might be, on his nightly rounds of every famous joint in New York, I was smart enough to head for the hat-check girl and leave him and Daddy to themselves.

Uncle Willie was famous as a second father, or godfather, to Frank Sinatra, the man who got Frank out of Hoboken to Hollywood, the man who freed him from his servitude to Tommy Dorsey and made him a star. The first time I met Frank was at Uncle Willie's lavish art deco Riviera supper club in New Jersey, atop the Palisades. There were floor-to-ceiling windows with the most spectacular view across the Hudson to the skyscrapers of Manhattan, and the roof opened so the stars of screen could see the stars of heaven. The Riviera was Vegas before Vegas ever existed. The talent had to be great to distract the audience from the view, which was up there with the one from the top of the Empire State Building. But Uncle Willie always had the best: Hope and Crosby, Martin and Lewis, Sammy Davis, Jr., and, of course, the pride of Jersey, hometown boy Frank Sinatra.

One night, when I was ten or eleven, Frank came over to our table after his set to say hello to Daddy and to meet little me with my bottle of ginger ale in a chilled champagne bucket. Again, how grown-up I felt, out with Daddy, out on the town, in a *nightclub*. Wow! I had never seen anyone so nervous, particularly a star who had all the teenagers in New York screaming for him. But Frank was more fidgety in Daddy's presence than any bobby-soxer would have been in his. He was so anxious that when he reached over to shake my hand, he knocked over the champagne bucket of ice right into my lap. He nearly died.

Maybe he was worrying about dying for getting me all wet. Maybe Daddy had given him one of his looks. Frank got on his knees, grabbed a bunch of napkins and frantically tried to dry me off. The only relief came when I started laughing and said that he was tickling me. The twinkle returned to Daddy's eyes. I rarely saw him laugh. The twinkle was as good as it got, but it was good enough for Frank to breathe easier. He gave me a big hug, as if I had saved his life by forgiving him, like getting a thumbs up from a Roman empress.

Frank, to make more amends, even sang a song for me. He improvised lyrics on "You're the Top." "You're the top. You're cotton candy. You're the top. You're a doll named Sandi." I can see him winking at me from the stage. No last names, naturally. But I was much more interested in Señor Wences, the famous Spanish ventriloquist with his puppets Pedro and Johnny, who was sharing the bill with Frank. When Daddy introduced me to him, that made my night.

There was Frank Sinatra, and then there was Uncle Frank. Frank Erickson looked just like Santa Claus, if you shaved off Santa's beard. He was a big, jolly, ho-ho-ho sort of man, whose high spirits concealed the fact that he was supposed to be, after Daddy, the biggest brain in the uncle group. Uncle Frank, like Daddy, was a largely unschooled math wizard and considered the biggest bookmaker in the country. He was the architect of most of America's betting systems, including the wire services where the odds on every race, every fight, every game, were communicated around the country to the delight of gamblers everywhere. Uncle Frank not only looked like Santa; he had the heart of Santa as well. He was one of the most generous of men, donating millions to children's charities, giving even more than Uncle Frank Costello gave to his pet cause, the Salvation Army.

No star, no performer at the Riviera was bigger, or more handsome, than my Uncle Bennie, Ben Siegel. The world knew him as Bugsy, a name that referred to his having been "crazy as a bug" in his hot-tempered youth, a past that he was always trying to obliterate by chasing success and glamour. Uncle Bennie had moved to Beverly Hills. I first met him there on a trip I took with Mommy and Daddy. We went on the Twentieth Century Limited to Chicago and then we changed to the Super Chief to California. I remember Daddy leaving us at the Chicago train station once to go a meeting that he was very secretive about. "Who are you meeting?" Mommy nagged him, "Al Capone?" My mother was joking; my father, as usual, did not laugh. Capone was out of prison then, in the early forties. Of course I had no idea what any of this meant until later, and it was just as well, because it would have scared me to death.

When we got to Beverly Hills, Uncle Ben did scare me to death, but not because of any of the Murder Incorporated stuff he was associated with in his wild and crazy young manhood. What frightened me out of my wits was the creepy stuff he did to stay young like a Hollywood star. The Siegel mansion in Beverly Hills was like a country club, with a pool and towering palms and vast gardens. Nothing in New Jersey, at its green nicest, could match this, especially the smell of the night-blooming jasmine. But when I was awakened early by the brilliant California sun, my new Eden suddenly became Hell. I had gone to bed in the huge bedroom of my Aunt Esther, Benny's wife (they had separate rooms), and suddenly I saw that the sweet woman I had gone to bed with had been replaced by a witch. Esther was wearing a black sleeping mask to block the sunlight, but I thought she had turned into a witch. So I screamed and ran into Uncle Benny's bedroom, and what I saw there was even worse. If Aunt Esther was a witch, Uncle Benny had become the devil himself. Not only was he, too, in a black eye mask, but he had this crazy black elastic vise around his cheeks and chin. It turned out to be some device Hollywood stars wore to bed to prevent wrinkles, and Uncle Benny had bought into it. But to me, he was Satan himself, and it took me a day to recover from my first brush with the vanity of the movie colony.

Mommy and Aunt Esther had been best girlhood friends growing up on the Lower East Side, when Daddy and Uncle Benny had had their own bootlegging gang, known as the Bugs and Meyer Mob, in the Roaring Twenties. They double dated, fell in love at the same time. Daddy and Benny were each other's best man at their weddings. Now they were both rich and wildly successful. Benny had gone Holly-wood, trading in my father's dark discreet suits for flashy plaid sport jackets and silk Hawaiian shirts decorated with palm trees and fla-mingos. When the two of them stood together, one looked like an un-dertaker and the other a circus clown. Growing up in formal New York, I had a hard time adjusting to how casual California was.

Aside from Benny's flashy wardrobe and the swimming pool, the Siegel family was very similar to the Lanskys. There were two daughters, Millicent and Barbara, a few years older than me, who went to exclusive private schools, rode horses, were outfitted by Bullock's of Wilshire, and generally led the kind of refined, pre-debutante finishing-school life that Mommy seemed to be preparing for me. It seemed like Mommy and Aunt Esther were reading the same child-rearing playbook. Although both my parents and the Siegels had grown up in Orthodox Jewish families, none of them made any effort to keep the faith. We always had a Christmas tree, as did the Siegels. We ate a lot of bacon. In fact, I had no idea I was Jewish, or what being Jewish was, until I was a teenager. I thought my grandparents' religion was some sort of exotic Old World custom. When my parents spoke what I later discovered to be Yiddish with each other, I assumed it was a special code to keep secrets from me.

There were dozens of uncles. What a big family I had! Half my uncles turned out to be Jewish. The other half were Italians. Daddy seemed totally at home in both camps, and, actually, one camp didn't seem any different from the other. Most of them had assimilated so well they all seemed like WASP businessmen, a big bunch of bankers. God knows what my uncles may have done as boys, but they had grown up into very serious, civilized gentlemen. The Al Capone image of the gangster as brutal, volatile and ignorant, propagated by such stars as James Cagney ("You dirty rat . . . ") and Edward G. Robinson (*Little Caesar*), simply didn't apply here.

Daddy's group, the Unclehood, I'll call them, were all about rationality and control. Their business wasn't murder. Their business was business, big business. High leverage, low visibility. Mob family warfare, Cicero rubouts, and Valentine's Day massacres were the stuff of medieval Sicilian peasants and maybe of Hollywood movies, but not of these modern men. Theirs was a new world where Longy Zwillman, a Jew from New Jersey, and Frank Costello, an Italian from Calabria, could embrace each other like brothers and get rich together under Daddy's brilliant guidance. That was the beauty of America. Or so it seemed.

The most important thing to me about my uncles was that they seemed to love me like one of the family. They hugged me, they kissed me, they picked me up, and I never felt more secure than in the arms of these powerful men. What did they talk about? How could I, at six, seven, eight, have any idea? It was all names and numbers. Mostly numbers. Sometimes I thought my father and my uncles had their own language of numbers. I was more interested in the scene, the noise, the action. Half the time I was running off to my friend the hat-check girl. Those big furs and the candies she gave me were much more fun than Daddy's numbers. Was I the mascot of the Mob? I had no idea. All I knew was that these were family men, in the nicest sense of what could have been an ominous term.

Aside from Benny Siegel, one of Daddy's best friends, particularly after Benny moved to the West Coast, was Uncle Jimmy. His real name was Vincent Alo, but he was known as "Jimmy Blue Eyes." The confusing thing about that was that his eyes weren't blue at all. They were dark brown. Uncle Jimmy apparently got his nickname from having survived endless beatings as a young man. The poor kid was forever black and blue. Why they didn't call him Jimmy Black Eyes, I'll never know. What I did know was that it was not for me to ask. Uncle Jimmy was tall and austere. In his dark suits, all he needed was a white collar and he could have passed for a priest.

In fact, film director John Huston went one better. He met Uncle Jimmy in Rome when he was shooting his epic *The Bible* and he offered to cast him as God Himself. No one I ever met, including Daddy, was more low-key and low-profile than Uncle Jimmy, who often joked with Daddy about the ludicrousness of the director's casting gambit. In the end, God proved impossible to cast, so the egomaniacal Huston took the part himself.

Whatever my father may have lacked in religion, he had the deepest faith in success. And he was inordinately proud of being American. He worshipped Abraham Lincoln; large bronze bookends of the head of Honest Abe dominated the bookshelf of Daddy's study. He refused to be limited by the ancient Jewish traditions of his parents, who had escaped the pogroms of the Russian czar in Grodno, on the Russian-Polish border. Daddy, who was born in 1902, came to New York with his mother, Yetta, in 1911, two years after his father, Max, had made the brutal voyage in steerage to establish a beachhead in the poor Brownsville section of Brooklyn and worked as a pants presser.

It was a long, long way from Brownsville to the Beresford, our palatial apartment house on Central Park West, across from the Museum of Natural History where a statue of Teddy Roosevelt astride his horse dominated the entrance. What could be more American than that? And what could have been more American than my favorite picture of my father, looking positively Roosevelt-like, jauntily astride his own horse on vacation in Hot Springs, Arkansas, my parents' favorite resort when they first got married.

Yet even on vacation in the South, even on horseback, there was something slightly off about my father. He was rich. He was success-ful. He had a beautiful wife. He was living the American dream. But he wasn't by any means all-American. Nor was Hot Springs. It was a lavish resort, the best in Dixie, but it was controlled by a famous New York gangster named Owney Madden, who had owned, among other Prohibition hot spots, Harlem's Cotton Club. Hot Springs may have looked like a magnolia paradise, but it was in fact a cesspool of illegal gambling, prostitution, and far worse.

Maybe all Daddy did in Hot Springs was relax, swim, ride, take the federally protected radioactive waters, but there was a sinister un-dercurrent in Daddy's very presence in Hot Springs. The water was just about the only thing that was legal there, and my parents sent the family postcards from the Arlington Hotel, where they stayed, which had been Al Capone's southern headquarters. Owney Madden wasn't exactly an uncle, but he went way back with Daddy. He was born in England, came to New York, and led a Hell's Kitchen gang called the Gophers. He went to Sing Sing for killing a number of his rivals. With a background like that you would think he'd be doomed for life, but Prohibition could turn abject notoriety into success and celebrity. Madden, paroled from Sing Sing, became an overlord of New York nightlife. His driver was the future movie star George Raft, or Uncle George, who didn't have to act when he played a gangster.

In addition to the Cotton Club, Madden was the money behind the Stork Club, where the most famous and powerful of all gossip col-umnists, Walter Winchell, held court in the Cub Room. Over two-thirds of all Americans listened to Winchell's radio show or read his column. And Winchell, arguably the most powerful man in the media, was Daddy's friend. Winchell lived in the art deco tower called the Majestic Apartments on Central Park West, where my parents had lived before they moved nine blocks north to the Beresford. Theirs was a small world, and after Prohibition, apart from movie stars and show people, no one could have been more high profile than my uncles, who seemed to be sitting on top of the world and making it spin.

After the Prohibition laws were repealed in 1933, Madden got into trouble in New York with still another murder, that of gangster Mad Dog Coll, and decided to bring his nightclub skills to the sunny South in Hot Springs, a spa town with a long history of corruption. President Clinton grew up there with a stepfather who had a gambling addiction that seemed to come from the town's supposedly magic waters.

In the twenties, a young Tennessee minister's son came to Hot Springs to coach football and teach math. He was so appalled by the decadence of this American Sodom that he fled north to Yale Law School, the first step on what would become a crusade against organized crime whose prime target was my father. Estes Kefauver was the man, who more than anyone else, demonized Meyer Lansky and my uncles. His "war on crime" in 1951 would upend my seemingly perfect teenage life and Daddy's life as well. Owney Madden's Deep South empire was headquartered at the Southern Club in Hot Springs, a fancy pre-Vegas casino-nightclub that became famous as the spot where Daddy's great friend and mentor Uncle Charlie Luciano was apprehended in 1935 in what became a love-hate affair with the American government. Uncle Charlie, who would host me in his exile in Naples on a European trip in 1955, had been the king of New York before Uncle Frank Costello. New York's wildly ambitious district attorney, Tom Dewey, saw his road to the White House paved with the scalps of my uncles.

Dewey couldn't have gotten a bigger one than Uncle Charlie, whom he sent to Dannemora prison for fifty years, not for murder, which he couldn't prove, but for promoting prostitution, which my uncles considered a joke. Prostitution was chump change for Gotham's Mister Big, but despite the best criminal defense lawyer money could buy, Uncle Charlie lost his fight with Dewey. Even though America sent him to prison, Uncle Charlie turned the other cheek and wouldn't turn his back on America during the war. As a kid, World War II terrified me. The air raid sirens for the drills made me think we were being invaded. The blackouts were even worse, because I thought the enemy had taken over and was going to kill us all. I was afraid to sleep in my room. I had to sleep in my parents' big bed, in Daddy's strong arms. He was fearless. He always reassured me. "Don't worry, darling, we're going to win." One thing we didn't have to endure during the war was rationing. Everybody else, even the rich people in the Majestic and the Beresford, complained about food shortages, clothing shortages, medicine shortages. The Lanskys had no shortages. It paid to be connected. Even as a kid, I sensed we were extra-special.

Daddy quietly put his money where his mouth was, though he refused to brag about it, or any of his accomplishments. First, even before I was born in 1937, he used some of his old Lower East Side Bugs-Meyer musclemen to break up Nazi rallies in Yorkville, on the Upper East Side. There were a lot of Germans in New York then, and a lot of them were loyal to the Fatherland. If they could be true to their roots, Daddy had to be true to his. If Daddy had a special nostalgia for his young life, he never showed it to me. Daddy never discussed the past and didn't dwell on the present. What inspired him was the future. What I learned of the past I got from Buddy. Daddy's youth was a time of bootleg booze and bullets and danger, cracking skulls and shoot-outs that I still can't imagine my buttoned-up banker-like father being a part of.

It was an era that provided still more uncles, Uncle Red Levine, Uncle Doc Stacher, and my *real* uncle, Jack Lansky, Daddy's younger brother, all a little rougher than the Dinty Moore elite. Unlike the others from "the old days," Uncle Jack Lansky seemed weak and timid, lucky to have a fearless big brother to protect him. The others seemed rough because they *were*, tough Jews to a man, living and laughing refutations of the brainy, nerdy, meek, rabbinical stereotype. These were Jews who could kill. Notwithstanding our Christmas trees, our liver and bacon, my brothers not being bar mitzvah'ed, Daddy would not abandon his pride in the faith of his parents and of his oldest friends, and he certainly would not give up his pride in being an American.

New York was in real danger. Those air raid drills weren't just for caution. The enemy was right here. This was brought home to me when the famous French luxury liner *Normandie* was sabotaged at the West Side docks and set ablaze. We could see the cataclysmic black clouds of smoke all the way uptown at the Beresford. If the blackouts were bad, this was worse. The sirens wouldn't end, and I thought the city had been bombed and that worse was coming.

Days later, on our way to dinner, Daddy drove his Oldsmobile (he refused anything show-offy like a Cadillac or Packard) down 10th Avenue to show me the wreck of the ship. The *Normandie,* he explained, couldn't sail the seas anymore with passengers, because the German submarines would sink it. So the French had given it to us to use as a troop ship and we renamed it the *Lafayette,* after the French general who helped us win the Revolutionary War against the British. For a guy who never got to high school, Daddy was a whiz on American history. Whatever we called it, the ship was finished, destroyed. It looked like a giant beached whale, lying on its side, its innards burnt out, smoke still billowing from its ruined carcass.

Why would Daddy take a five-year-old to Dinty Moore's during wartime? Because I was too scared to stay at home without him. Plus I loved to go out with him. That night we had dinner with Uncle Joe, who was the big boss of the Fulton Fish Market downtown and as the head of the seafood workers' union, one of most powerful men on the waterfront. His name was Joseph Lanza, but everyone called him

"Socks," I guess because he must have socked a lot of tough guys in the nose on his way to the top of this super-tough field.

You'd think Uncle Joe would have been a big fish eater, but I never saw him touch anything but big steaks. At dinner, Daddy was even more serious than usual, and he and Uncle Joe kept talking about "Salvatore" who turned out to be the famous uncle Charlie I was yet to meet, because he was otherwise engaged at Dannemora prison. Uncle Joe and Uncle Charlie had both been born in Sicily, and Uncle Joe, who had a heavy accent, stuck to the Old World lingo. Of all my uncles, Uncle Joe was one of the rare ones who didn't affect the custom-tailored style of a Wall Street banker. Somehow his bullish presence made me feel even safer during wartime.

What Daddy and Uncle Joe cooked up at Moore's was a patriotic Irish stew crafted by a Jew and an Italian. Uncle Charlie would use his still-massive influence, which no prison bars could contain, to mobilize dockworkers up and down the East Coast to root out the kind of sabotage that had sunk the *Normandie* and that conceivably could sink America. Of the thousands of Italian longshoremen, many might be as loyal to our enemy Mussolini as some of the Yorkville Germans could be to Hitler, and Uncle Charlie had the immense power to find out who the traitors were and stop them before more harm was done. But Meyer Lansky and Socks Lanza had an ulterior motive, which was to free Salvatore Luciano from Dannemora. Daddy was all about deals, and this was a big one, involving naval intelligence and Governor Dewey, who agreed to pardon Uncle Charlie in return for his inside information, his vast influence, and his high-level detective work. Although Daddy dreamed up the deal, it was brokered by Daddy's lawyer, Moses Polakoff, a grand and scholarly man I would call "the Professor." As with most of Daddy's deals, all the parties—Governor Dewey, the new New York district attorney, Frank Hogan, the navy, the entire war effort—got what they needed and wanted. Many Axis agents on the waterfront and beyond were identified and arrested. No more ships were sunk. Plus Uncle Charlie provided valuable intelligence to the Allies for their invasion of Sicily.

Knowledge was power and also a gambling chip. Once the war was won, Governor Dewey kept his word and pardoned Charlie in 1946. And Daddy was key in concluding the deal in which Luciano, in return for his liberty, had to agree to be deported back to Italy. It may have seemed like a raw deal for a would-be patriot who had helped America win the war. But it was freedom, and better to dress in the elegant silks of the Via Veneto than in the rough prison stripes of Dannemora. "You always have a friend in Italy," Daddy told me many times, once I was old enough to figure out where and what Italy was.

Did I really want friends like that? As a little girl, as Daddy's girl, I had no idea what Daddy and my uncles were really up to. Whatever it was, they seemed great at it, and I was living like a little queen.

The Unclehood had seized a golden opportunity in Prohibition, a law that very few Americans liked or respected. In fact most Americans liked the people who broke the Prohibition laws way more than those who tried, in vain, to enforce them. And when America gave up its crazy dry experiment in 1933 Daddy and my uncles leapt into this void, turning the speakeasies—that for the prior decade had sold their bootleg liquor—into legitimate nightclubs. Illegal gambling still went on in the secret rooms of these glamorous roadhouses and talent emporia across America. The gambling was where the big money was, because Americans liked to gamble just about as much as they liked to drink.

Just as Washington, D.C., had foolishly tried to keep people from drinking, now the legislators' puritan efforts were focused on gambling, which, as time as shown, has become as American a pastime as baseball. Daddy and my uncles were just as puritan as the men in Washington. They hated drugs. They hated prostitution. But the Washington party line was that if you had liquor and if you had gambling, then drugs and whores were sure to follow, and Tom Sawyer's America would turn into Owney Madden's Hot Springs. As we have seen from Atlantic City to Las Vegas, the puritan doomsday has been a false alarm.

The Unclehood was in the entertainment business, giving the people what they wanted, up to a point. There were other elements in gangland who might have catered to "true crime," but not the Unclehood. As one of my uncles, Uncle Doc Stacher, often said, the main difference between Meyer Lansky and his old Prohibition friend Joe Kennedy was Kennedy's rosary and his Harvard degree. If Daddy and my uncles had had those degrees (forget the rosaries), they probably would have ended up on Wall Street. Without them, they ended up in Havana and Las Vegas. But what really is Wall Street, anyway, but a fancy casino whose croupiers have MBAs?

None of my uncles had gone to Harvard, or anywhere near it other than maybe to pull some heist in Cambridge or Arlington. They hadn't gone to any college. In fact, I think my father's eighth-grade education was the equivalent of a Ph.D. in the Unclehood. He was the scholar of the group, the wise man. But look how far they had come with nothing but their brains and their fists. It was all a matter of perspective, a matter of opportunity, a matter of respect. Whether Kennedy or Lansky, the key to success was all about taking risks. Daddy wanted his children to be armed with degrees, rather than the pistols and brickbats that he and Uncle Benny and all the others were armed with. That Buddy and I, true to the Unclehood, never finished high school, that we were millionaire dropouts, was one of the great tragedies and heartbreaks in the life of a man who never displayed his emotions. But I can guarantee you that no daughter of Wall Street had as privileged a girlhood as the one Daddy arranged for me. That I blew it has always haunted me, the thought that maybe there was a Lansky curse, that we were all genetically programmed to take the wrong turn, to miss the yellow brick road, and to choose the dark highway to oblivion.

CHAPTER TWO

AMERICAN PRINCESS

For a girl whom many assumed to be a Jewish American Princess, I had absolutely nothing Jewish in my upbringing. It started with my birth, on December 6, 1937, at New England Baptist Hospital in Boston, where a Catholic priest my mother had befriended—later the famed Cardinal Cushing, the Archbishop of Boston—blessed the event. I was raised by an Irish nanny named Minnie Mullins and a Filipino butler/chauffeur named Tommy, who was a devout Catholic. My mother made a big deal of celebrating Christmas, with a huge tree and more gifts than any Santa could handle, and an even bigger one of celebrating Easter, with Easter egg hunts and baked hams and custom-made hand-painted dresses for me that I could have worn in the Easter Parade if Daddy had only let me.

We lived in one of the most expensive apartment houses in Boston, on Beacon Street in Back Bay, in the heart of the Mayflower aristocracy, with a view over the Charles River and the Esplanade where the Boston Pops Orchestra played their summer concerts. This was WASP country, Harvard country, the land of Cabots and Lodges. And Lanskys. Meyer Lansky was precisely the kind of man the Puritan New England preachers would have given angry sermons against. Yet here he was, the merchant of pleasure in the land of pain.

But pain was why we were in Boston, a pain that may have caused my parents to lose their Jewish faith. My brother Buddy was Meyer Lansky's firstborn son, whom he hoped would become a Harvard man, a great man, a straight man. But Bernard Irving Lansky came into the world of the Depression in 1930 with the birth defect of cerebral palsy, which basically rendered Buddy a cripple at birth. The name of the condition implies a disorder of the brain and in most kids manifests itself with both mental and physical impairment. In that sense, my brother was lucky. Buddy's brain was fine. It was his body that had betrayed him, and with it, my parents' big dreams for him. Mother spent a lot of time by herself in the great Reading Room of the gigantic Christian Science Church (Boston was the home of Christian Science) looking for answers she could never find, as to why God had let her down like this over Buddy.

Daddy had already made his first fortune in bootlegging, and he threw all of it at trying to cure his son, who could not walk and could barely use his arms. Daddy and Mommy took him to the best doctors in New York and all over the country, wherever there was a lead. They were the wandering Jews. They even tried the magic healing waters in Owney Madden's Hot Springs. They would have travelled to Lourdes if they had thought there was a chance of a miracle. But when miracles did not appear, both of my parents seemed to give up on their own parents' devout Judaism.

However, they didn't give up on life. They tried again, and, two years later, in 1932, they hit the genetic jackpot with my brother Paul, who was not only the picture of his beautiful mother but also the picture of health. That same year, they also heard of a medical miracle worker at Boston's Children's Hospital who promised them that, like Jesus, he could make the lame walk. They kept their apartment at the Majestic and took a place in Boston. Daddy lived and breathed business, but it would still come second to Buddy. Daddy was on a mission. Mommy believed in the new doctor, Dr. Carruthers, and at the same time, with the support of Father Richard Cushing, she began believing in Jesus.

———————

If anybody deserved the title of Jewish American Princess, it was my mother. Anne Citron had been a real catch for Daddy, who had definitely married "up" in 1929, from his father Max's grinding job pressing pants for slave wages. My parents had their honeymoon in Atlantic City, where Daddy characteristically mixed business and pleasure by attending a kind of summit conference of all my future Italian and Jewish uncles to plan the future of the liquor business while the end of Prohibition was in sight. It would be naïve to ignore the fact that part of Mommy's allure to Daddy was that her family represented a way for Daddy to get out of bootlegging and go legit.

Mommy's father, Moses Citron, was a major produce wholesaler in New York, who also had a chain of markets, Universal Fruit and Produce, in New Jersey. They lived on an estate in New Jersey near the Zwillmans in ritzy South Orange. Grandpa Citron looked very grand in his pinstripe suits. Daddy may have gotten some of his style ideas from him. Grandma Citron was enormously fat. She looked like she had devoured all of Grandpa's produce.

Grandpa Citron had been born in Moldavian Romania to a fine family of produce barons. Romania was apparently something of a land of opportunity for Jews, at least compared to Russia and its pogroms, where the Lanskys didn't have a fighting chance. He and Grandma Citron, whose first name was Shelma, had married into a world of culture, breeding, and wealth. They were not your typical immigrants.

Grandpa was a college graduate, and when he and Grandma came to America, they didn't go to Ellis Island, like the Lanskys, but travelled by clipper ship to California, where they had purchased a big plot of land to create a vineyard. However, when they arrived, they found that the land they had bought in Europe was in the middle of the Pacific Ocean. Welcome to real estate in the New World. They quickly decamped to New York, where Grandpa Citron built his major produce business to mirror that of his family back in Romania.

Grandpa Citron had wanted my mother to go to college like he did. However, she was the baby in the family, the fourth of four children, and according to Old World tradition, she was expected to marry, and to do it as soon as possible. She was all of eighteen, and her parents always regretted that they had sacrificed her to those ancient traditions, rather than insisting that she get the higher education she clearly would have loved. Instead she married a "hoodlum." Grandpa Citron didn't care. He embraced his new son-in-law and gave him a job, so he would have a legitimate salary.

Daddy didn't want a job with anyone. Once my parents were married, Daddy charmed his way into a partnership with Grandpa Citron, forming, along with future Uncle Moe Dalitz, an enterprising bootlegger who would "own" Cleveland and be a major force in Las Vegas, a giant corporation called Molaska, Inc., which would manufacture molasses out of which the soon-to-be-legal-again liquor could be distilled. Grandpa Citron invested what today what would be millions of dollars in Molaska, which had huge plants in New Jersey and Ohio. The idea was that, with Citron backing, Meyer Lansky could become a Joe Kennedy–style big businessman, even without the Harvard degree. Molaska had all the potential to become the next Seagram's and make the Lansky-Citrons the American version of the Canadian Bronfmans.

But Daddy must have had a gambling gene that even the loftiest ambitions to respectability could not overcome. You don't run the casinos in Las Vegas, Havana, and London without that inner high roller. Instead of playing it totally legit, totally Wall Street, with the Molaska Corporation and making legal whisky, Daddy and Moe Dalitz decided to make *illegal* whiskey, so they wouldn't have to pay the government's new heavy "pleasure" tax. They thought they could get away with it, just like they had gotten away with it during Prohibition. But they didn't.

By 1935, the taxmen had descended, raiding the plants, serving subpoenas, looking for ways to "get" Daddy and Uncle Moe. But Daddy was as elusive as Harry Houdini. He had Molaska declare bankruptcy and hid behind an impenetrable maze of shell corporations that made the credit default swaps that nearly bankrupted America in 2008 look like a kid's game. But the price he paid was losing his big chance to go straight. He also cost Grandpa Citron a fortune, which surely didn't sit well with Mommy, who had enough stress with Buddy's illness.

When the Molaska dream turned to ashes, Daddy embarked on what became his great trademark skill, casino gambling. Alas, this was before casino gambling had been legalized, so you could say Daddy was way ahead of his time. He had cut his casino teeth during Prohibition in minor gambling operations, from numbers running to crap games to bookmaking. Once liquor became legal, he quickly became a nightclub impresario—the clubs, filled with stars, becoming the lure and the front for the back-room gambling that was where the serious money lay. These clubs were called "carpet joints," because carpets were a shorthand for the lavish luxury that awaited the high rollers.

Daddy was involved with such clubs all over the country, usually outside the limits of big cities whose upright fathers could look the other way once the fun went to an adjacent county, places like the Riviera, just over the new George Washington Bridge in Fort Lee, where Frank Sinatra spilled the ice on me. Daddy, who had a "piece" of the Riviera, had similar pieces of most of America's prime nightclubs. His main operations were in Saratoga Springs, the horse racing mecca in upstate New York, and Broward County, just above Miami and its American Riviera. But he was also the mastermind, if not on the masthead, of similar operations near New Orleans, Cincinnati, Council Bluffs, Dallas, and Phoenix—all of which were joint ventures with uncles all over the country. I had a *huge* family. Daddy was always on the road, which caused Mommy endless loneliness that the money that was pouring in couldn't compensate for.

Mommy's best friend, Esther Krakower, who married Uncle Benny Siegel, was from a much poorer family. Esther had a brother, Whitey, who was a genuine gangster of the old brass knuckle school, a charter member of the Jewish gang known as Murder Incorporated. Whitey was shot to death in a gangland assassination on Delancey Street in New York in 1941. Such violence was never even referred to or even whispered about when I was growing up, unfit for my ladylike ears. Despite Mommy's friendship with Esther, in the eyes of her parents, people like the Krakowers and the Lanskys would have normally been considered "not our kind." However because the Citrons loved their daughter, they put aside any class prejudices and embraced not only the Lanskys, but also the Siegels as "family."

Mommy, probably in reaction to her mother's behemoth weight, was extremely skinny and stylish. She had a beautiful, cultured voice, not at all a harsh Brooklyn accent. Then again, her parents weren't New Yorkers. They were transplanted Californians, and Mommy and her siblings sounded neutral and very American. With her slinky dresses and her Pall Mall cigarette always in hand, she gave off a sultry Hollywood glamour, a little like Rita Hayworth in *Gilda*, except Mommy couldn't sing.

Mommy was about five three, a few inches shorter than Daddy. She was taller than he was when she wore high heels, so she kept the heels low, as Daddy didn't want anyone to think he was weak enough to fall for some big showgirl, as the foolish rich men in his nightclubs and casinos were wont to do. That was for suckers. Above all, Daddy was dead serious and wanted to be regarded as such. Mommy loved beautiful clothes and jewels and had closets and closets of them. She seemed to live at beauty salons. Before the kids were born, I don't know where she found time for Daddy between all her shopping and her styling. They were lucky he travelled so much.

So this was the world I was born into in 1937. The Citrons had one son-in-law, the husband of my mother's sister, Sadie, in the very legitimate produce business, and another, my father, in the very illegitimate gambling business. But they didn't judge Daddy for it, or if they did, given their patrician background, they suspended that judgment. They loved their daughter, and what was good for her was good for them. The Lanskys, on the other hand, were mystified that their son had become a criminal, no matter how much money he was making and how much of it he lavished upon them. Plus Meyer had brought his younger, weaker brother Jacob, Uncle Jack, along for this illegal joy ride. Grandpa Lansky, whom I never knew, was a cautious man like his son Jack and would have been happier if Daddy had stayed in the tool and die factory where he had held his first and last conventional job. Grandma Lansky, on the other hand, gave Daddy unconditional love, and he gave it back. The real shame, or *shonda,* as the Lanskys might wail in Yiddish, was that none of their grandchildren were being raised as Jews. They could call the Christmas trees Chanukah bushes until they were blue in the face, but they were still Christmas trees. Grandpa Max Lansky died in 1939, a very sad and unfulfilled man. Grandma Yetta would go on and on and help raise me when no one else was able to.

Daddy, having moved the family to Boston for Buddy's health, was impatient at his slow progress and, I later learned, a little depressed over the loss of his best friend in Boston, Charlie Solomon, who had given him aid and comfort when Buddy was born and made the connections to Dr. Carruthers. Before I was born, Solomon, who was known as King Solomon, owned Boston the same way Charlie

Luciano owned New York. He had made his fortune in bootlegging alongside Joe Kennedy and owned Boston's grandest nightclub, the Cocoanut Grove. But Solomon had been shot to death by rivals from another club. I had no idea until years later that murder could be an undercurrent in the business-y world of Daddy and my uncles. That was the key difference between Wall Street and the Vegas Strip. Big shots on Wall Street were rarely assassinated.

Uncle Hy Abrams took over King Solomon's vacant, bloody throne. He and Daddy would take long walks along the Charles River Esplanade. I used to watch them from our windows, or when I was playing in the park by the Charles with Nanny Minnie and my one friend, Wendy, whom I named my very first doll after. Wendy was always my favorite name, long before I even knew about *Peter Pan*.

Notwithstanding Buddy's daily therapy with Dr. Carruthers, we seemed to be travelling all the time. In family scrapbooks, I have pictures of myself as a very little girl in Florida, Arizona, California, and Cuba, all hot spots to escape the icy Boston winters and, more important, for Daddy to do his endless deals. He understood how much Americans loved betting, and he was betting his own career on it. I remember fondly one train trip to Phoenix, where we visited Daddy's dog track there. He had chimpanzees dressed as jockeys riding the dogs on their backs. That made a huge impression on me. I also had a wonderful trip to Cuba, my first international journey. Mommy made a scrapbook with a bunch of press clippings of me in 1940 at the legendary Hotel Nacional in Havana, where the Cuban daily *El País* wrote that the Lanskys were in residence there for ten weeks. A world war was erupting. Europe was freezing and dying. Most of America was still getting over the Depression. And here we were amidst the palms and the hibiscus, the happiest kids on earth. Charmed lives.

Even with Daddy's philosophy of staying under the radar, he was front-page news and a VIP all the way. There were pictures of me with my curly blonde hair in a white bonnet and white sundress confidently pushing my own stroller, the little golden girl. And there was my brother Paul at the racetrack, dashing in a rep tie and white Bermudas, a pair of binoculars around his neck so he could see the precise result at the finish line. But for all the copy about Daddy, he and my mother and Buddy were never photographed for the paper.

Even when we were in the Cuban paradise, education always took precedence for Daddy. He sent Buddy and Paul to the American School in Havana, figuring a few months of lessons were better than none at all. For all his limitations, Buddy could still use his hands a bit. He spoke beautifully. And he walked by holding on to you. Under the circumstances, he had amazing poise.

What was Daddy doing in Cuba? In his travels, Daddy had become good friends with Cuba's military ruler, Colonel Fulgencio Batista. Batista, impressed with Daddy's success in the carpet joints across America, offered him a plum contract to renovate and manage Havana's famed Oriental Park racetrack and its two casinos. Oriental Park had been a haven for American millionaires in the Roaring Twenties. But the Yankee millionaires had gone home in the Depression, and Batista wanted them back. Daddy brought in a New England friend named Lou Smith, one of the disciples of King Solomon, who ran horse and dog tracks in the Boston area, to run the racetrack at Oriental Park for him.

Daddy was like a business consultant, the McKinsey of the Mob. However, where gambling was legal, there was no Mob stigma to running a casino, only the huge prestige that got Daddy written up in the papers. The respect must have felt good, so good that he took his family to Havana for the whole season to bask in it. The millionaires started coming back: the Vanderbilts, the ice-skating star Sonja Henie, who had been the obsession of Adolf Hitler and had rejected him cold. But she liked my father, who wore a white dinner jacket and ran the places just like Humphrey Bogart did as Rick in *Casablanca*. Being the *patrón* of Oriental Park was a dry run for creating Vegas a decade hence and for turning Havana into the Las Vegas of the Caribbean, another decade after that. Meyer Lansky would soon own the Nacional, where we were staying. That was like owning the Waldorf in New York.

In 1941, we faced the reality that medical miracles were not going to happen in Boston. We moved back to New York City, to a grand art deco high-rise at 411 West End Avenue. The feature I remember most was the sunken living room, like the dance floor on an ocean liner. I had to share a room with my brothers, who both liked to tease and torment me. But it didn't last long. At the tender age of nine, Paul was sent away to boarding school at the New York Military Academy (NYMA), a "feeder" school for the U.S. Military Academy at West Point, further up the Hudson, where Daddy's friend, Philadelphia publisher and *Racing Form* owner Moe Annenberg, had sent two of his grandsons. A lot of Daddy's friends, in the upper world as well as the underworld, were sending their sons and grandsons to military schools. That was the big thing in those days. Instead of preparing Paul for Harvard, Daddy had decided that West Point was the pinnacle of American education. It was wartime, and the military had way more prestige than big business, which had spotted its blotter in the 1929 crash.

Moe Annenberg had just pled guilty to tax evasion to save his only son (he had seven daughters), Walter, Reagan's future ambassador to England, who had also been indicted, from prison. NYMA would later be the alma mater of director Francis Coppola, mogul Donald Trump, and John Gotti, Jr., the son of the gangster. A number of my uncles' sons ended up there as well. There was nothing like a military education to counter charges that a family was "un-American."

After Buddy was sent to a rehab school in Cockysville, Maryland, outside of Baltimore, under the care of another supposed miracle worker, Dr. Phelps, I was home alone in New York and had my parents all to myself. The problem was that they were never around. Daddy was always on the road, and Mommy was shopping on 57th Street, often with Flo Alo, Uncle Jimmy's wife, and Aunt Esther Siegel, before she moved to Beverly Hills.

She was shopping her lonely blues away at a store called Wilma's, a more exclusive version of Bonwit Teller, just down the block. She bought hand-embroidered linens at an expensive place called Leron. If they had actually served breakfast at Tiffany's, Mommy would have been there to eat it. One time her sister Sadie told Mommy to buy herself a "little" birthday present and send the bill to Sadie. Poor Sadie nearly had a heart attack when the bill came for over $200, which was a fortune for silk pajamas in the Depression. Mommy had expensive tastes; she couldn't help herself.

Mommy also was addicted to beauty salons. Elizabeth Arden, one of her favorites, was like something out of Marie Antoinette and the French court at Versailles. It was a long way from the men's barbershop on the Lower East Side where she and Aunt Esther had gotten their hair cut as girls. I still can't imagine what Mommy was doing there. Slumming, I guess. Taking a walk on the wild side. Maybe she wasn't always so refined and proper. After all, she did marry Meyer Lansky.

Please don't get the idea that Mommy was selfish, sending my brothers away and shopping all the time. She shopped for me as much as she shopped for herself, buying me clothes at the Saks children's shop, getting my hair cut at Best & Co., and spending more money on dolls at the enormous toy emporium FAO Schwarz on Fifth Avenue than any other customer in its history. I was the doll queen: my room was filled with at least fifty dolls. I had a whole set of Jane Austen dolls; a collection of Alice in Wonderland dolls; Red Cross war nurse dolls; Princess Elizabeth English royalty dolls; and Cinderella dolls, all from the famous doll designer Madame Alexander, who was to dolls what Chanel was to clothes.

I thought Madame Alexander, with a fancy name like that, was royalty herself, but it turns out she was just a Jewish princess like my mother, although one who created a big business. She was born in the same part of Russia as Daddy. If I had known, I would have begged him to get out of the gambling business and into the doll business. I had dolls from other doll makers than Madame Alexander, boy dolls, too, General MacArthur dolls and Rhett Butler dolls to go with my Scarlett O'Hara dolls and a whole city of dollhouses, the nicest one fully lighted, an electric dollhouse. Plus I had enough big stuffed animals to fill the Central Park Zoo.

Mommy bought me books, too, and lots of them. The first one I remember was "The Goops and How to Be Them: A Manual of Manners for Polite Infants," which she would read to me until I could read myself. Mommy was raising me as a little lady, and she wanted to be sure I behaved like one. Perfect manners were essential. As was generosity, at least from Daddy's point of view. When Buddy was a therapy outpatient at Bellevue Hospital, Daddy thought it would be nice to give something to the kids on the children's ward. "It'll make them feel good, and it will make you feel even better," he promised me.

At first I didn't want to give away my dolls. They were my friends, my only friends, and they were real to me. But you didn't say no to Daddy. There were twenty-one kids, and I picked out twenty-one dolls, one for each. Daddy was right, that it was better to give than to receive. The smiles of those kids will stay with me forever. I wish I could have brought them all home to be my friends. I would have rather had real people than dolls to play with. For all the stuff I had, I couldn't have been lonelier.

One of the reasons Paul had been sent to military school, aside from Daddy's West Point dreams for him and the fact that Daddy's friends' sons were being sent to such places, was that he was a little rambunctious. On a visit to the Citrons in New Jersey, Paul had broken some things in the tightly ordered house, a boy being a boy. That wouldn't do. If he needed discipline, who better to instill it than a military school? Not wanting to get sent away myself, I took the Goops to heart and memorized its illustrated etiquette rules as insurance against deportation. My little world was too good to lose.

Nanny Minnie Mullins had stayed behind in Boston. So Mommy sent me to a French nursery school for four hours a day. Mommy wanted me to have European culture the same way Daddy wanted Paul to go to West Point and become a general. I hated French. At five proper English was hard enough. It was like being on Mars, and I didn't last very long.

The best part of the boys being gone, aside from having the room all to myself, was travelling whenever Daddy took Mommy with him, like the trip to California to see the Siegels. Until 1945 my childhood summers would be spent on the beach in Deal, New Jersey. Deal, and the neighboring towns of Long Branch and Elberon on the Jersey Shore were known as the Jewish Riviera, where many of the old German Jewish families who had become the pillars of Wall Street at the turn of the twentieth century had imposing Victorian summer homes. From the post–Civil War days until the 1929 crash, this part of the Jersey Shore was as grand a resort as Newport, Rhode Island, frequented by seven presidents, from Ulysses S. Grant to Woodrow Wilson. There was even a Church of the Presidents in Long Branch, where all the chief executives worshipped.

By the forties, the Jewish Riviera had become the Gangster Riviera. In addition to Daddy, many of my uncles owned or rented great estates there—Willie Moretti, Ben Siegel, Jerry Catena, Doc Stacher. These were the people who controlled the nightlife of the Garden State; it was only fitting that they summered in the state that was making them rich and not running up to Maine to cool off. They lived in homes that decades before had belonged to such important American families as the Hartfords of the A&P food stores, the Woolworths of *those* stores, and the Seligmans, one of the Jewish investment banking baronies of Wall Street who financed the railroads that we took out west to visit Uncle Benny Siegel.

Thomas Edison had lived here, and, most important to Daddy, Robert Lincoln, the son of Daddy's revered "Uncle Abe." I could only hope Daddy and my uncles could become as respected in their business as these Jersey Shore predecessors. I played with the children of all these powerful men, my "cousins." It was simple, swimming and sunning and riding bicycles, going to Asbury Park, now famous for Bruce Springsteen, then famous for its boardwalk, its carousel, its imposing casino, which was a beach club that had nothing to do with gambling and was designed by the same architects who built New York's Grand Central Station.

I normally never liked to eat very much, but the salt air made me hungry for the cotton candy, the toffee, the popcorn, the hot dogs, the all-American junk. Daddy couldn't have picked a more all-American spot to celebrate his birthday on the Fourth of July. His idea of relaxing was sitting outside overlooking the sea, drinking scotch, smoking cigarettes, and playing gin rummy with my uncles and other men like Uncle Benny, visiting from California. Here in the Jersey breeze, America's highest rollers would get all worked up over their hands as they played for a penny a point. Daddy and Benny also enjoyed fierce handball competitions. You could see how intense they could be. In those games, you could see how these men could rule their world.

Despite my summers in Deal and my travels with my parents all over the country and to Cuba, as a little girl my New York was a very limited slice of Manhattan, bounded on the north by 96th Street, the south by 42nd Street, the west by the Hudson, and the east by Fifth Avenue. I never visited the Statue of Liberty or the Empire State Building or Gracie Mansion, never saw Wall Street or Greenwich Village, never was taken to Macy's or Gimbels. Daddy did take Paul and Buddy to Yankee Stadium to see baseball, but not me. They said I was too little.

I certainly wasn't shown my Daddy's roots on the Lower East Side, where his gang had gotten its start running garages of hot cars that transported illegal booze. Occasionally we would go to Brooklyn to visit Daddy's mother, Grandma Yetta. But this was fancy Brooklyn, not poor Brooklyn. Daddy had set his mother up in a luxurious apartment on Ocean Parkway, the grandest boulevard in the borough, supposedly modeled on a street in Paris. It went all the way out to Coney Island, where they never took me, either.

Grandma Yetta was very sharp, and she didn't seem very Old World at all, like Grandpa Lansky was supposed to have been. I was too young to remember him, but Grandma Yetta would later become a great friend to me. She knew everything and about everyone, and I could see sometimes how all her chattering, especially about Uncle Benny in Las Vegas and all his *tsuris* (trouble, I learned to translate), would make my reserved father very nervous.

That, and stories like how her sister had also immigrated to the States and raised a family. This sister's immigrant husband was so proud of his kids that he then took them back to Poland to show them off to the relatives who stayed behind. But his timing was terrible. Just on his visit, the Nazis invaded, and they took him and his kids to a concentration camp and killed them all. Neither Mommy nor Daddy had wanted my tender ears to hear horror stories like that, but Grandma had a mind and a mouth of her own. I could see where Daddy got his drive and power. Everyone said his brother Jack, who seemed weak and passive, was much more like their father.

Some of Yetta's horror stories turned out to be comforting. Yetta told me how she had lost two daughters, Lena and Rose, who would have been my aunts, Lena to walking pneumonia in 1915 and Rose in 1928, to skin cancer, just before Daddy married Mommy. That's why he needed a wife, she told me. That's why he treasured his daughter, she assured me. And that I would always be Daddy's pet, the most important woman in his life. "More than Mommy?" I wondered.

"More than anybody," Yetta declared, in the same sweepingly confident tone that Daddy had when he made his pronouncements.

Grandma Lansky liked to talk to Daddy in Yiddish, not to keep secrets like Mommy did, but because that was her first language, and Daddy's, too. When Mommy was there with us, I think that made her uncomfortable. But she often let Daddy take me alone. The only old world she liked was France, not Russia. Yetta was a wonderful cook; all her Jewish classics, like lokshen soup, latkes, blintzes, and gefilte fish were, to me, better than Dinty Moore's. Somehow with her, I had a big appetite, but nowhere else.

My first inkling that I was Jewish came from Yetta. I was totally confused, going from her world in Brooklyn back to our world on West End, from blintzes to bacon. Somehow I had a sense that Brooklyn, even fancy Brooklyn, was more real than West End. In a few years I would see exactly how right I was, how the Beresford, the ultimate New York building where we would soon move, was one big mirage.

CHAPTER THREE

MAKE BELIEVE BALLROOM

In 1942 we moved to the Beresford at 211 Central Park West, on the corner of 81st Street. This was a real castle in the sky, built in 1929, just before the crash, when rich people thought that the sky had no limit. Our apartment on the 19th floor was vast (Jerry Seinfeld lives next door today), with a huge terrace overlooking Central Park and an army of doormen and elevator men in fancy uniforms to wait on us.

Our unit, 19J, was as close to a palace as you could have in New York. There were four bedrooms, two maid's rooms, a restaurant-sized kitchen and pantry, a breakfast room, a dining room, a marble foyer, a paneled library for Daddy and clothes closets Mommy could live in, a vast living room, and more bathrooms than I could count, with black tiles and stall showers with multiple shower heads. The bathrooms were so art deco that I wouldn't have been surprised to see Fred Astaire coming out of one of the showers. Daddy's library was my favorite. It looked like it came from a European university. He had walls and walls of books and three sets of encyclopedias: *Colliers*, the *Book of Knowledge*, and the *Britannica*. There was nothing he didn't want to know about. For an eighth-grade dropout, he was the most learned man I ever saw.

I had a huge room where I could see the spires of the new George Washington Bridge in the distance over the water towers of the Upper West Side. They sort of looked like space ships. The room was blue and white with fleur-de-lys wallpaper and French provincial furniture. Throughout the apartment were priceless Oriental rugs and silk carpets that the maids took up in spring to display the parquet floors. Summer was too hot for rugs. Mommy got her help from Mrs. Gooding, who ran an employment agency in Harlem. She looked just like Aunt Jemima on the pancake mix boxes. Mommy kept Mrs. Gooding very busy, because no maid could get the apartment clean enough. She was always on her hands and knees cleaning up after the maids. A microscopic amount of dust would drive her crazy, and she would be on the phone to Mrs. Gooding to find her someone new.

If I thought Mommy was away all the time buying clothes and getting beauty treatments, decorating this apartment would take her away forever. Mommy loved to decorate, to design built-in furniture and discover rare pieces. Her impeccable, refined taste ran to French antiques, hence my French nursery school. I later learned that the buildings across Central Park on Fifth and Park Avenues were more "exclusive" than the Beresford, which was another way of saying they didn't accept any, or many, Jewish families, not with poor Russian roots like Daddy's. In the 1950s bestseller *Marjorie Morningstar*, Herman Wouk's Jewish princess heroine lived in the Eldorado. Given that my parents didn't see us as a Jewish family, I'm surprised, particularly given my mother's Francophile cultural fantasies, that she didn't have us living on the WASPy Upper East Side.

Maybe the Lansky name was a deal breaker. Or maybe it was the Lansky deeds. But Mommy was a cultural striver, rather than a social climber. She wasn't conflicted about her roots. She didn't try to conceal her Jewish background. She didn't want to become a WASP. She didn't care about getting her name in the columns. She just wanted to live like a queen, and her children to live like princes and princesses. And in this regard, at least in the material sense, Daddy made her dreams come true.

No sooner had we moved in than the lessons started. At age five I was taking ballet lessons, piano lessons, ice skating lessons at the rink in Rockefeller Center. Mommy would watch from one of the two cafés beside the rink. The best part was Mommy taking me for hot cocoa at Schrafft's after the lessons. I could actually ice skate on our terrace; it was that big, so the lessons had some utility. The ballet lessons were Daddy's idea. He was a good friend of Leon Leonidoff, a Russian-born ballet master and impresario who staged all the shows at Radio City Music Hall. He did the "Living Nativity" Christmas show, with live camels and elephants, re-creating the Holy Land on stage.

We had the best seats at that show and at the equally famous "Glory of Easter" show, which re-created St. Patrick's Cathedral and the Easter Parade right on stage. It was funny how all these Christian spectacles were created by Jewish men like Mr. Leonidoff and his boss Roxy Rothafel, another friend of Daddy's who had built the famous Roxy Theatre. Mr. Leonidoff also created the Rockettes, and we'd see them, too, dressed as daffodils with the longest legs on earth.

Daddy didn't want me to be a Rockette, but he would have liked if I had become a ballerina. To that end, Mr. Leonidoff set me up in the best school in the city, right behind Carnegie Hall. The main reason I went was because I wanted to get the ballet shoes. I wasn't that great at the dancing part, though I lasted there longer than the French nursery school. Mommy herself took me into Central Park and taught me to roller skate. I had never thought of her as athletic. I assumed she was too delicate and pampered for any sports. But she really surprised me. Mommy loved taking me to parks, Central, Riverside, and she loved the Central Park Zoo, probably more than I did. She was big on chimps. One of them she named "Jimmy," and he responded to her whenever she called his name, coming over and reaching his hand to her out of the cage, pure beauty and the beast.

The fall before I turned six, in 1943, Mommy enrolled me at Birch Wathen, a fancy finishing school twelve blocks away up on 93rd Street. The school building was a limestone townhouse that looked like it belonged in Paris. Maybe that's why Mommy picked it. She took me up there each day in the morning and picked me up in the afternoon, either driving Daddy's Oldsmobile or in a cab. She refused to let me go by myself, even though the school was so close to us. All she could ever talk about was the Lindbergh kidnapping. Although that crime took place in 1932, Mommy treated it as if it had happened yesterday and could happen again to me tomorrow. Most of my new classmates were WASPy debutantes in training, though not every girl was in the *Social Register*. One who wasn't was Barbara Walters, who was closer to Buddy's age. Her father, Lou, owned the Latin Quarter nightclubs in New York and Miami and was a friend of Daddy's, as both men were working the same beat. Barbara would have been a perfect match for Buddy. I wish my parents had fixed them up.

When we moved into the Beresford I got my first dog, a smart and elegant fox terrier. He could have been a double for Asta, the dog in the *Thin Man* films who was as much of a star as William Powell and Myrna Loy. The *Thin Man* movies were selling the same art deco damn-the-Depression fantasy as the Astaire/Rogers films. Mommy bought it hook, line, and diamond tiara.

That year that I started Birch Wathen, Mommy took me to a movie that she surely thought was the Hollywood fantasy version of her life. This was the romantic comedy-drama *Mr. Lucky*, starring Cary Grant as Meyer Lansky, or rather as a devious gambler-promoter-criminal named Joe "the Greek" Adams who plans to rob a war-charity casino that he is running. Laraine Day played the glamorous East Side socialite who falls for him. Of course there was a happy ending; Cary Grant goes straight and love conquers crime. If only. Mommy loved it and sat through it again with Flo Alo, and maybe even more times with her other friends, as if to say, see, I married Cary Grant. Not bad, eh?

Our Asta, whom we named Petey, for God knows whom, was a gift from one of my uncles, Uncle Nig Rosen, whose name I should have been ashamed to say in front of our two black housekeepers. Uncle Nig's real name was Harry Stromberg. They called him Nig because of the dark tropical tan he cultivated to cover his terrible acne scars. Nig looked scary. Nig and his brother Dan Stromberg were major Philadelphia mobsters. The Rosen boys had succeeded their mentor Max "Boo Boo" Hoff, who had been the preeminent bootlegger in the City of Brotherly Love, sort of what King Solomon was to Boston.

Unlike Daddy, who made a big point of abjuring drugs, Uncle Nig, according to Buddy, my fount of inside information, was said to have made his post-Prohibition fortune in trafficking heroin through Mexico. Maybe it wasn't true. Maybe the tan came not from the Mexico drug routes but from Florida or somewhere innocent. Nig and Dan seemed too nice to be doing anything bad. But then again, so did Daddy. I wasn't about to call Daddy on the carpet. Mommy, too, was willing to look away from the possibly awful truth.

We all adored the dog, even when he would invariably bite any deliveryman who happened to cross our threshold. At first Petey would be docile, tricking the deliveryman into saying what a cute, sweet dog. Then Petey would spring and bite. Petey cost Mommy a fortune in tips. We even sent him to obedience school, but he failed. Daddy and Mommy both took turns walking Petey in Central Park, and I would always tag along. Petey never bit any of the family.

The only time we all enjoyed our palatial apartment as a family was in our ritual six o'clock dinners. It was just Mommy, Daddy, Buddy, Paul, and me at this big table, waited on by our cook and maid, always in crisp black and white uniforms. Mother was too spoiled to have ever learned to cook. Most people would have found our cook's southern-style cooking, with lots of hot biscuits and sweet potatoes and collard greens delicious, but I didn't really like any of it. All I wanted were Kellogg's Rice Krispies, followed by a bowl of applesauce. Kids . . .

Daddy, the epicure who knew all the best restaurants in America, was as appalled at my lack of interest in fine food as he was at Mommy's. Never forgetting her mother's weight, she picked at her dishes and shuffled the food around on her plate. I tried to give my food to Petey under the table, but when Paul was home he would eat my food for me. He said the military school was starving him to death, and he made up for it in New York.

Mommy liked being super-organized. She hated any surprises. Aside from holidays, when we'd have ham and turkey, every night had a set main course, roast chicken Mondays, lamb chop Tuesdays, roast beef Wednesdays, liver and bacon Thursdays, meatloaf Fridays. Thank goodness we never had fish. For dessert there would always be a big cake baked by Mrs. Gooding, who ran the employment agency but who was also a great cook. Saturdays my parents went out, and Sunday the maids were off, so we'd go out together for Chinese or Italian. The coolest thing at dinner was watching Daddy carve the food. He had the hands of a surgeon. You should have seen what he could do to a chicken, or a turkey on Thanksgiving. He couldn't bear seeing anyone pick up a wing or a drumstick with his hands. When his brother, Uncle Jack, did that, he called him a "savage."

I didn't learn to cut up my own food until I was ten. I saw Buddy's food being cut up for him by the maid, and I didn't think it was fair that I should have to cut my own. I was too self-centered to realize that Buddy wasn't strong enough to cut his food. As I said, I was that spoiled. Not that Buddy wasn't spoiled himself. Daddy had Julie Fink, one of his Baltimore sales representatives from the national jukebox company he owned, install a Wurlitzer in Buddy's dormitory room at his school in Maryland. Julie became Buddy's valet and took him to his row house in Baltimore on weekends to join his wife and family. I visited a few times and couldn't figure out how to tell one house from another except by the numbers. They all looked exactly alike from the outside. I was glad we didn't live in Baltimore.

I'm sure Buddy was the only boarding school student in America with his own private jukebox. No one begrudged him the luxury, and he became a great expert on popular music. Daddy was frustrated that he wouldn't spend half the time on his studies that he did on the big bands, but Buddy could tell Artie Shaw from Glenn Miller from the first few notes, and he was a big fan of Sinatra, Tony Bennett, Rosemary Clooney, and all the other big stars who worked in Daddy's nightclubs. Buddy did get stronger (miracles did happen!) and was able to walk with braces. Daddy would urge him on, "If Roosevelt can do it, so can you!"

I never thought of Buddy as handicapped. I got so used to his disabilities that I only could admire his many abilities. He was a master at board games, and strong enough to move the pieces. I could never learn chess, but Buddy was great, a real Bobby Fischer. He must have had Daddy's strategy gene. But Buddy's prime passion was show business. Once Buddy could go out, Daddy would have George Wood, who knew them all, introduce Buddy to the singers or take him to their shows, usually at the Copacabana. I was so jealous, but my time would come.

When we were all home together dinners were formal affairs, Daddy in a suit, Mommy in a fancy dress, Paul in his uniform, Buddy in jacket and tie, and me in one of my custom dresses from Saks. Daddy would run the show, constantly asking my brothers about history and geography, and, most importantly, mathematics. He would come up with all sorts of math exercises, addition, multiplication, division, and the boys were supposed to answer. Dinner was like a quiz show, with the reward being Daddy's satisfaction. Paul always won. He was a great student. Buddy couldn't seem to care less. He might not have been able to beat Paul at math, but Buddy ruled the table in current events and sports. Buddy was smart as a whip. He might have made a great agent, like George Wood, and maybe that's why Daddy cultivated George so much, to be Buddy's mentor when he finished school and started a career.

As Buddy got older, he also became a walking encyclopedia, with information gleaned from relatives and lesser employees, about my father's secret life, about gangland yesterday and today. This, alas, was a knowledge that, in the eyes of my father, was a very dangerous thing. It was an unspoken commandment at the Lansky home that Daddy's underworld associations were never to be spoken of, or even suggested. Buddy didn't dare flaunt his acquired knowledge in my father's presence, but as I grew up, he became the source of endless rude awakenings and disturbing suspicions that Daddy's business and normal business were much different than they seemed to be on the surface.

While Buddy loved gossip about celebrities both high and low, Paul was always very, very serious. He denounced Mommy at the table for spending so much money on me at FAO Schwarz, which he declared was "owned by Nazis." The Schwarz family was German in origin, Daddy, with judicial restraint, pointed out, but just being a German didn't make you a Nazi. During the war years, that argument was probably a hard sell to many other New Yorkers.

Paul tried his best to be a big brother to me, taking me to *Bambi* and *Dumbo* and *Song of the South* at the Broadway movie palaces, and across the street to the Hayden Planetarium and to the Museum of Natural History to see those amazing dinosaurs. But Buddy was more fun. He educated me about pop culture—the music, the movies, the shows, the stars. While I read comic books, *Mickey Mouse, Archie, Richie Rich, Little Lulu, Wonder Woman,* he read magazines like *Photoplay*, which were full of gossip about "Daddy's employees," as Buddy called them.

We spent hours together listening to the radio, especially the music program *Make Believe Ballroom,* a great show where America's premier disk jockey, Martin Block, played the best dance music and jazz, enabling Buddy to introduce me to the wonders of Duke Ellington and Cab Calloway. Block was famous for coining the phrase "LSMFT" for his show's chief sponsor Lucky Strike cigarettes. "Lucky Strike Means Fine Tobacco." Buddy and I tried to come up with our own secret letter codes, like BLLBG, Buddy Lansky Loves Beautiful Girls. He had his dreams, if not his body. When I grew up I wanted to be one of the Beautiful Girls that Buddy loved, a living version of the beautiful dolls I collected. *Make Believe Ballroom*'s other big sponsor was a line of diet pills called Retardo. I filed that away. Retardo could make me beautiful. It would come back to haunt me.

Buddy and I were riveted to the radio soap operas like *Stella Dallas,* inspired by the Barbara Stanwyck movie, about a mother who sacrifices everything in her life for her daughter. Buddy would say things like, "Can you see Mommy doing that?" Mommy didn't have to sacrifice, because Daddy took care of everything for us. We also liked the detective series *Boston Blackie.* I wanted Buddy to become a private eye, because he seemed good at figuring out clues. But it was sad that he couldn't chase down the bad guys.

As a big shot in the jukebox business, Daddy was connected enough to get us one of the very first black and white television sets. But there wasn't very much to watch, except boxing. Buddy liked it and always wanted to bet me as to which guy would win. The names were great: Sugar Ray Robinson, Willie Pep, Jake La Motta, Manny Ortiz, Rocky Graziano, Joe Louis. I tried to show some interest. I got Mommy to buy me my own boxing ring from FAO Schwarz, where I'd have boxing matches with a punching bag on a stand that kept snapping back and knocking me down. I couldn't even beat a punching bag, so boxing got old fast. For Buddy, though, his early desire to wager turned out to be a seed of destruction. Betting would become one of his many roads to ruin.

I loved being friends with my brothers, as long as they wanted me. I had buck teeth, and they called me "Bucky" like in the Westerns.

They also reported me to Mommy when I didn't brush my teeth. I think I subconsciously wanted them to fall out. I was grateful to be noticed by my brothers, good or bad, but one day I fought back. I found a naked baby picture of Buddy in Mommy's china cabinet and displayed it in the living room when my parents were having a holiday party. After that I used to bribe Buddy for five or ten dollars to hide the nude shot before his friends came over. Eventually Buddy figured out where I was hiding it, and the picture disappeared

I loved money. I used to go into Daddy and Mommy's bedroom during the day after school. There were piles of cash everywhere. Twenties were the smallest bills. Hundreds were abundant. It was like Monopoly money, but it was real. I knew it worked because I would help myself to some of the twenties, knowing they wouldn't be missed. I wasn't stealing. Mommy gave me anything I asked for. I was just playing banker. This was my way of learning math. Then I took my American Flyer wagon and went to the newsstand on 81st Street, where I stocked up on comics. I had seen my Daddy tip the doormen, so I imitated him and gave the doorman a dollar to keep his mouth shut that I had gone out all by myself, which was supposedly a no-no. I was like a little gangster girl.

Maybe I was my father's daughter after all. But then I had no idea what my father was all about. All I knew was that I was his pet, that after dinner, he'd hold me in his arms in his paneled library, door closed, and read to me wearing his silk Sulka robe over his silk Sulka pajamas and smelling like Benson and Hedges and English lavender. For some crazy reason, he liked to read to me from Thomas Paine, the Revolutionary War writer, *Common Sense* and the *Rights of Man*. He said that Thomas Paine was his favorite writer and these were brilliant ideas, ideas that made America free.

Paine said unforgettable things like "the summer soldier and the sunshine patriot" and "these are the times that try men's souls" and "the duty of a patriot is to protect his country from its government," things that would hit close to home for Daddy years later when the government was dead set to ruin our lives. Some things kind of spoke to me, or us: "If there must be trouble, let it be in my day, that my child may have peace." But it was all very heavy stuff, hardly bedtime stories.

Obviously these were way over the head of a six-year-old, or even a twenty-six year-old. I think Daddy was reading them for himself and just taking me along for the ride. Whatever, I didn't care. The ride was enough; if I wanted to read, I had my comic books. I just loved Daddy's strong, quiet voice, which, like Mommy's, had no trace of a New York accent. I loved being in his arms. Too bad Daddy was gone most of the time, and tortured by them or not, I felt very sad and abandoned when my brothers would leave, too. Until I started school, I didn't have anyone else.

But then I began making friends, though not exactly the ones my mother assumed I would connect with in my fancy school. One day when one of the maids had taken me to play in Central Park, I met a girl my own age named Terry Healy, who was a brilliant roller skater. She lived on 82nd Street across from the back of the Beresford. I brought her home to play, and she was amazed at our apartment. When I went to her house, I understood why. She lived on the second floor of a big, twenty-unit old brownstone where her father was the superintendent. We liked to hang out with him when he was fixing the boilers and the pipes. It was like an adventure movie, and I loved it, even when we saw a big rat.

For all her aspirations to glamour and culture, Mommy was anything but snobbish about my friendship with an Irish Catholic janitor's daughter. She was delighted I had such a nice companion. She just didn't want me running around outside by myself. Maybe it was her Lindbergh kidnapping fear. Not that I paid much attention to her. I would sneak out of the apartment and cross 82nd Street by myself to go play at Terry's. The Healys took me to mass with them. I liked it almost as much as Radio City. One day a yellow cab almost hit me running across 82nd Street. It had to screech on its brakes. And who was in the cab? Mommy. She threw a fit and confined me to my room.

In 1943, Mommy decided to turn me into a fancy horsewoman. To add to all my other lessons, she began taking me for riding lessons at the Aldrich Stables between 66th and 67th Streets on Central Park West. Mommy herself had liked to ride, but she lost her passion for it after a horse threw her down in Hot Springs. She tried to brainwash me into the sport by getting me kids' horse books, like *My Friend Flicka,* and dragging me to see *National Velvet* at least three times.

The books and movies didn't inspire me, but the horses did. At first I hated the lessons as punishment, but I quickly took to riding and all the cool outfits, leather boots and hats, and saddles and riding accessories. Daddy was so proud that I could ride and had the potential to become a sportswoman that for my seventh birthday he bought me a horse. I named her Bazookie, not my misspelling of the bazooka weapons that I'd constantly heard about because of the war, but rather a tribute to an older girl neighbor named Sookie in the Beresford who was nice to me. Grandpa Citron was so amazed that I could ride, and so proud, that every week he'd send his chauffeur, Major, in his limousine to deliver a case of the freshest carrots to Bazookie, straight from one of Grandpa's produce suppliers in New Jersey. What luxury!

At the stables, which became my second home, and sometimes more like my first one, I also made another less-privileged friend, who, like Terry, would become a pal for life. This was Eileen Sheridan, whose father was a trainer at the stables. The family lived in an unfancy part of the Upper East Side, all the way over near the Third Avenue El, the elevated line that was torn down in 1955. Eileen, who was there to help her dad, was rough and ready and afraid of nothing. I wanted to be alone with Eileen, but my overprotective mother always came with me to Aldrich. I had to figure out a route to independence, and eventually I did. One day Mommy and I were riding together, and I used my riding crop to startle her horse, so it would run off in the opposite direction. After that, Mommy stopped riding with me. She would drop me off and pick me up, and I felt free for the first time in my young life. Like Terry, Eileen was also a Catholic and went to parochial school. Daddy liked both Terry and Eileen and was impressed that both were hard-working students at Catholic schools, which he held in high regard. That man had a huge thing for education. I think he was hoping, against hope, that some of it would rub off on me. Eileen's parents, like Terry's, took me to their Catholic church. However, after the priest did something to bless my throat, sprinkling holy water or crossing it with candles, I came down with a terrible case of the mumps. I stopped going to any church after that. I thought God was trying to tell me something, giving me a sign.

After our summers in Deal, we spent our winters in Miami, travelling down to Florida on trains with names like the Havana Special. Courtly black porters waited on us in the luxurious Pullman cars. I loved sleeping on the trains, although I never slept, too excited to look out the window all night as Baltimore became Washington became Richmond became Rocky Mount became Columbia and on through the swamps down to Miami, sunny and perfect, while New York was gray and cold. The one thing I didn't like about Miami was seeing two lines of people at the water fountains, with big signs "White" and "Colored." That seemed mean and wrong. It was just water. I wondered where Nig Rosen would be allowed to drink.

Otherwise I loved Miami Beach. And the Roney Plaza Hotel where we stayed. The Roney Plaza was also the winter headquarters for Walter Winchell, who broadcast from the lobby and always said hello to me in the nicest way, although I gathered he could be very nasty to everyone else. My favorite restaurant was a place called Pickin' Chicken across the street from the Roney Plaza. The place wasn't fancy, like the clubs Daddy owned, but the food was great there. Daddy might have preferred that I go to a grander, Lansky-style restaurant, but he was so grateful to see me eat that he endured sitting through our excursions there.

If Dad co-owned New Jersey, he had an even bigger stake in Florida, with a number of grand nightclubs in Broward County, just over the line from Miami's Dade County. That line was significant, because the officials of Broward were much more enlightened toward entertainment than their compatriots a little to the south. They welcomed Daddy with open arms, and probably open wallets, which was one of the costs of doing business with them. Bribery was normal when gambling was involved. Daddy's two great clubs were the Colonial Inn, which looked like Tara in *Gone with the Wind* but served fancy French-style cuisine and Hollywood-level stage shows, and the Club Boheme in the former mansion of the founder of the beach town of Hallandale. Big stars and high stakes were the attraction. Meeting Ginger Rogers was a special treat.

All the travel was great for my suntan, but it wreaked havoc on my early education. Daddy and Mommy seemed to think that a school was a school was a school. They'd take me out of Birch Wathen in December and send me to the Colonial School in Miami Beach for three months, then come back to Birch Wathen in March. Wherever I was I was always out of sync, and I couldn't make any friends, because I was the stranger everywhere. That's my excuse for not even trying to be the great student Daddy would have liked. I wasn't much at reading, writing, or arithmetic, but I enjoyed the colonial stuff, like learning to make candles and churn butter. To be fair, Daddy never pushed me about school the way he pushed the boys. That only worked with Paul, anyway.

Maybe Daddy didn't place much of a premium on a woman's education. Maybe he just expected me to get married young like Mommy and shop all the time. In his own family, his sister Esther had majored in French at Brooklyn College. Daddy had gotten her a great job at Schenley Whiskey in the Empire State Building, through the company's owner, Lewis Rosenstiel. An old friend of Daddy's from Prohibition, Mr. Rosenstiel was from a distinguished German Jewish family from Cincinnati who had been in the distilled spirits business long before the Eighteenth Amendment in 1920 made it illegal. During the dry era, Rosenstiel kept his fortune by starting Schenley as a legal, medicinal whiskey company, which made a still bigger fortune in bourbon once Prohibition was repealed.

For Daddy Rosenstiel's success surely represented the road not taken, playing by the rules, absurd as they may have seemed. For all his legitimacy, Rosenstiel was branded as a gangster simply by being in the liquor business, a label that Joe Kennedy managed to avoid by using his wealth and patronage with President Roosevelt to get appointed chairman of the Securities and Exchange Commission and ambassador to England. Then again, Kennedy had the leg up with his Harvard degree. The Lanskys would have to wait for Paul, Daddy often said. He never said anything about waiting for me.

Even if Daddy didn't think of me as being the family's future messiah, I took comfort in being his pet. When he was in New York, he'd take me everywhere with him, and not just to Dinty Moore's and to the theatre. He took me to his gym, a place called George Brown's Gymnasium and Health Club on West 57th Street, to watch him play handball and paddleball, rarely with my uncles, whom Daddy ridiculed as being lazy, but with young pros from the club. He was good, fast, strong, and very competitive, always beating the much younger and bigger pros. And no, they didn't let him win because he was Meyer Lansky. Both he and they sweated way too much for that. After school, he would also take Paul to Brown's for some sweaty father-son bonding.

After his workouts, Daddy would often go for simple food, and not the grand restaurants we'd go to at night with my uncles. We'd often go to Jewish delicatessens, so brightly lit, smelling so strongly of garlic, and so New York. Daddy was very specific about his order: a hot corned beef on seedless rye, extra fatty, with just the tiniest smear of hot mustard. Anything else and back it would go. If we went to a coffee shop counter and ordered a hamburger, it had to be medium rare on a toasted, buttered bun. One of the few times I saw him get angry was when the waiter or waitress dared to garnish his burger, even with the best of intentions. The worst mistake a coffee shop could make was to put a pickle, slices of lettuce, tomato, or onion on the plate. Daddy was a purist and he wanted things nice and simple.

He'd give the wait staff a vicious lecture that would inevitably leave them near tears and trembling. Dessert also had to be just so, either a chilled bowl of precisely half chocolate and half strawberry ice cream, or a heated plate of warm apple pie with a small wedge of cheddar cheese. Dessert mistakes didn't provoke the same rage, probably because the hamburger had taken a bit of the edge off. One thing I noticed about Daddy, who may have loved eating good food more than he loved making money, was that he'd always be talking about his next meal while he was eating the one at hand.

After lunch, we'd go to Daddy's office, which gave me my first tangible look at what he did as a businessman. Emby Distributing Company was the name elegantly stenciled on the big oak door in the office on West 43rd Street, just down the street from the headquarters of the *New York Times,* which is how Times Square got its name. Inside was a huge space with several secretaries and walls of files and a big office for Daddy. What did Emby Distributing mean, I asked him. He told me: The first letter "E" was for a partner, whose first name was Edward; the "m" was for Meyer; and the "by" was for another partner whose last name was Bye. And what did they distribute? He took me towards the back of the office and then opened a door, like a magician saying "Presto," to reveal a whole illuminated showroom full of Wurlitzer jukeboxes, just like the one Buddy had in his room in the school in Maryland.

The machines were beautiful and futuristic, something from another planet, chrome and glass and with neon tubes of all different colors. They reminded me of the pinball machines I'd seen on the boardwalk in Asbury Park, but instead of noise, they made beautiful music. Though not at Daddy's office. There they stayed silent, just on display. Bye had worked for Wurlitzer as a salesman, and now he and another former Wurlitzer representative were working for Daddy, selling or leasing these magic machines to bars and restaurants all up and down the East Coast.

Talk about cash cows. Teresa Brewer's number one song of 1950 "Music, Music, Music" would say it all: "Put another nickel in, in the nickelodeon . . . " captured the essence of what enormous money machines these jukeboxes were. And here was Daddy at the heart of it all. Daddy was the king of the party America was throwing for itself for winning the war. I found out that these jukeboxes cost over a thousand dollars apiece, and since every bar and every restaurant seemed to need to have one, the sound of music seemed to add up to the sound of money. Daddy had huge Christmas parties at Emby, and he always hired a Santa Claus to give out gifts, as well as to pour champagne. I had never seen a Santa pour champagne, but Daddy had a way to get people to do what he wanted them to.

All Daddy's businesses seemed to make lots and lots of money— the nightclubs, the dog tracks, and the casinos, which I never saw. Actually I did see one once. It was at the Riviera, where Frank Sinatra had spilled the ice, and which was primarily owned by Uncle Willie Moretti, even though they had another guy's name on the door, first Ben Marden's, then Bill Miller's. Spotlights were for the stars, the "help," Uncle Willie would joke. The owners didn't have to show off. Daddy was asked to meet someone unexpected and he didn't want to leave me alone at the table, so he took me with him. It was like a maze in an amusement park, up stairs, down stairs. Then we went into a janitor's storage closet, full of mops and light bulbs and cleaning supplies.

A big bouncer, who was sitting there, plugged in an electric fan. I had no idea why, until, like in the movies, a secret wall opened, which led down another corridor into a big bright room with chandeliers and men dealing cards in tuxedos and roulette wheels spinning. It was a real casino, my first one. Daddy met his friend, who was so wrapped up in his gambling he couldn't leave the table. I had a ginger ale and got a lot of smiles and winks from the pretty showgirls sitting with their dates. They seemed bored to death.

Aside from his outbursts at waiters or waitresses who served him his hamburger the wrong way, I never saw my father lose his temper. Nor did he and my mother ever fight. Except once. Mommy was angry with me about something and she slapped my face in front of Daddy. I'm sure she didn't mean to whack me very hard, but my ear turned all red. Daddy went crazy, jumped up and grabbed Mommy's arm. I thought he would break it. "You fool!" he raised his voice to a pitch I had never heard. "Do you want her to end up like *you*?"

Daddy stormed off to his library, maybe to read Thomas Paine and calm down. Mommy begged *my* forgiveness. She hugged me and put ice on my ear. I was easy. "Sure, I forgive you. You can even hit me again. It didn't hurt. I love you. You know I do," I comforted her. She smiled a little. I liked seeing what words could do. Mommy explained to me how her brother Julie had hit her as a child and punctured her eardrum, causing her to have surgery and all sorts of problems. Then Daddy came out, all calm himself, and we all hugged and kissed like a normal all-American family. The next day Mommy took me to the doctor, just to make sure my ear was all right. It was. She never hit me again.

I had a hard time forgetting my shock at that fight. I had an even bigger shock one day when Daddy came to pick me up at Birch Wathen instead of Mommy. "She's gone away for a rest," was all he would tell me. Rest? She was tired, he explained. Women did that all the time. No big deal. When would she come back, I pressed him. I had never been without her. "Soon," he said in a tone that told me not to continue the questioning. Back at the Beresford, our regular maids looked after me, as Daddy drove me to and from school. He also had another maid come in, just to help out.

Mommy did come back, a week later, but not the way I ever expected to see her. She showed up in the middle of the afternoon, just as Daddy had dropped me off from school. She was wearing a night-gown in the middle of the afternoon. But it wasn't one of her fancy silk gowns from Saks or Wilma's. It was gray and made of some rough fab-ric. Her normally perfect hair was all scraggly and a mess. She had on no makeup. Her eyes were all bloodshot. Some "rest" she had gotten!

"Don't make me go. Don't let them take me," she begged me. I had no idea what she meant, but I was terrified to see her like this. No sooner had she issued her plea than the door to the apartment opened. The elevator man and the doorman were there. Four men in white coats rushed in. They looked like waiters. But I knew they couldn't be waiters. Mother screamed and ran to the master room and locked herself in. Soon Daddy arrived. He pounded on the door. She refused to come out. Daddy ordered me to go to my room. "What's wrong with Mommy?" I begged him to tell me.

"She's sick," he said. "I'm here now. She'll be fine."

Ha! I thought. I went to my room and heard the terrible banging noise of the men breaking down Mommy's doors. "Don't let her jump," I heard Daddy instructing them. "She could jump."

Oh, no, I despaired. I wanted to go out and plead with Mommy not to kill herself, to tell her I loved her, and that whatever bad things I had done to make her feel this way, I would never, ever do again, whatever, making her horse run away, not studying, playing with Terry, anything. As afraid as I was *for* Mommy, I was just as afraid *of* Daddy, of disobeying him. Finally, I couldn't stand it any longer. I ran out into the hall, just as the men in white coats smashed open the great French double doors to her room.

When I saw Mommy, I was somehow vastly relieved. She hadn't jumped. But I've never seen anyone so haunted, so tormented. She just looked at me, almost as if I had betrayed her. "You . . . you?" Was she accusing me? I don't know. She just went limp, and then the men put her in her own white coat, one with lots of straps that made her their prisoner. It was a straitjacket. I hated it. Then they took her away.

I couldn't stand the pitying looks the doorman and elevator man gave me. I guess they felt sorry for me. They had always been so nice. The whole place, the Beresford, had always seemed so perfect. I'm sure they weren't used to this. I felt like a trespasser, a part of a crazy family that didn't belong in this royal residence.

I truly thought I would never see my mother again. But once the men in the white coats left, Daddy appeared and did his best to comfort me. "She's going to be okay, darling."

"Liar!" was what I thought, but couldn't bring myself to say the word.

Daddy couldn't read my mind, but he gave me that dark look anyhow. But then he hugged me. He kissed my forehead. He wiped away my tears. "I'm sorry," he said, and then, big businessman that he was, he made his forecast. "Your mother will be home in a few weeks. She'll be fine. We all get a little crazy sometime. I'm taking care of it."

I don't know why, but I believed him. And Meyer Lansky was as good as his word. In about four weeks, I came home from Birch Wathen, and there was Mommy, not in a straitjacket, but looking as good as new, rested, fresh, in her Wilma finery. She took me in her arms and gave me a huge kiss on the lips, something she had never done. She gave me a sailor doll that she had actually made for me. They must have had an arts and crafts workshop at Mommy's "spa." Her craftsmanship was amazing. I had no idea she could do that. But there were no explanations, no apologies. It was as if the nightmare had never happened. It was don't ask, don't tell. I wanted to will away the whole episode, the worst nightmare I ever had. And so I did. And nothing happened again. It was the Lanskys as usual, Daddy mostly gone, Mommy mostly shopping, me mostly riding. That was as good as I could hope for, and good enough for me. About a year later, however, Mommy hit me with another big one: Daddy had moved out. He was gone. She had asked him for a divorce.

CHAPTER FOUR

HOMELAND INSECURITY

Three remarkable things happened to me between 1946 and 1947, though I'm not sure any of them were related. But they could have been. First of all, I saw my father's penis. Seeing your father's penis at age nine isn't particularly remarkable in itself, but given how private my father was, my accidentally stumbling into the master bathroom while he was getting out of the shower was a pretty big shock for both of us. Our life at the Beresford was pretty buttoned up, and anything but a nudist colony. I'm not sure I ever saw Mommy naked either. But what was remarkable was the enormous size of Daddy's penis. You couldn't help but stare at it. It was the first thing you'd notice, like the trunk of an elephant.

I had seen my brothers' penises before, when we shared a room together, and off and on. These were nothing out of the ordinary. Boy stuff. But Daddy! Talk about separating the men from the boys. This was something that belonged across the street in the Museum of Natural History. This was the most embarrassed I'd ever been, way worse than falling off my new horse Time Clock when showing off for Paul. I turned bright red, was stunned speechless, and then ran out of the bathroom. Like most controversial things at the Lanskys,

Daddy never brought it up, nor did I. However, the image stayed in my mind forever.

The second remarkable event of my ninth year was getting my period. I was about nine and a half, and from what I later learned from my girlfriends, this was happening about three years early. Of course no one had ever told me about the facts of life, the birds and the bees. Talking about sex at our house would have been like talking about crime. Both were unmentionable. There was no warning for me. I was a little horse-riding tomboy. I didn't have breasts; I didn't have anything. I didn't have a clue. I thought I was bleeding to death, so I showed Mommy, thinking she would take me to the hospital. Instead, she flashed the biggest smile I had ever seen, and gave me a huge hug and kiss, as if I had won a riding competition, or gotten a great report card.

She soon told Daddy, who gave me a pat on the backside, I'm sure to feel the sanitary napkin Mommy had gotten for me. That was almost as embarrassing as seeing him naked. But he, too—dead serious Meyer Lansky—lit up with a huge smile. Still, nobody told me what it meant, other than "it's part of growing up." Mommy told me it hadn't happened to her until she was sixteen. I guess that was supposed to mean I was a precocious, gifted child, or something like that. Instead, I just felt weird and confused. So I had to turn to Terry and Eileen, who clued me in. I never told them about the penis-sighting episode, but I couldn't help but wonder if that accidental encounter with Daddy's great white whale was so traumatic that it accelerated my adolescence.

Finally, the third remarkable thing of the 1946–1947 period was Daddy's sudden disappearance from the Beresford, like a thief in the night. In one day, we went from happy family to nonfamily, just as suddenly as seeing my naked father or getting my period, out of nowhere. As it turned out, my parents has been planning the divorce for a long time—a year or so—but in the most cordial way, they kept it from me and my brothers. Like everything else Daddy did, the divorce was a deal, a negotiation. Just business. Yet for me, it wasn't business as usual, and it shook my ordered little world.

The divorce business had its origins on the long-distance telephone line to Beverly Hills. Even though Mommy and Aunt Esther Siegel were separated by a whole continent, they seemed to lead copycat lives. They were like the Bobbsey Twins of the aristocracy of what would soon be referred to as "organized crime." Mommy and Esther both lived in splendor and raised their children like pampered little lords and ladies. On the other hand, they were equally miserable in exactly the same way, singing the same blues over their absentee husbands.

If Mommy went away for a "rest," as Daddy had called it, you could be sure Esther had gone to at an equally posh sanitarium, Esther's Malibu to Mommy's Riverdale. And if Mommy had electroshock therapy, which Buddy claimed she had, you could bet that Esther had it, too. Although electroshock sounds like some kind of terrible treatment, in those days it was cutting edge—technology, not torture. Daddy never complained about Mommy's huge bills at Wilma's and Saks, but I did hear him complaining about her huge long-distance bills. She was on the phone to California day and night with Aunt Esther, bemoaning their mutual mistreatment by their husbands. The American gambling empire that Daddy and Uncle Benny were creating in the mid-1940s was probably the world's most jealous mistress.

Uncle Benny, who was always considered one of the world's great ladies' men, had also acquired a flesh-and-blood mistress who was giving him even more aggravation than the new wagering mecca of Las Vegas that he and Daddy were laboring to turn into a desert version of Monte Carlo. The challenge was just as absurd as it sounds, trying to turn sand into gold. They pulled it off, although at a horrible cost to both of them; Daddy, his family, Benny, his life.

One thing Daddy did not seem to have was a weakness for women. In all our nights out on the town, whether in New York or

New Jersey or Florida, I never once saw Daddy's eyes lingering on the hat-check girl at Dinty Moore's or a showgirl at the Riviera or the Colonial Inn. Broads were for suckers, was how Damon Runyon might have put it, and Daddy was the last guy on earth to be hoodwinked by a doll. However, given what I had seen of Daddy's huge "asset," there may have been more romance and intrigue to Daddy's life than met the eye. Daddy was the master of never showing emotion or weakness. God knows how many showgirls there might have been.

On the surface, Uncle Benny was just the opposite of Daddy, a true romantic. My brother Buddy, who was the ultimate Hollywood fan, loved to read the movie magazines and recount Benny's exploits with likes of Jean Harlow, Mae West, and Wendy Barrie, the elegant British actress who got her stage name from her godfather, the author of *Peter Pan*. Uncle Benny was Buddy's hero. Uncle Benny's mistress, or at least his chief mistress, was named Virginia Hill. She had also been the mistress of Uncle Joe Adonis, just as Jean Harlow had also been the mistress of Uncle Abe Zwillman. It was all very incestuous; the family that played together, stayed together. My brother Buddy had met Virginia Hill with either Benny or Joe, or maybe both, at Dinty Moore's. I guess there was no such thing as too close for comfort.

Buddy always went on and on about how beautiful Virginia Hill was and how she had kissed him on the lips. What a teenage fantasy that was. He was maybe fourteen at the time, in 1945, and had just moved back with us at the Beresford. He showed me his red lips, and he didn't want to wash the lipstick off for days. I was reminded of the fairy tale where the princess kisses the frog and turns him into a prince. Poor Buddy just wanted to be loved. I guess we all did.

Virginia Hill had kissed a lot of frogs. She was a voluptuous, brassy redhead who had escaped Georgia poverty to become a waitress in Chicago. There she had become the pet of the Al Capone mob, ferrying money and jewels around the country for them, hidden in the linings of expensive mink coats they had bought her. She was a real gun moll, a cool character, and a Hollywood character, and Buddy told me how she had gone west to be in movies. There, through Uncle George Raft, who had become the "family star," she connected with other stars like Errol Flynn and, most dramatically, with Uncle Benny, much to Aunt Esther's deep dismay. His nickname for her was "Flamingo," the name he would give to the new resort in Las Vegas that he would build and Daddy would finance, when Benny's money ran out.

Sometime in 1946, Esther decided she couldn't take it anymore. She got a lawyer and demanded a divorce. She got what she wanted and moved her daughters back east to their Scarsdale estate. At exactly the same time, Mommy did exactly the same thing, though I had no idea until the divorce was final in 1947 and Daddy moved out, virtually overnight, that things had changed between them. I still can't understand why Mommy asked for the divorce, other than to copycat Esther Siegel. Maybe it was a ploy to get Daddy to stay home more. There certainly weren't other men in Mommy's life, nor would there ever be.

That divorce had been the greatest trauma of my life so far, and it was impossible, as usual, to get Daddy, or Mommy, to explain what had happened. Only Buddy would provide some clues. Mommy had apparently been going to psychiatrists several times a week after that terrible trip to the sanitarium. The doctors, Buddy said, had told her a divorce was a good idea, and Daddy was simply giving Mommy what she asked for, as he always did.

When they went to court to get their divorce, it was more like a business closing than a war. In those days, people couldn't just get a divorce because they wanted to. They had to show cause. So Daddy got Uncle Jack and Mommy got Aunt Sadie as their witnesses, all very amicable, and they went as a group before the family judge and said how they simply couldn't get along and how they made each other unhappy. And the judge said fine, if you're unhappy, I'm happy. Divorce granted. Bang went the gavel.

Buddy had sneaked a peek at some of the divorce papers, which Mommy had left lying around. They said that Daddy didn't like the rigid order of meals and everything else Mommy had planned to the split second, like a cruise director, or a drill sergeant. Why did it have to be liver and bacon only on Thursday? Why couldn't we have it Wednesday, too? I hated it any day, but Daddy liked it. I couldn't believe that they'd split the family up over liver and bacon. The problems obviously were a lot deeper than that.

Until Daddy left, everything had seemed fine, now that Mommy was home again after that awful incident with the men in the white coats. Mommy was back. Paul was back, after years at the military school, enrolled in high school at Horace Mann, the very exclusive boy's prep school up in Riverdale, where everyone went on to some great college, be it Harvard, Columbia, or West Point. By 1945, the war was over, and somehow the great American victory had not only liberated Europe from Hitler, but had also liberated Paul from the New York Military Academy.

One of Daddy's proudest possessions was a memorial book commemorating the Japanese surrender on the battleship *Missouri,* personally autographed by General MacArthur and Admiral Nimitz, as well as by other dignitaries. It was a gift to Daddy from the U.S. Navy for his secret wartime service in purging the waterfront of Axis saboteurs. Daddy treasured that book, and, even if Paul had decided that he now wanted to be a corporation president instead of a general, Daddy would have still pushed him to West Point. The Lanskys, in Daddy's mind, had a duty to our country, and he wanted Paul to pay our family's huge debt to America. Still, I'm pretty sure that Paul was also so caught up in our winning the war that West Point would have been his choice under any circumstances.

Buddy was back, too, freed from his handicapped boarding school in Maryland. Now he went to a tutoring day school on the Upper East Side, but Daddy had pretty much given up on Buddy as a student. The important thing was that Buddy get well, that he learn to stand on his own two feet. Quite literally. To that goal, Daddy put him in a therapy program at Bellevue Hospital, with another famous doctor named Howard Rusk.

Daddy had met Dr. Rusk through his good friend, the singer Jane Froman, who had often been a headliner in Daddy's nightclubs around the country. Jane had come to New York from a small town in Missouri and become the lead singer in the Ziegfeld Follies. Her trademark song was "Blue Moon." During the war, while on tour in Europe entertaining the troops, her plane crashed in Portugal. She barely survived; everyone thought she would be crippled for life. Daddy had taken me to visit her in the hospital in New York. Aside from the crash injuries, she had giant shark bites on both her legs. Despite her pain, she was always cheerful and kissed me and smiled when we came to see her. She seemed to adore Daddy.

Dr. Rusk, a fellow Missourian, saved Jane's life, and made her walk again, with crutches, like Buddy. She rallied and went back to Europe and serenaded the troops on those crutches. With the war over, she was ready to get back out there and serenade Daddy's customers. Jane naturally took a deep interest in Buddy and introduced Daddy to Dr. Rusk, who became our newest medical messiah. Buddy had a much bigger crush on "bad girl" Virginia Hill than "good girl" Jane Froman, but that was a different story.

Howard Rusk was a no-nonsense, aw-shucks Midwesterner, sort of like Harry Truman, who had developed a renowned rehabilitation program for severely injured airman in World War II. But this master of rehab, known as "Doctor Live Again," was aided by a team of equally crack physicians, all affiliated with New York University. If anybody could make Buddy walk on his own, this was the place, on the cutting edge. How I prayed that Buddy could one day throw away his "Canadian crutches," which wrapped around his frail forearms, and walk like a man.

A few times, I rode down to Bellevue with Daddy to take Buddy to therapy. In the city, we now usually took cabs rather than the Oldsmobile, because the traffic and parking had gotten so difficult, with everybody buying cars after the war. One day I overheard one of the doctors talking to another. "What's the point of all this?" the doctor groused. "The kid won't *live* that long." My heart totally sank. I wanted my brother to *walk*. I didn't want him to *die*. Doctor Live Again? What a lie. I wanted to tell Daddy about how cruel these doctors were. They were taking his money for a hopeless case. Again, I didn't dare. But it made me treasure every second with Buddy, whose amazing bravery I learned to appreciate the older I got.

Almost in anticipation of the divorce Daddy and Mommy were planning but keeping a secret from me, Daddy found me a permanent nanny to serve as a mother substitute. In the back of his mind, he must have worried that Mommy might have another nervous breakdown. What made Daddy such a brilliant businessman was that he thought like a lawyer, anticipating everything that might go wrong, no matter how long the odds. His was a worst-case scenario mentality.

My new nanny's name was Nancy Attina. I think Daddy thought of her as potential family as well, the idea being that she would have been a great wife for Buddy. We had met her in the winter of 1945 on our three months' stay in Florida. That season, instead of the Roney Plaza, we stayed a short ways up Miami Beach at the equally exclusive and right-on-the-sand Spanish colonial Wofford Hotel. It was Uncle Augie's headquarters and Nancy worked there as a waitress.

She was a very pretty, wholesome Italian girl in her early twenties from Bayshore, Long Island. The men were crazy about her, and she was always going out on dates, often to Daddy's Colonial Inn, which was the hot ticket in Miami, having just opened that season. Her dream was to go out with Frank Sinatra, a dream Daddy could have made come true if he didn't subconsciously think she'd make a great wife for Buddy.

"Little Augie" Carfano used to "own" Brooklyn and now, with my father's guidance, he was in the process of "owning" Miami. The western half of Florida was owned by Uncle Santo Trafficante in Tampa, who was always sending Daddy handmade cigars that Daddy refused to smoke because they smelled so strong. Instead he saved the cigars as collectors' items and gave them to his friends on special occasions, like births, weddings, and casino openings. Uncle Augie, who smoked Uncle Santo's pungent stogies with macho and gusto, dressed nearly as well as Uncle Benny Siegel. He was very proud of the huge scar down the whole side of his face and considered himself just as handsome as his best friend, Uncle Joe Adonis. Buddy told me he had gotten the scar in some gangland battle, but Uncle Augie, who had a great sense of humor, liked to call it a "dueling scar" incurred in a fight for the favors of an Italian countess. Suffice it to say, Uncle Augie had an eye for women and had married a series of showgirls.

One girl Daddy insisted Augie keep his hands off of was Nancy, saving this bobby-soxer for Buddy. He had hired her, I assume, at a very generous salary. I thought of her more as a big sister than a caregiver. During that winter, Nancy would drive me to my favorite restaurants, Pickin' Chicken, where we would eat outside, and the Lighthouse, a seafood palace you got to by crossing a rickety wooden causeway that was on the verge of collapse and always made the trip there an adventure. I didn't like fish, but I loved that bridge and the giant turtles that lived in a pond that was part of the restaurant.

During the day, Daddy would play cards with assorted friends or play golf with Jimmy Alo and other old buddies. But mostly he worked, up all night at the Colonial Inn. Mommy never went with him. I'm not sure what she did. She shopped a lot and slept a lot. Her best friend there was Flo Alo, Uncle Jimmy's Irish wife. The Alos had moved to Florida to a big house in Hollywood right on the water. Uncle Jimmy said New York was finished, overcrowded, falling apart, a decade before its urban problems became obvious; Miami to him was the shining future.

Mommy hated Uncle Jimmy for his endless womanizing, a continual slap in Flo's face. Flo and Jimmy didn't have children, so the marriage lacked that focus, though she did have two of her own with a previous husband. Flo never felt secure with Jimmy, no matter how many jewels and antiques and dresses she bought. But somehow they stayed together, thick or thin. Though Daddy didn't insult Mommy with open affairs like Uncle Jimmy did with Flo, Mommy felt her pain. She even threw a drink in Uncle Jimmy's face once, Buddy told me, and the two never spoke again. Flo was loyal to Mommy, and they kept their friendship, while Daddy and Jimmy kept theirs, separate but equal.

When Nancy came back to New York with us, Mommy seemed much more relieved than jealous. The divorce was already in the planning stage, and the jealousy days, if they ever existed, were behind her. The only thing that bothered my mother was when Daddy began buying expensive jewelry for Nancy. That didn't stop him, though Nancy swore me to secrecy. In New York, Daddy moved an extra bed into my bedroom and Nancy slept there. It was like having a big sister. I loved it. Nancy really opened up the city to me, driving me everywhere in her brother's roadster. I claimed the rumble seat in the back as my own. She'd take me to Bayshore to stay with her old-fashioned Italian family for weekends. I'd sleep in her bed with her, and go with the Attinas to the wrestling matches to see Gorgeous George. I had no idea the whole thing was staged. The spectacle was the thing.

The Attinas would eat pizza and spaghetti and meatballs and exotic Italian delicacies like the fried scungilli, which Mommy would probably have had quarantined if she had seen them. And somehow, around all this food, I developed an appetite. I couldn't help thinking that this simple family in this simple home was infinitely happier than my rich one back at the Beresford, just like Terry's family was happier and Eileen was happier. Everyone was happier. What good was being rich? I often prayed Nancy would fall in love with Buddy. Alas, it was not to be. She was saving herself for Frank Sinatra.

Nancy lived with us for a year and a half, until the divorce. Then Mommy let her go, to my great sadness. I think she thought Nancy was Daddy's spy. She certainly was Daddy's hire. If Daddy had to go, so did Nancy. We stayed friends, and I was greatly honored years later when she named her first child after me. But Mommy decided that she couldn't delegate my upbringing to a young stranger, however kind. Whatever her depression problems, she was my mother, and she was going to rise to the occasion. After the divorce, in early 1947 (I believe it was on Valentine's Day, of all times), Mommy, Buddy, Paul, and I had the huge Beresford apartment all to ourselves, with the two live-in black maids that Mommy had hired.

That same year, Mommy had decided to take me out of Birch Wathen and try public school. P.S. 87 was just a few blocks from the Beresford, but every morning Mommy would take me there in a cab. She would pick me up for lunch in a cab, take me back in a cab, then pick me up at school day's end in a cab. We were making the Yellow Cab Company rich. The public school was very crowded, and I didn't get much attention, not that I wanted any.

One day I ran away from school to play hooky and go swimming at Coney Island with my friend Terry. I had asked Mommy if I could go and she had said no. So I vowed to teach her a lesson. I took the subway to meet Terry all by myself. I felt like a big African explorer. It was wonderful. Mommy freaked out when she came to school to pick me up and I wasn't there. I doubt she called the police, because Daddy didn't believe in *ever* calling the police, because it would always back-fire and hurt him in some way. So she probably just went crazy for a few hours until I came home. She gave me a lecture on the dangers of the city and what foolish risks I had taken, then confined me to my room for two days. I still loved what I had done.

The next year, Mommy gave up the public school experiment and put me back in private school, briefly at the nearby Riverside School, and then at the more exclusive Calhoun. Mommy liked Calhoun, a fancy girls' school on West 74th Street that catered to fancy Jewish girls, like myself, although I still wasn't fully aware of my heritage. The art collector Peggy Guggenheim had been a Calhoun girl, as had lots of Strausses, Gimbels, and Morgenthaus, all rich German Jewish banking and mercantile dynasties. It was an old money, old Europe, Citron kind of place. Lansky, not.

To me Calhoun was just another school. Public, private, it didn't really matter. Despite my father's wish that I could be an academic star like Paul, academic stardom wasn't in the cards for me. The only place I was happy was at the Aldrich Stables, my home away from home. Eventually Mommy gave up on the ballet and other lessons, and let me devote myself to riding. Even though I had technically hit puberty, I had no thoughts, and no idea, about boys. I was a little nature girl, and Central Park was my domain. I got to know so many of the park's denizens. My favorites were a pair of squirrels whom I named Oscar and Oscarette.

The only man in my life was my riding instructor John, who dressed like an English country squire. When we rode through the park, I thought we were in some Camelot time warp. I did meet another boy at the stables who would become my first husband eight years later, but you would have never guessed it at the time. This teenager, who was Buddy's age, had the nerve to steal my horse. Not steal, precisely, but he did take Bazookie out on his own without getting my permission.

His name was Marvin Rapoport. He was tall and fair-haired and snazzily dressed. I hated him. He seemed like a spoiled rich entitled brat, a real Jewish prince. Imagine how upset I was when I got to Aldrich and found Bazookie gone. Mommy was with me that day, looking very regal in her jodhpurs, leather boots, and black riding coat. You would never have guessed she had a care in the world. But she threw a fit at Marvin and gave him a tongue lashing. Marvin smiled and tried to charm Mommy out of her rage, profusely apologizing to her and to me and offering to take me riding, anything I wanted. Mommy said Marvin's family was in the restaurant business, so he knew how to soothe the feelings of angry customers. She saw him as insincere, a flatterer, something of a con artist, and I think she scared him to death. Suffice it to say he never touched Bazookie again, and I didn't notice him for years, until he decided to reappear as my Prince Charming. As it would turn out, my mother was a good judge of character.

Although Daddy vanished from the Beresford, he didn't by any means vanish from the lives of his children, only the life of his now ex-wife. At first he moved in with Uncle George Wood, the famous William Morris agent, at George's apartment at 40 Central Park South. George was one of the ultimate playboys in New York, with unequalled access to the top models and ambitious actresses. He was also one of the city's sharpest dressers. The only thing wrong with him was his filthy mouth, which would have gotten an X rating or a "condemned" by the Legion of Decency.

If fame was an aphrodisiac, George Wood was a one-man Spanish fly dispensary. His legend was that he could make any girl a star. By milking that legend, Uncle George could "make" any girl, and his conquests were legion. His apartment, with its dramatic views of the park and the twinkling lights of Fifth Avenue and Central Park West, had to have been one of Manhattan's top bachelor pads. What in the world was my straitlaced, all-business Daddy doing there? Flashing on what I had seen that time in his bathroom, maybe I didn't want to know.

Daddy would often come get me at the Beresford and take me out on the town, just like old times. Except now he would usually wait for me in a cab or in the Oldsmobile downstairs and drop me off with the doorman on the way home. If he and Mommy talked, it was usually over the phone, if he could ever get past the busy signal caused by her endless chats with Aunt Esther and Aunt Flo. Daddy had his own friends, and now that he was single again, he spent more time with the bachelor types like George Wood and other great characters like Champ Segal and Swifty Morgan.

Champ, who was from a well-to-do Jewish family, had shocked his parents by becoming a boxer and then a major fight promoter. He was the right hand of boxing czar Frankie Carbo in a group of powerful promoters who were believed to have fixed most of the fights we watched on television. Champ, as you might have expected, was a superb athlete, and Daddy, very scrappy for a man in his forties, loved to compete with him in handball games at George Brown's gym.

Swifty Morgan's only exercise was running his colorful mouth. Swifty, who looked just like Colonel Sanders, string tie and all, was the inspiration for Damon Runyon's "Lemon Drop Kid," the loveable racetrack tout later played by Bob Hope in the movie. Swifty was the best friend of comedian Joe E. Lewis, who had been mentor to Frank Sinatra and Dean Martin, so Swifty was their best friend as well. His friendship knew no bounds. Swifty used to cruise from one nightclub to another—whether in New York, Miami, Las Vegas, he was everywhere—selling hot jewels to rich men for their expensively kept women. Always in money trouble, he loved telling the story of how, in one moment of deep distress, he had telegrammed Frank Sinatra asking his pal to bail him out. With his own wicked sense of humor, Frank sent Swifty a parachute.

Eventually, life at Uncle George's must have gotten too hectic. Daddy got his own place in a fancy doorman building in Murray Hill at 36 East 36th Street, right across the street from the august J. P. Morgan Library. He hired as his interior decorator Dorothy Hammerstein, the wife of composer Oscar Hammerstein, who had done *Carousel* and all the other shows I loved. No wonder Daddy got such great seats. Dorothy Hammerstein, who was from Australia and had a funny accent, had been an actress and was very theatrical. She was one of the first bi-coastal decorators, doing homes of the stars in both Los Angeles and New York. But what she did for Daddy seemed more appropriate for the Morgan Library, more for admiring than living in. I was always terrified I would rip some silk slipcover or break a priceless vase. I was confused by Daddy's hiring such a fancy decorator. At first I assumed that he must have missed the splendor of the Beresford; splendor was Mommy's thing, not his. Daddy was a no-frills, no-nonsense guy. But this place had a woman's touch. Little did I suspect there was indeed another woman involved. That mystery, however, took a while to solve, particularly with my inscrutable father.

There were certainly lots of women around. Next door to Daddy was an apartment that housed each year's Miss Rheingold, the winner of a beauty contest sponsored by the Rheingold Brewery. That was the New York equivalent of Miss World, and there were more gorgeous creatures coming in and out of that unit than George Wood's apartment. Again, Daddy never seemed to notice them, but that may have been for my benefit.

Another famous neighbor and friend to Daddy was Arthur Godfrey, the ukulele-playing redheaded radio superstar and host of the television show *Talent Scouts*. I got the biggest kick out of Godfrey's number one single, "The Too Fat Polka." I would sing the verse, "You can have her, I don't want her, she's too fat for me." Godfrey once sang it to me and gave me an autographed record. He was a pilot who flew the big Constellation planes and helped popularize air travel. And he was a horse fanatic and would always talk to me about my riding. Daddy, who was also good friends with that other impresario Ed Sullivan, was totally in the loop.

Once it became clear that Buddy was not going to be heading for college, Daddy arranged for him to get a job. Because Buddy seemed to love show business, that was the business Daddy put him in. He started on the ground floor, answering the phones at the Hollywood Ticket Agency, right across the street from Dinty Moore's. The connection, as usual, was George Wood, whose sister Annie was married to George Haden, who owned the agency.

The agency was in the lobby of Edison Hotel, which was filled with ladies of the evening, and the afternoon, but Daddy took Buddy to Saks Fifth Avenue and dressed him up in a wardrobe worthy of a Wall Street tycoon. The agency was actually a fancy front for book-making and where Buddy got his first exposure to gambling. That bite of a poison apple would lead to Buddy's addiction to a pastime that Daddy regarded as harmless entertainment. When his own son got hooked, Daddy, the Lord of Gambling, was as helpless as Buddy to stop the damage.

My brothers were home, but not home. With Buddy selling tick-ets and Paul up at Horace Mann or locked in his room studying night and day, and without Nancy to keep me company, I depended on my best friends Terry and Eileen. But they were each in different paro-chial schools, so I couldn't see them as much as I would have liked and needed. Mommy was spending a lot of her time at psychiatrists. Though she was certainly attractive and eligible, Mommy was nearing forty, and being in your forties in the forties was like being in your sixties, or more, today. There wasn't a lot of dating among the "desper-ate ex-housewives" of Central Park West. Besides, despite her divorce, Mommy was still, in her mind, married to the great Meyer Lansky. She couldn't imagine a life with any other man.

The biggest shock after Daddy's departure was the brutal murder of Uncle Benny in Beverly Hills in June 1947. He was shot to death in an unsolved rubout at the home of his moll Virginia Hill, while she was away in Europe. My "cousins," Benny's daughters Barbara and Millicent, had just left Scarsdale to spend the summer with their fa-ther. They were on the Super Chief when the train came to an unex-pected stop in the desert a hundred miles from Las Vegas. Several of Benny's friends were in a big black limousine to pick them up and break the terrible news and to avoid the reporters descending on them at the Las Vegas depot.

I was away at camp for the first time that summer, so Mommy didn't tell me until later, just as she had spared me the news that her own father had died that year on Daddy's birthday, July 4. When she finally did tell me, at the end of the summer, it was just that Uncle Benny had passed away, just like Grandpa Citron. No mention of bullets, not for my tender ears. Daddy was even more vague, and Buddy, who loved to tell hair-raising stories, kept the ones about Benny to himself, maybe on Daddy's orders. Some of those stories, I learned much later, suggested that Daddy had had advance knowledge of the planned mob hit on Uncle Benny for going grossly over budget on the Flamingo. It was supposedly "just business," and the idea was that Daddy, the ultimate businessman, had his eye on the bottom line and harbored no sentimentality about his deepest friendship. I never believed that. Benny was pretty much Daddy's brother.

I'm not sure how sad Mommy, or even Aunt Esther, were at Uncle Benny's death, but they must have been concerned about the terrible violence of his being riddled with bullets in Hill's living room affecting Barbara and Millicent. The girls had surely seen the grotesque photos, with Benny's eye blown out of its socket, on the front pages of every paper in the land. When I got older, Buddy went into full-disclosure mode and told me the gory details of the rubout. He also said both Mommy and Esther had the "he got what he deserved" attitude, for all the pain Uncle Benny's Hollywood romances caused his wife. There was something to that.

In the early fifties, Millicent Siegel married Jackie Rosen, whose father, Morris Rosen, worked for the syndicate of gangland financiers that supposedly ordered the hit on Uncle Benny for his wasteful extravagances with their money, mostly in the name of his obsession with Virginia Hill. This syndicate suspected that Virginia Hill had gone to Europe to hide money stolen from them and they feared that Uncle Benny was going to skip the country and join her. The termination orders had come from the very top, which meant Uncle Charlie Luciano, then in exile in Italy, was still pulling the strings—and the triggers.

As a token of remembrance to Uncle Benny, and perhaps of remorse over being unable to stop Luciano's edict, Daddy gave Millicent and Jackie their gala wedding party at the Waldorf-Astoria. That Daddy could have endorsed the union of Benny's daughter to the son of someone connected with his assassination raised endless troublesome questions. The day Uncle Benny was killed, Morris Rosen and two other syndicate-appointed overseers seized control of the Flamingo and turned it into a huge success.

Jackie Rosen, like Paul, was a graduate of New York Military Academy, though he didn't make it to West Pont, just Las Vegas. We were all one big family. The idea that one of the family could kill another, or countenance the killing of another, would have blown my mind, so I was happy to be young, innocent, and sheltered from reality. Thinking of it now just haunts me. How could Millicent marry into the family that so bloodily replaced her father, unless she hated her father, way beyond hatred? How would Paul have felt if Daddy had run off with Virginia Hill? The odd thing was that Buddy would have loved it.

My own father was unable to save his best friend, a man who was more a brother to him than his real brother. Daddy couldn't help but have guilty feelings, being the man who arranged the financing to bail out the Flamingo, getting in business with Morris Rosen and ending up making a fortune on the ashes of Uncle Benny's lost dream. Plus Daddy gave that wedding bash for Millicent and Jackie. How could Daddy have forsaken the man he loved above all others? I'll never know, because nobody ever kept his feelings more to himself than Meyer Lansky.

Without Daddy to care for, Mommy devoted herself to me, more than ever. She got me braces for my buck teeth, but she kept cancelling appointments when the orthodontist planned to extract a tooth. Mommy couldn't bear the thought of my losing a good tooth, so her delays pushed back getting the braces for months. Meanwhile my brothers continued to tease me. I was ready for the dentist to pull all the teeth if he wanted to.

Mommy and I seemed to be spending all our time at doctors' offices, either for her mind or my body. I had awful sinus problems. Whenever I had sinus headaches, which was often, she'd put sandbags on my bed to keep the mattress from making any movements that would cause me pain. In the process, I developed a big crush, my very first, on the sandbag-prescriber, Dr. Max Eagle, a general practitioner whose offices were downstairs in the Beresford. I liked his moustache for some reason, and what really drew me to him was the fact that his shots never hurt. I thought he was Jesus.

Now that my parents had broken up, going to Deal, New Jersey, for family summers was a thing of the past. Mommy now sent me away to camp. For two years I went to a place called Highland Nature Camp, up in Naples, Maine. I hated it because of the mosquitoes and because I seemed to be allergic to everything. My poor sinuses. And I was too timid to ask the camp for sandbags. I refused to see the camp doctor and began writing letters, love letters I guess, to Dr. Eagle, asking him to miraculously cure me by mail. He never replied. Instead, he gave all my letters to Daddy, who drove up to Maine with Nig Rosen's brother Dan to bring me home. I felt betrayed.

On the way home we stopped in Boston to have dinner with our old Filipino houseboy Tommy, who was working in a Chinese restaurant. On the road, we almost got killed when Dan ran a blinking red railroad crossing light and we came inches from being crushed by a speeding train. When we got out of the car to catch our breath, Daddy, who was fuming, noticed that Dan's socks didn't match. He gave him a quick color quiz and found out that poor Dan was color blind. That blinking red light had looked green to him. Daddy turned volcano red and cursed Dan out, using even more expletives than George Wood, words I never heard Daddy use before, or again. "You shit-eating idiot! You goddamned fool! You almost killed my daughter!" These weren't businessman words; these were gangster words. Daddy was tougher than I ever thought. I'd never seen Daddy lose his temper like that; it was much worse than if a coffee shop garnished his hamburger with lettuce and tomato. The next summer Daddy paid for my friend Terry to go to Highland Nature with me. I enjoyed it a lot more that time. Misery loved company.

A measure of how close Daddy held his cards to his chest came in June 1949, just before I left for a new summer camp, this one in the Hudson Valley, much closer to home. There, splashed on the front page of the mass-circulation *New York Sun,* was a big photo of my father under the banner headline "Lansky Sails in Luxury for Italy." The article was about my father's departure on the ocean liner *Italia* for a European trip. But the big news wasn't that my father was on the front page described as the "underworld big shot" or the speculation that he was going to Europe to confer with his big business partner Uncle Charlie Luciano, now living in Rome. No. The big, big news was that he had "sailed with his wife."

Wife? What wife? Mommy was at home in the Beresford, getting me ready for camp. This was no Mommy. This was, as the *Sun* described, "a slender, attractive brunette, whom he married last winter." The paper described how Daddy and this new mystery wife "departed in an atmosphere of champagne and orchids, in the manner befitting Lansky's reputation as a powerful and wealthy underworld figure. The Regal Suite, which they occupied, is the most luxurious that the *Italia* affords . . . Lansky's passage for himself and his wife cost him a cool $2600, one way."

Luckily, I didn't find out for quite a while, not until I came home from camp in the fall, and I never saw the paper until many years later. Thank God for that; ignorance was bliss. Those were the pre-Internet days of "yesterday's papers," when one day's headlines became the next day's wrapping paper, when most news, good or bad, was quickly forgotten. Besides, at age eleven, I wasn't a newspaper reader. I was a comic book girl.

Daddy never told me about his trip. I guess he figured I would be away at camp. I didn't care about his trips. He was always away. But what was horrible to me was that he didn't tell me about his *wife*. The amazing thing was that Mommy was spared the news by Buddy, who took cabs all over the city buying up all the copies of the *Sun* at just about every newsstand from Times Square to 96th Street, to keep this awful truth away from Mommy and from me. Buddy loved Mommy, and he knew how weak she was. It took one to know one. Buddy sensed that the news would devastate Mommy and did everything to keep it from her. That was remarkably thoughtful of Buddy, who was as big a gossip as Walter Winchell. Holding no grudge about the secret marriage, Buddy would move out of the Beresford and in with Daddy and his new bride on 36th Street that fall. Ah, and that explained the Dorothy Hammerstein décor. This romance was no spur-of-the-moment infatuation. It had been going on for years. That apartment was a woman's place. Now we had the woman.

Her name was Thelma Schwartz, but she called herself Teddy. With a name like that, I thought she was a boy. She and her husband had a young son and had lived in the same building at 201 West 85th Street as my parents did when they first got married and had Buddy. Thus Teddy and Daddy went back, way, way back, to 1931. They had history. Teddy's husband had been in the fashion business, but Teddy pushed him into starting a nightclub, and with Daddy being the king of clubs, she naturally sought all the advice she could get from him for free. Because her husband had worked on Seventh Avenue, Teddy had nice clothes. Still, there was something cheap and flashy about her, more Virginia Hill than Jane Froman. Buddy later told me she had been a manicurist. Once I saw her, I saw what Buddy meant. She looked like a manicurist who would do Mommy's nails. She didn't look like Mommy.

After my parents' divorce, I had actually seen Teddy a couple of times at Daddy's new 36th Street apartment. I didn't think much of it.

I assumed she was this old acquaintance, there for a visit. How blind I was! I didn't feel threatened. She wasn't Miss Rheingold. She wasn't a chorus girl, not even a hat-check girl. Yes, she did have a very pretty face, with nice features and blonde highlights in her brown hair. But she had ugly legs, like fire hydrants. And she totally lacked Mommy's quiet, ladylike refinement, which even at my age I associated with class and beauty. Whatever she was, she was persistent, and she was as secretive as Daddy.

My mother may have missed the papers, but eventually that same day she got the news. Paul got it by reading someone's paper on the subway home from Horace Mann. That Daddy had gotten remarried was the biggest hurt of all in Mommy's life with him. That destroyed her pride as a woman. To divorce Daddy was her idea. But when he chose someone new, it was as if he had rejected Mommy for that person. If that seemed a little crazy, there was some method to Mommy's madness. Teddy was indeed someone whom Mommy had known, and who worked on Daddy for a long, long time, spinning her web.

The scandal of it all was overwhelming for Paul, who referred to Teddy with quiet, contempt, as "that woman." He left New York and went for a year to the Sullivan School, a prep school in Washington, D.C., that specialized in placing graduates in the service academies, to prepare for West Point.

In the winter of 1948, the year before the Teddy romance went public, with Mommy staying home, Paul and I had gone to Miami to spend the Christmas holidays with Daddy. Teddy was there then, too, basically stalking our father. She had just divorced her husband, whose nightclub had failed. Imagine how she must have looked up to Daddy, whose Florida nightclubs, the Colonial Inn and the Club Boheme, were the talk of the town, and of the whole country, packed with stars and millionaires who were reveling in postwar affluence. Daddy didn't seem the type to be susceptible to flattery, though Teddy must have helped him feel good about himself and feel less bad about having lost Mommy. Whatever, Daddy never mentioned Teddy. Instead, he arranged flying lessons for Paul and trips for me to Pickin' Chicken and the Lighthouse and the fancy toy store on Lincoln Road. Sometime in the midst of all that activity, Daddy managed to find time to secretly marry Teddy Schwartz. Buddy came down that January, after the marriage and was let in on the secret. He was the last person to be sworn to secrecy, but somehow he managed to button his lip.

Aside from Buddy, no one in our family knew that secret until the papers hit the stands that day in June 1949. When Mommy found out, she got furious with Buddy for concealing the papers from her. She never forgave him, and I think her anger had a lot to do with Buddy leaving us and moving in with Daddy, and Teddy, on 36th Street that fall. The friendship between Buddy and myself suffered from that move. I was Mommy's girl, and he was Daddy's boy, and never the twain could meet. But the presence of Teddy resulted in Buddy cutting me off as "the other side" if not the enemy. I missed having him to play and talk with. I didn't want to choose sides; I didn't really have a choice.

In the summer of 1949, I went off to the new camp, Camp High Point, in Ulster County, New York, up on the Hudson above West Point. I went with a friend named Natalie from the stables. Her family was rich from owning parking garages. I didn't think that was a particularly good way to get rich, not compared to Daddy's cool nightclubs and jukeboxes. Cool or not, those garages bought them a big black Cadillac, a fancy home in New Rochelle, and a nice horse for Natalie. High Point was known as a "Jewish" camp. At first that sounded scary, like a concentration camp in the war. But most of the campers were from prosperous Jewish families. There were no prayers or other religious stuff. And the food was really good compared to the junk at Highland Nature.

I still didn't think of myself as Jewish, or Christian, for that matter. I didn't have a label. I was just going to a Jewish camp. Like going to a Chinese restaurant. Natalie and I became pals with two of the boy campers whose fathers were famous singers at the Metropolitan Opera, Jan Peerce and Richard Tucker. The boys were good singers, too, but nothing fancy. We'd all sit by a campfire and sing songs from the Hit Parade, like "'A'—You're Adorable" and "Some Enchanted Evening" from *South Pacific,* which Daddy had taken me to see that spring on Broadway, right before he left on that secret European "honeymoon" with Teddy.

I was having a good time at High Point until I had a nasty accident, tearing the ligaments of my hand while getting out of the pool. Mommy came up to rescue me. Instead of going back to hot and sticky New York, she took me to stay at a fancy resort hotel nearby at a pretty place called Lake Mahopac. We stayed for a whole month, until school started in September.

I'm not sure what the name was, but, like the camp, it was the first "Jewish" resort I had ever been to, this place with lots of rabbis and kosher food and comedians like you'd see on television on Milton Berle's *Texaco Star Theatre* and handsome counselors and dance teachers (like the Patrick Swayze character in *Dirty Dancing*) who clearly weren't Jewish. Mommy seemed depressed and barely spoke. All she would eat was cold borscht three times a day and an occasional hot knish. She must have found out about Teddy by then and was staying away from the city, ashamed to show her face. Mommy wasn't there because she had rediscovered her heritage. She was there to hide out.

I did my best to have fun at the hotel. One night I went out on the lake with some girls I met without telling Mommy. She would have said no. She was totally overprotective, particularly with my injured hand. The boat flipped over and sank. Somehow we made it back to shore. I was a good swimmer, bad hand and all. Luckily Mommy was asleep when I came in. She would have gone crazy.

Aside from my boating accident and until I met "that woman," my stepmother, face-to-face that winter in Florida, the most eventful thing that happened to me that year was meeting a hotel kids' counselor whom we called Jimmy C. Tall and rugged, Jimmy was more like a young dockworker than the fancier boys who rode at the Aldrich Stables. You might say he looked like what people in a few years, inspired by the likes of James Dean and Marlon Brando, would call a juvenile delinquent. He had a big, Cheshire cat grin, and I liked him. Jimmy took me for a ride in his car, parked in the woods under a full moon, and asked if he could kiss me. I said yes. Why not?

Jimmy was eighteen. I was eleven and a half. Theoretically, though, I was a woman. This was the first time I was treated like one. I got an even bigger crush on Jimmy C than I had on Dr. Max Eagle. This one was flesh, the other fantasy. But not too much flesh. Consumed with guilt over my transgression, I went to Mommy to confess. "Mommy, I think I did something wrong," I said, very sheepishly.

"What did you do, Darling?"

"This guy kissed me."

"Which guy?"

"Jimmy . . . " I told her all.

Mommy wasn't particularly excited. She was distracted by her own miseries. "If that's all you did, you didn't do anything wrong," she rendered her judgment. "But," she added, "Don't do anything else. Kissing is enough," she declared, and I followed her dictates. Sadly, it was not enough for Jimmy C. He stopped taking me out. Thanks for the memories.

CHAPTER FIVE

THE MAN IN THE COONSKIN CAP

My brother Paul was a perfect gentleman who would never say an unkind word about anyone. That he said absolutely nothing about Teddy, other than calling her "that woman" spoke volumes to me. Although Paul's loud silence about "that woman" had led me to expect the worst, my new stepmother turned out not to be as horrible as I had feared. I think Daddy could have married Eleanor Roosevelt, and Paul would have resented him for it. Teddy Schwartz—I could never come to call her Teddy Lansky—was perfectly nice to me, though I never told Mommy that. In the winter of 1949, the year after their European love cruise on the *Italia*, I flew down to Miami to spend the Christmas vacation with Daddy. It was just a two-week break, and Mommy didn't come. She didn't want to be in the same state as Teddy if she could help it.

Mommy, perhaps distracted by her own depression over the marriage, somehow was much less smotheringly protective of me. She even let me fly to Miami by myself, on a big Eastern Airlines Super Constellation. Her brother Uncle Julie, who lived near us on the

Upper West Side and was in the family produce business, drove me to Idlewild Airport. They put a little tag around my neck in the shape of a teddy bear that said "Unaccompanied Child," but I took it off the minute I got on the plane. In my mind, and actually in my body, I was no "child." I had just turned twelve. I may have looked like a little tomboy, but there was something starting to stir in me. I had just been kissed. I was flying to the tropics all by myself, to be alone, or kind of alone, with my famous Daddy. Some child!

Daddy picked me up at Miami airport in a rented Chevrolet. No big Cadillacs, no sporty convertibles for him. No show. Though I wondered what had possessed him to get that flashy suite, fit for an emperor, on the cruise ship. I guess Teddy possessed him, that's who. This winter he wasn't staying at the Wofford or the Roney Plaza. Instead he told me he had rented a house. Given his lavish New York apartments, I thought he might have installed Teddy in a mansion like the Firestone Estate that would soon be torn down to build the Fontainebleau Hotel. Showy cars were a no-no for Daddy, but showy homes were okay. Was I ever surprised when we pulled up to this flimsy little cottage in Hollywood. It was about as fancy as Nancy Attina's family home in Bayshore, Long Island. This one wasn't even on the water. Inside was just as plain as outside. Instead of being decorated by Dorothy Hammerstein, it seemed to have been decorated by the welfare office. Maybe Daddy was doing this to test Teddy, to see how much of a gold digger she really was. If she could stay in this dump without complaining, her love for Daddy was been more genuine than Paul gave her credit for.

True to form, Daddy didn't say a single word of explanation about who Teddy was or that he had a new wife, and certainly not why. The expression, "Never complain, never explain" could have been Meyer Lansky's motto. This was just life as it was, and my only choice was to accept it, to go with the flow, as they say now. So I did. There Teddy was, amidst the indoor wicker garden furniture on the lawn.

She didn't hug or kiss me like my new mother. She shook my hand, a little nervous and a little standoffish. Under Daddy's unforgiving microscope, she didn't want to seem too familiar. At the same time, she didn't want to seem too cold. I felt for her. I thought she was pretty, though I couldn't help but keep noticing her heavy legs. With all the showgirls who worked for Daddy, he could have had Betty Grable, the wartime pinup who had the most famous legs in America.

Teddy had to have something more, something special. I couldn't figure it out. I was just happy to have my own room. She gave me whatever I wanted to eat, and gave Daddy and me a lot of time to ourselves, only joining us for big dinners with all my "uncles" at the Colonial Inn and Club Boheme. It was as if Dinty Moore's had transferred their whole clientele south for the holidays, Broadway on the sand. Until then, I only got to go to nightclubs, the Riviera in New Jersey or the Copacabana in New York, on rare occasions. Now I was right at center stage, with the best seat in the house.

One night at the Boheme, Daddy caused a big stir when he threw out Howard Hughes, the millionaire aviator and film producer who owned Trans World Airlines. Daddy had no idea who he was. He thought he was a bum. Hughes was wearing tennis shoes and a stained open shirt, and everyone else was in black tie and fancy jewels. Daddy didn't recognize him, and even after someone pointed out who he was, Daddy said to throw him out and keep him out. Hughes left without a fight. He wouldn't mess with Daddy. Daddy ran a tight ship.

People dressed up then, and so did I, in clothes Daddy bought me at Burdines, the Saks of Miami. All I needed was a cocktail and not my ginger ale, but I felt very grown up. It was good to be twelve. Oddly, at these dinners, nobody, uncle nor aunt, ever asked about Mommy. Not Uncle Doc Stacher or Uncle Jimmy Alo or even Aunt Flo Alo, Mommy's dear friend. It was as if Mommy had never existed. Teddy was the new queen, the only queen. I felt bad for Mommy. As always, I kept it to myself.

Back in New York, Mommy didn't ask me a single thing about my trip. If my uncles didn't mention Mommy, Mommy didn't mention my uncles. However, the sounds of silence at the Beresford got louder and louder. Buddy had gone, to 36th Street, and Paul was still in Washington, at the Sullivan School. It was just Mommy and me. Paul enrolled in West Point in July 1950. This was Daddy's dream come true, and a lot of people said he had made sure it would come true by putting the pressure on Representative Arthur Klein to secure Paul's appointment. Klein was the congressman for New York State's 19th District, where West Point was located. Daddy's dear friend and colleague Uncle Frank Costello, who used to be my parents' neighbor in the Majestic, also had a lot of influence on Congressman Klein, who was elected by the Tammany Hall democratic political machine that Costello was said to control.

I had met Congressman Klein with Daddy at Uncle Frank's famous annual Salvation Army Christmas children's party at the Copacabana in 1949, before I flew to Florida. Paul, the object of Klein's supposed charity, refused to go, as always, even though he was applying to West Point and may have needed Klein's help. Paul had no interest in nightclubs or in any inside connections. He just wanted to be his own man. He and Buddy both knew Daddy was a gangster, maybe *the* gangster, but they were both kind enough to keep me in the dark. Little ladies like me were not supposed to know such things. I probably wouldn't have believed it, anyway. For a million reasons, Paul didn't want his help.

A nightclub may have been a strange place to raise money and give toys to the orphans of New York, but it certainly got the job done. Frank Costello may have made more city kids happy than Santa Claus. And Santa Claus couldn't have given Paul a better gift that his fat letter of acceptance to the U.S. Military Academy. When the press soon focused on the Lansky-Costello-Klein connection, it tarnished Paul's achievement. He wanted to do it his way, and he had worked so hard that he surely would have made it there all by himself.

That Daddy was seen to have greased the wheels of power, that he may have "fixed" one of the country's noblest competitions, had to be hurtful to Paul. If Paul suffered, he suffered in silence. I wouldn't have blamed him if he told us all to stay away. One Lansky at the academy was enough. Nevertheless, he showed no hard feelings and opened the doors of West Point to us. For all his militariness, Paul was at heart a spiritual hippie before his time. He was a rebel against his family's materialism, which I must admit was extreme even in the highly materialistic postwar times. He liked living purely, like a monk, and if that monk had to be a soldier, so be it.

With Daddy, Buddy, and Paul all gone from the apartment, Mommy, for all her own conspicuous consumption, eventually decided we had more room than we needed, even with our two live-in maids. She made plans to leave the Beresford and move into a brand new building, the Schwab House, which was going up on Riverside Drive between 73rd and 74th Streets. If Paul could overlook the Hudson, so could we, from this spectacular building, one of the first and finest luxury residences to be built in Manhattan after the war. This was an era when modern was better, so the Beresford, grand as it was, seemed obsolete, like a medieval castle, compared to the space-age Schwab House. The Beresford was also a castle haunted by the ghosts of Daddy. Time to go. Mommy was excited to move, and the transition seemed to lift her spirits and alleviate her depression.

Unfortunately, the Schwab House construction, like most construction, took far longer than anyone anticipated. By the end of 1950 we were all packed up with no place to go, so we moved into the St. Moritz Hotel at 50 Central Park South, basically next door to the building where Daddy had lived with George Wood. I liked having Uncle George there as my "boy next door." Daddy always assured me that George could fix anything. He could, and, in time, he did. Not that Mommy would have asked him. She saw him as the serpent in the garden, a dreadful influence, and she was probably right.

The St. Moritz was a thirty-six-story skyscraper designed by Emery Roth, who was the architect of most of New York's ultimate luxury buildings built during the Roaring Twenties, before the stock market crashed. Aside from the antiques-filled rooms and the stunning park views of our two-bedroom suite, plus room service from the hotel's fancy dining room, the Café de la Paix, the best thing about the hotel for me was Rumpelmayer's, the ice cream parlor of the rich and famous. Mommy said she saw people there like Greta Garbo and Marlene Dietrich, though I was much more interested in the stupendous hot fudge sundaes and nearly life-size stuffed animals that I would make Mommy buy for me.

At this stage, however, I was moving beyond dolls to guys. Unwilling to pine away for Jimmy C, I found a Jimmy substitute at the Aldrich Stables, which had been renamed the Manhattan Riding Club. I still called it Aldrich, though. The boy's name was Curtis, a rich young socialite whose family split its time between New York and Santa Barbara, California. He was so handsome, again, in that blond, insolent, James Dean way, but very charming and polite, especially when Daddy sold Bazookie and bought me a new gelding named Time Clock. T.C. was one of the top horses at Aldrich. If anything, Curtis was too polite. He'd ride horses with me, but that was as far as it went. No Jimmy C make-out session in the hidden glens of Central Park, no scandal in the Ramble (the thick park underbrush area). I didn't feel rejected, because Curtis didn't notice any of the girls at Aldrich. Today, I'd probably say Curtis was gay. But then I didn't have any idea what gay was. I would soon enough.

Even if Curtis, who was at most twenty-one, had made a move on me, I probably would have said no. You see, I was saving myself for my true love. Who was that? Gordon MacRae. The movie star. I was crazy about him and turned my room at the St. Moritz into a Gordon MacRae shrine, messing up the silk-papered walls with Scotch tape putting up every photo of my idol I could get my hands on. Of course

George Wood could have introduced me to Gordon MacRae with one call. He probably could have gotten him to take me for a sundae at Rumpelmayer's. But I didn't dare speak my love, because George would tell Daddy, and Daddy would have not approved.

I first became aware of Gordon (our fantasy first-name basis) when I saw him starring in the movie *The West Point Story* in 1950. Paul had just gotten in, and the Lanskys had gone West Point–crazy. We assumed that the movie was written for us. The story had echoes of the Lansky life. A Broadway impresario played by James Cagney gets involved in a scheme to convince a cadet with a fabulous voice, played by Gordon, to give up his dreams of generaldom for the certainty of stardom on Broadway, where his father, Cagney's friend, is a major mogul. Sounds like Daddy wanting Paul to give up the army for the Mob. Here, however, was a case of life not imitating art. The last thing Daddy wanted was for his brilliant son, his golden boy, to follow in his footsteps.

Gordon had just become a big star opposite Doris Day in *Tea for Two*, a remake of the musical *No, No, Nanette*. It was still playing when *The West Point Story* came out, and I must have gone down to Broadway five times to see the films at after-school matinees, skipping Curtis at the stables for my new true love. When Gordon sang "I Only Have Eyes for You," I was convinced he was singing to me. I was turning into a little bobby-soxer. Probably the West Point connection was the aphrodisiac. Paul was the idealized boy, but since I couldn't have my brother as my boyfriend, I would find a cadet of my own. There was Gordon MacRae, waiting in the wings.

Gordon was anything but a rough boy like Jimmy C. He was a gentleman, the son of professional musicians, educated at the posh Deerfield Academy, a prep school football hero, a navigator in the Air Force during the war, and now a movie star—at twenty-nine. Sure, he was a little old for me, and he had been happily married since 1941, but those were only details. We could work it out. My fantasy romance, however, came to a crashing halt in the spring of 1951, when I came face-to-face with the hard reality of my father's life in crime.

I was coming home from Calhoun by myself, in a cab. Mommy was not only trusting me on my own, but giving me tons of cash, just to be "safe." I took yellow cabs everywhere. They were my magic carpet. I arrived at the lobby of the St. Moritz and stopped at the newsstand to look for the newest *Photoplay* and *Modern Screen* in hopes that Gordon's marriage had suddenly unraveled.

Instead, what I saw on the newsstand was my father. There he was, the title *Meyer Lansky,* over his picture on a softcover magazine-sized book. Next to him, in big piles, were two other titles: *Frank Costello* and *Joe Adonis,* with my uncles' pictures on the respective covers. I bought all the copies and jammed them in my book bag, crazily trying to prevent guests or employees in the St. Moritz from seeing them. I had no idea what was in these books, though I had a pretty good idea that whatever it was couldn't be good.

Luckily, Mommy was away at the psychiatrist's. She was gone most afternoons. If she hadn't been going to these headshrinkers, as they were called, she would have surely needed one after she read the books I brought home. Basically, the three books accused Daddy, Uncle Frank, and Uncle Joe of being the kingpins of crime in the New York metropolitan area and portrayed them as three of the most powerful men in the world. The problem was that the books made the point that their power was *evil,* that they were the lords of crime, the pinnacle of a sinister aristocracy. There was one aristocracy of the Roosevelts and the Cabots and the Lodges and all the old names I heard in Boston and of the parents of my classmates at Birch Wathen and Calhoun. Then there was *our* aristocracy, the aristocracy of Deal and the Jersey Shore and South Orange and Ocean Parkway in Brooklyn. There was a war going on between the good people and the bad people. And the Lanskys were not only bad people, we were the worst of the whole bad bunch, the brains behind the brawn, the ones who gave the orders. And sometimes, orders to kill.

The books were short, and I read each one, cover to cover. I had
no idea what most of it meant. There were a lot of legal terms and lots
of police and FBI jargon that was beyond my thirteen-year-old vocab-
ulary. In summary, the books were three long rap sheets outlining
the crimes and misdemeanors of Daddy and his friends. They talked
about Daddy and Uncle Benny and their gang in the twenties, with all
these allegations of terrible violence and murders and corruption that
got them all to the top so they could live at the Majestic and the Beresford and eat at Dinty Moore's with the distinguished mayor of New
York, William O'Dwyer, whom the books claimed Daddy and Uncle
Frank basically "owned."

Mayor O'Dwyer had just resigned his office to become ambassador to Mexico, which was highly unusual, because mayor of New
York was a much more important job. The books made it clear that he
went south of the border because the heat was on over his gangland
associations. They called Uncle Frank "Prime Minister of the Underworld," and they called Daddy "Chancellor of the Exchequer." Whatever that was. The books implied that the law was after Daddy and
company the same way it was after the fallen mayor, that justice was
near. I was actually worried that Mommy and I would be arrested ourselves. I felt like a teen version of Virginia Hill, whom everyone had
blamed for Uncle Benny's downfall and death. The books went one
step beyond that and blamed Daddy for ordering Benny's assassination. Heavy stuff. And I thought all Daddy did was sell jukeboxes and
own nightclubs.

I glued myself to the television to see the news, and I quickly got
an education in what was going on. Something called the Kefauver
Hearings were just getting under way, and they were drawing a bigger
television audience than the World Series or the heavyweight championship fights. This was like the heavyweight fights, the Feds versus
the Crooks, and guess who the bad guys were? Us! Kefauver, Kefauver,
Kefauver. That was the weirdest name I ever heard, and when I saw
the man himself, he was the weirdest guy.

Estes Kefauver was the senator from Tennessee. His trademark was his coonskin cap, something that Daniel Boone had worn to fight the Indians and the symbol of the all-American, all-natural, God-fearing, homespun, good guy. A few years later, in 1955, Walt Disney had one of his biggest hit series, *Davy Crockett, King of the Wild Frontier,* about a heroic Tennessean in a coonskin cap. Every boy in America had to have one of those hats. It was Estes Kefauver who ignited the craze. He was the king of a new frontier, the frontier of crime. In the movies, before Davy Crockett, they said you could tell the hero by his white hat. In 1951's real life, you could tell him by his coonskin cap. To me, the senator didn't look like any hero I had ever seen on screen. With his cap and his thick glasses and long anteater-y nose, he looked like a cross between a furry mammal and a funny Martian.

Kefauver was with a big team of lawyers and other Washington lawmakers down at the federal courthouse in Foley Square doing what was known as the "Mafia Roadshow," which was kind of a legal trav-elling circus, a rolling witch hunt. This was the last stop on a national tour of fourteen cities, Los Angeles, San Francisco, St. Louis, Detroit, Chicago, New Orleans, Miami, and more, where Kefauver held public hearings on "organized crime" and interviewing my "uncles." I had no idea what "organized crime" was. Yet I found out that the main guy who organized it was Daddy!

If I thought about it, crime seemed pretty disorganized, guys rob-bing banks and eventually getting shot. Kefauver, however, had this new theory that crime was a lot more complicated than that, much less the shoot 'em up that you saw in the movies and more like mak-ing lots of money by controlling the labor unions and not paying taxes on it. The reason they didn't make movies on organized crime was that it was so *boring,* like banking or accounting. I nearly fell asleep watching these hearings and was amazed that the public had tuned in in such massive numbers. They were getting a real-life cops-and-robbers drama, or at least a white-collar version of one, and I suppose the thrill was to see powerful men like Daddy and Uncle Frank burned at the stake.

Uncle Frank was on television when I was watching. He seemed nervous and fidgety and incredibly uncomfortable. He testified to Kefauver that he was too sick to testify. I believed him. He wasn't his normal self. At Dinty Moore's and elsewhere he had always seemed so cool and controlling. Later it was said that with his tailored clothes and the gravelly voice, he was Marlon Brando's role model for *The Godfather*. To me, he always seemed like Secretary of State Dean Acheson, quiet and commanding and even better dressed. That's surely why they called him the prime minister. Maybe Uncle Frank had stage fright. Very few people were used to being on television. Here was Frank Costello, one of the most intimidating men in America, intimidated by the camera, if not by Kefauver. He may have controlled the biggest city on earth but on the small screen, he was no match for Arthur Godfrey or Milton Berle.

There wasn't much Italian about Frank Costello. Not anymore. After all, he had a Jewish wife and an Irish name and my Daddy as his good friend. He was pure American, which went against the point of the Kefauver Committee that organized crime was an Italian thing, and that Daddy was the exception who made the rules for a bunch of Sicilian trigger men. That was the image in those books I bought. Maybe in the Roaring Twenties, the Sicilians, just off the boat and known as Moustache Petes, for their Old World facial hair, had treated New York like an East Coast version of the Wild West, but now it was all business: Big Business, the Irish mayor, and Daddy and Abe Zwillman and Frank Costello all worked together. Estes Kefauver had a big problem with that. To him that was un-American.

"What have you done for this country, Mr. Costello? What contributions have you made?" Kefauver, in his southern drawl, attacked Uncle Frank. The senator's attitude seemed clear that the only good and pure Americans were the founding fathers and Daniel Boone. If you were a later immigrant, you were a freeloader to begin with, and you usually got worse. Italians, Irish, Jews, they were all sinister, up to no good. Kefauver was practicing racial or ethnic profiling long before they had a name for it. "Come on, Mister Costello, tell me one single thing you have done for this great country of ours in return for us giving you citizenship. You can't, can you?" Kefauver kept pressing.

"I pay my taxes," Uncle Frank finally replied, and the entire courtroom broke out laughing, as loud as the black-tie audience at the Costello-owned Copacabana might have laughed at a Joe E. Lewis one-liner. That shut Kefauver up.

But only for a while. Uncle Frank's lawyer made a big speech denouncing the televising of these hearings as making a "spectacle" of justice akin to feeding Christians to the lions at the Roman coliseum. How could his client get due process of law if he was inhibited by the camera to speak to his counsel? Kefauver offered the compromise of forbidding the televising of Costello's face. The lawyer took the deal. It was a dreadful mistake. Instead the camera stayed close-up on Uncle Frank's hands. What beautifully manicured hands they were. However, they were terribly nervous, shaky hands, fidgeting, twisting fingers, pouring glass after glass of water, reaching for his fine silk handkerchief to wipe away the endless sweat on his brow. That handkerchief was the equivalent of worry beads and, boy, was Uncle Frank ever worried. The public naturally assumed that he had something to be worried about. They didn't write it off to performance anxiety.

Frank Costello looked shifty and guilty as sin. And sin, in the form of gambling and connections to elected power, was what Kefauver was driving at. He wasn't trying to call him a murderer or a drug trafficker. His questions, or the ones I could understand, were fairly simple. Were you convicted of possessing a weapon back in 1918? Did you ever travel to Cuba? Did you ever meet with Meyer Lansky? Did you ever meet with Mayor O'Dwyer? Did you ever meet with Benjamin Siegel? Did you ever meet with Charles Luciano? Of course he had. Yet

Uncle Frank refused to answer the questions, and his refusals were accompanied by the endless wringing of his hands. Worried about looking bad to the television audience, he ended up looking terrible.

I was upset by Uncle Frank's awful performance, one that would have closed a Broadway show on opening night. When Mommy came home from the psychiatrist, I couldn't control myself, spilling the beans about the books I bought and the show I'd seen. I was worried they were going to take Daddy off to jail, and all of his family along with him. Tell me that it isn't so, I was begging her, in effect. And that's exactly what she did. "Please, honey, do not believe *anything* you read!" she insisted emphatically. "Do not believe this stuff. It's all lies." She tore up the paperback books and threw them in the trash. Then she called room service to come and take out the trash baskets so I couldn't fish the pages out and read them again.

"What about what I *see*?" I asked her.

"What did you see?"

"I saw Uncle Frank. He was right there on television"

"Did you see him do anything?"

"No . . . But he looked . . . scared."

Mommy just laughed. "Uncle Frank isn't scared of anything."

"He looked scared. He looked like someone who just got caught doing something he shouldn't."

"Like you at Lake Mahopac?"

I blushed, remembering Jimmy C. "A little."

"Uncle Frank was just acting. So they'd leave him alone."

"But he lied. He said he didn't know . . . Daddy." I was nervous now even mentioning Daddy's name around Mommy. After Teddy it had become an unmentionable.

Mommy laughed again. I think she had seen the hearings, too. The whole city was watching them. "He didn't say he didn't know him. He didn't lie. He just didn't answer. That's a big difference, honey. Why give those people anything? They are no good."

"They say *we're* no good," I replied. "They're the law."

"They are not the law. They are *politicians*," Mommy said, as if "politicians" was the dirtiest word in the dictionary. She explained that whatever Uncle Frank had done in the past were petty crimes, that everybody had something bad in their past they didn't want to talk about.

"Not me," I said. "Not Paul. Paul's perfect."

"Knock on wood," Mommy answered. "It was hard in those days, hard if you had just come to this country from Europe."

"Did Grandpa Citron do anything bad?"

Mommy didn't answer that one. "His family was rich."

"Isn't Uncle Frank rich? He's really rich."

"He didn't start that way," Mommy said.

I was perplexed. If you weren't rich to begin with, was it okay to do bad things, crimes, to get rich? Is that what everybody did? "Did Daddy do terrible things, too?" I blurted out.

Mommy kept silent for a while. She held her breath. Then she spoke very deliberately. "Your father is a good man, a very fine man. There's nothing, absolutely nothing wrong in what he did. You know Uncle Frank. You know your Uncle Joe. Do they seem like bad men to you?"

I didn't answer.

"Do they?"

"They seem nice."

Mommy sighed. "These awful politicians, they just want to get rid of good people like General O'Dwyer and put their own people in." She called the mayor General. He had been a general, a war hero, before winning election as mayor. By a landslide. She seemed right. He was a general. Paul was going to be a general. So was Gordon MacRae, at least in the movie. Generals couldn't be bad.

Mommy went on defending a world she was no longer part of. Did she want to be? I didn't know. Probably anything to be back with

Daddy. That, sadly, was a lost dream. "You don't hear them talking about all the good things these men do. They help the poor. They get them food. They get them jobs. They pay their hospital bills. They pay for college. They pay for funerals. And they keep this country safe. Just think how your father saved this city, the waterfront thing . . . Please, Sandi, please don't watch this garbage," Mommy begged me.

"It's just sensationalism." she continued. "Honey, newspapers and television make money by scaring people. They scare people about what they call the Cold War, they scare people about the Communists, they scare people with the atom bomb. Now they've found something new to scare people with. They're scaring people with your father. They're scaring people with Uncle Frank. Please . . . It's just to sell newspapers and stupid books like those." She waved her arm at the trashcan and called room service once more to come up and take it away.

I promised Mommy I'd ignore the hearings. Ha! I lied through my teeth. How could I ignore something that called my entire identity into question? This was my initiation into adulthood, even more than Jimmy C. That I was the daughter, not of a great businessman, but of a great gangster, was the stuff of the greatest identity crisis a teenager could ever have. And I certainly couldn't discuss it with Daddy. Mommy had given her last word on the subject. Paul was at West Point. Buddy might rat me out to Daddy for asking. And I was too ashamed of the whole thing to mention it to my friends Terry and Eileen, and never to the girls from school. So I bottled it all up, but couldn't stop listening. It was like Sodom and Gomorrah. I wasn't supposed to look or else I'd turn into a pillar of salt.

I'd find appliance stores on Broadway and just blend in with the crowd gathered inside. I'm sure those hearings sold more televisions than Milton Berle and Ed Sullivan combined. They made New York TV-crazy. The number one song was Patti Page's "Tennessee Waltz." My eyes would be filled with images of the coonskin cap–wearing man from Tennessee in one part of a store while over in the record department my ears would be bombarded by Patti Page's warbling " . . . the beautiful Tennessee waltz." At one hearing, I was especially thrilled to see Virginia Hill in the flesh. She lived up to her reputation for sex appeal, a brunette bombshell with a fabulous body to go with a fabulous mouth. I had heard from Buddy all about this "bad girl," the endless stories of wild high living with Uncle Benny that nobody wanted me to hear. She wore a big hat and a big mink coat. She had the goods, and she liked showing them off. Nothing shy about this lady. I really liked her. She was gorgeous and sassy, just the opposite of proper and demure Aunt Esther. I could see why Uncle Benny and Uncle Joe both fell for her. She seemed like one of the guys. What an aunt she would have made.

Virginia Hill told Kefauver and the self-righteous senators to go jump in the lake. When Virginia left the hearings, she slugged a nosy woman reporter. Then she cursed the rest of the press, wishing an atomic bomb would wipe out all of them. She called them "goddamn bastards." When, in one final closed session, the Kefauver people asked her why these powerful men gave her so much money, her answer was basically "because I'm worth it." Her precise answer, which could not be reported in the papers or heard on television, was that she gave the world's greatest blow jobs. Although this didn't make the official news, it somehow got out and got the whole city whispering about it, even the older, more sophisticated girls at Calhoun. Miss Hill's forte was way over my young head; I would have been thrilled just to be kissed again, the old-fashioned way.

Virginia Hill had star quality. The camera loved her. None of my uncles had it. Uncle Joe Doto (Adonis) was handsome enough to be a star but stiff. Uncle Willie Moretti tried to be funny, a real Milton Berle. How could he be in the Mafia, he quipped. He didn't have a membership card. But Estes Kefauver and his colleagues were hardly a comedy audience. He even invited Kefauver to visit him down at the shore in Deal. Kefauver declined. Mayor O'Dwyer ended up looking bad. Just to ask him if he had ever met Daddy branded the once-beloved mayor with a scarlet letter. That he was friends with Uncle Frank spurred the most dire assumptions that he was bought and paid for. Name an uncle, give the mayor cooties, that was the Kefauver game.

When I couldn't see the hearings on television, I'd listen to them and the endless commentary on the radio in my room, playing it very low so Mommy wouldn't hear it. The worst was a show hosted by the Hollywood actor Robert Montgomery, who would say the meanest possible things about Daddy and his circle, far worse than what Kefauver was saying. Narcotics, prostitution, murder galore. He had a beautiful voice, but a vicious tongue. He made me so angry and so protective of Daddy. I later found out that Montgomery was a right-wing, anti-Semitic Republican, a Red Scare fanatic who had denounced a lot of his Hollywood colleagues as pro-Russian Communists a few years before and destroyed their careers. Because he was a skilled actor, he spoke with the greatest authority, so what he said sounded like it had to be true. How I wished that Gordon MacRae, with his own beautiful voice, could come to Daddy's rescue.

I dreaded the day Daddy would be called to the stand, but in the end, to my great surprise, that day never came. Daddy didn't play chess, but he would have been a champion if he had. He knew every move. He knew that Kefauver was out to get him, maybe more than any of his associates. He had to get Kefauver, and he did, by finding out everything he could about this sainted senator from Tennessee. Yes, his grandfather had been a minister, yes, he taught high school, yes, he went to Yale. But, from his vast network of information from uncles around the country, Daddy found out that the coonskin man also went to the track. He didn't go there just to watch the pretty horses. He went there to gamble.

Estes Kefauver was a compulsive gambler, maybe even an addicted gambler. And it wasn't limited to horse racing. Tennessee, the entire South, was full of gambling emporia, road houses, carpet joints, nightclubs, bookmaking centers, owned by Daddy's associates and sometimes part-owned by Daddy himself. Daddy knew who the important clients were. If Big Brother was watching Daddy, Daddy was also watching Big Brother. The year Kefauver had spent school teaching in Hot Springs, Arkansas, Owney Madden's gambling town, was his introduction to Sodom. But he didn't look away. He jumped in. The Holy Roller was the ultimate hypocrite.

That year may have turned Kefauver into a crusader; it also turned him into a gambler. He had a terrible conflict. He never told the public he was fighting his own demons. The only demons he acknowledged were Daddy and Uncle Frank and Mayor O'Dwyer, and he was out to get them. Estes Kefauver didn't take his road show to the places he frequented. He didn't "expose" Memphis and Nashville and Chattanooga and Atlanta and Little Rock. Those were too close for comfort. Daddy, all by himself, had gone to see Kefauver, armed with log books from the race tracks and other information and quoted the Bible to him: "Let he without guilt cast the first stone." Plus he had a thick sheath of Kefauver's gambling IOUs. Those were Daddy's ultimate trump.

Daddy had several meetings with Kefauver, at first by himself, then accompanied by his famous criminal lawyer, Moses Polakoff. Polakoff was a tough, powerful man who looked more like a boxer than a lawyer. Maybe that's why his most famous client, Jack Dempsey, liked him so much. Polakoff also was the lawyer for Lucky Luciano and many of the big nightclubs in Manhattan. Despite his tough façade and louche clients, Polakoff was a real intellectual. As I said, I always called him "Professor" because he was so scholarly. Before the divorce, Daddy and the Professor used to sit for hours in Daddy's study at the Beresford talking about American history, Thomas Paine, and democracy. I'm sure Daddy would have loved to scrap the jukebox business and just go and enroll in West Point with Paul and lead a life of the mind. If anyone would have appreciated a college education, it was he.

Even if Daddy hadn't gone to Yale Law School like Estes Kefauver, he wasn't at all intimidated by Kefauver's education and by his power. Daddy got exactly what he wanted, which was to *not appear* at the official hearings, and to *not* be photographed or televised. In most businesses, the rule was that any publicity was good publicity. But as we saw with Frank Costello, for Daddy and my uncles, any publicity was bad publicity.

Although Daddy's meetings with Kefauver were behind closed doors and supposedly top-secret, word leaked out, just as it had with Virginia Hill's famous line about her special amorous skills. There were just too many assistants and reporters snooping around the Kefauver road show. What captured the public's imagination was the exchange that leaked out between Daddy and Kefauver about the senator's passion for gambling. Kefauver reportedly admitted that he liked to gamble, but he didn't like the idea of "you people," as he said to Daddy, running the gambling show in the U.S.A. "You people." In New York City, those were fighting words. In the capital city of America's melting pot, right versus wrong, cops versus robbers, may have mattered less than us versus them. The immigrant population of New York was "you people" and on the other side was a drawling, arrogant, white churchman from Tennessee, of the Old Confederacy, the birthplace of the Ku Klux Klan.

Southern nativists were often equal-opportunity bigots. They hated blacks, Jews, Asians, Catholics, whom they called "Papists," whether Irish or Italian, all with equal venom. I had seen the separate water fountains in Miami, and I just knew they were wrong. Kefauver may have been a liberal Democrat, but he was still a southern man, a Dixie man, and New Yorkers didn't trust him anymore than he trusted them.

Daddy was quoted in the papers as having said to Kefauver, "I will not let you persecute me because I am a Jew." Those words made him something of a folk hero in New York City. They made him my hero as well. Until that moment, I had never even thought of him, or myself, as a Jew. Suddenly I realized what I was, what we were, and that anti-Semitism was worth fighting against, whether in World War II, or in America. Moses Polakoff, the Professor, was also a master of public relations. He let it slip to the press that not only had Daddy thwarted Hitler's agents on the docks in the war, but he was a major financial supporter of Israeli independence in 1948, by buying Israel bonds and providing arms for Israel's freedom fighters. Daddy could not stand back and allow the country where his own refugee grandparents were buried to be extinguished by the Arabs, who were being supported by our ostensible friends, the British.

Polakoff also played on the sympathy that New Yorkers had for their beloved but deposed mayor, Bill O'Dwyer, who had done so much for so many poor citizens, but whom self-righteous politicians like Kefauver had driven from office. Daddy was standing up to Kefauver, who was shown to be just one more bully. This man Meyer Lansky was tough, a living rebuke to anyone who said Jews were meek and weak. In a lot of local circles, Meyer Lansky, previously under the radar, or if known, then feared, was now embraced as a hometown boy, the pride of the Yankees.

Now I knew my father was a gangster. Now I knew he was a Jew. Wow! What was I going to do with this knowledge? I was still too scared, too polite, too intimidated, to speak to him about it. Or to speak to Mommy. I didn't speak much to Buddy now. I rarely spoke to Paul. I didn't dare talk to my friends. This was family stuff; it had to stay in the family. So I just tried to keep living the life I had, Calhoun, Aldrich Stables, Lake Mahopac, Gordon MacRae.

Then once again, a big event shook up my world. I was back in New York after another summer with Mommy at Lake Mahopac. I had come back, without a Jimmy C this time, to find out that I would be uprooted. Mommy decided to move us out of the St. Moritz. The Schwab House still wasn't ready. I had gotten spoiled at the grand hotel. I was Eloise before *Eloise*, the series of books about a pampered brat at the Plaza Hotel that first appeared in 1955. I may have been the inspiration. All the doormen and maids and concierges and bellmen knew me, and I adored room service from Rumpelmayer's, ice cream night and day.

I'm sure the hotel luxury was horribly expensive, even for Mommy, even with her family money and her Daddy money. We moved to the Westover Hotel on 253 West 72nd Street, off Broadway. If I thought Daddy's rented home in Florida was a dump, this place was dumpier. The Westover was a residential hotel, nothing like the St. Moritz, with a lot of European refugees who had fled Hitler on the eve of World War II. The place smelled like a deli, and the furniture was ratty.

Mommy had all her fancy antiques and carpets in storage waiting for the Schwab House; I assumed this was very temporary. It was funny that, after spending a lifetime not even realizing I was Jewish, now I was surrounded by Jews, at the Westover, at all the stores and kosher markets on Broadway, at a kosher eatery called Steinberg's Dairy Restaurant. In the past, Mommy would take me to Schrafft's and Longchamps and Rumpelmayer's, where we ate among stars and socialites. Now we always went to Steinberg's where I ate scrambled eggs, and Mommy ate borscht amidst old, sick people, many of whom had suffered in concentration camps. I went to Calhoun, with all the rich girls, but the huge contrast now between my fancy school, my fancy stable, and my unfancy home was giving me a split personality. The way Mommy was headed, I might have been better off in a girls' *yeshiva*, or special Jewish school. However, whenever I asked her anything about all the Jewish people around us, she'd brush off the question and say she didn't know.

I obviously had much more fun with Daddy, who, alas, was spending much more time in Florida and elsewhere than he was in New York. And because of all the publicity at the Kefauver hearings,

Meyer Lansky was now a household name in New York, even though he hadn't appeared. Daddy didn't like going out and being recognized. Our nights at the theatre dwindled to an end. One of the last musicals he took me to was *Call Me Madam* in 1950. We went backstage to meet Ethel Merman, whom I had loved in *Annie Get Your Gun* and who always made a big fuss over Daddy and me at Dinty Moore's. *Call Me Madam,* in which she played a wacky ambassadress, was all I knew about Washington, D.C., until I was rudely awakened by Estes Kefauver. The play had made me think politics was great fun, one big party. Was I naïve.

Despite his new notoriety, Daddy still frequented Dinty Moore's, which is where he had most of his business meetings. In early October 1951, he took me there to dine with Uncle Willie Moretti. We met him out front of Moore's. As a young prizefighter he had been known as Willie Moore, and he often joked that he was Dinty Moore's Italian cousin. He was the funniest of all my uncles. He lived in high style, arriving in a chauffeur-driven white Packard convertible, the kind of entrance stars would make at Hollywood premieres.

Speaking of which, Uncle Willie was all abuzz about his new protégés Jerry Lewis and Dean Martin, who were becoming the biggest stars in the country. His old protégé Frank Sinatra had hit the skids and was at a low point in his career. He had just released a dumb song called "Mama Will Bark," filled with yapping sounds. "Song's a dog," Uncle Willie wisecracked, expecting Daddy to laugh at his joke. That was expecting way too much of my always somber father, who was more somber tonight than usual.

We ordered our meal, and they began talking business, mostly about Kefauver. While the senator had wrapped up his road show months before, Daddy expressed concern about all the damage the hearings had done to his nightclubs in Florida. Until the hearings, Daddy had expected Miami to vote to legalize gambling in Dade County. Now the spotlight Kefauver had shown on Daddy's hugely successful, tolerated, but technically illegal gambling operations in adjacent Broward County was about to bring the whole party to a crashing end. The waiter, in his Eisenhower jacket, brought my broiled chicken, all cut up for me, even though I could have done it by myself at this point in my life. I ate the bite-size pieces.

The men kept talking over their big steaks. Although everyone loved to gamble, nobody liked the word "crime." The main crime Kefauver was after was his own vice of gambling. Daddy was certain Miami would vote down any referendum. Uncle Willie regretted to agree. "It's like asking a broad to go to bed with you," he said, "She may do it, but she sure as hell won't agree to it in advance." That comment was my cue. I went to hang out with the hat-check girl. Jack Benny came in the restaurant. I thought it was Uncle George Wood, because they could be doubles for each other, their thinning hair combed straight back, professorial eyeglasses, great clothes. "Hi, Uncle Georgie," I said.

"This is how George steals all my women," Jack Benny said, and the hat-check girl laughed out loud. I blushed at my mistake. "And she's just my type." He winked at me.

"I'm sorry, "I apologized.

"That's okay, sweetheart. If I had a nickel for every time that happened, I could afford a date of my own." The entourage with the comedian, famous for jokes about his own cheapness, roared with laughter.

When I returned to the table, Daddy and Uncle Willie were talking about Havana. "If Florida goes down, there's always Havana," Uncle Willie said. Daddy was quiet, thoughtful, and a little sad. Uncle Willie liked to reminisce about old times, about how he taught me to ride his nephew's two-wheel bike at Deal, our day trips down to the Boardwalk in Atlantic City. "Remember our first convention in Atlantic City, Meyer?" he asked Daddy. "Me and you and Charlie Lucky and Waxey G. and Nig Rosen and King Solomon. All yids and wops, yids and wops. And your bride, what a honeymoon." Willie turned to me. "He took your beautiful mother on her honeymoon with Dutch

Schultz. Is that any way to treat a lady?" He turned back to Daddy. "Meyer, Meyer, where is the romance?"

Daddy was growing very uncomfortable. "Willie, you talk too much," he said and asked for the check.

The next day at Calhoun, during outdoor play period in the early afternoon, one of the school janitors was reading a newspaper. On the cover was Uncle Willie. I wanted to brag to my classmates that I had had dinner with him just last night. Then I saw the other half of the paper. "Dead!" it read. "Mob Boss Exterminated in N.J." There was a photo of a man on the tile floor of a bar, a pool of blood around his head. There was a café sign above the body: "Chicken in the Rough. $1.50."

I couldn't see his face, but I could see his tie with the diamond stickpin gleaming. I knew from the tie it was Uncle Willie. I ran to the bathroom and threw up. I got an excuse to go home. But I had the cab drop me at a Broadway appliance store first so I could see the news. The story was everywhere, on every channel. Uncle Willie, on his way to lunch with Martin and Lewis, had stopped for a quick meeting with someone at a place called Joe's Elbow Room in Cliffside Park, New Jersey, right on the Palisades near the Riviera, where Willie's godson Frank Sinatra spilled the ice on me. Daddy had taken me there before to meet Willie, before we would go to Palisades Park. Whoever Willie met that day had shot him to death. Newsmen speculated that Willie was hit because he had run his big mouth to Kefauver, to the press. I thought of Daddy's sad last words, "Willie, you talk too much." The news shows reported that Martin and Lewis thought he had stood them up.

Back at the Westover, Mommy was out. She was always out, at the psychiatrist's. Every month it got harder and harder to talk to her. Uncle Willie was family, but he wasn't *her* family anymore, so I didn't bring it up. If only Daddy had called me, to calm me down, to tell me why. In Daddy's mind I was still too innocent to even know what happened. What could I understand about murder?

Uncle Willie's murder, like Uncle Benny's murder, was never solved. But for me, Uncle Benny was a death, while Uncle Willie was a killing, my first real murder. I hadn't seen what happened to Ben Siegel. I only heard about it, and much later. Uncle Willie's violent demise was right in my face, alive and laughing one night, blown away the morning after. What Daddy didn't get was that television had been the end of innocence, for me and everyone else. You couldn't keep secrets from kids anymore. However, Daddy had me trained. Never complain, never explain. And never, ever ask to be explained to. Although Mommy had assured me during the Kefauver assault that Daddy was a good man, I began to have my own nagging doubts. What kind of business, what bloody business, was my father really in?

CHAPTER SIX

TEENAGE WEDDING

I knew Mommy was dangerously depressed because she never wanted to go up to West Point and visit Paul. Her son had achieved an American citizen's holy grail by getting into the U.S. Military Academy and walking in the footsteps of legendary leaders from Grant and Lee to MacArthur and Eisenhower. Now Mommy wouldn't go to see her own legend being made. To get out of it she'd say, "He doesn't want us there. Would *you* like it if I came to Calhoun? You don't even want me at the stables." "Mommy, that's not so," I said. And she knew I was lying. I didn't want to hurt her feelings.

Daddy, on the other hand, went to West Point twice a month. The unspoken deal between them was that Daddy could come up as much as he liked, as long as Teddy wasn't in tow. So Daddy would drive up to West Point by himself, sit in the reviewing stands, and watch Paul and the other cadets drill for hours. Daddy knew how Paul felt, and he didn't inflict his new wife on him. Instead Daddy began taking me with him on weekends.

We'd get a suite at the Thayer Hotel right on campus, with an amazing view over the Hudson. Daddy refused to use the phones. He once said that the biggest stool pigeon in the world was the telephone.

He was convinced that since we were on federal property they must be tapped. And there was no way any of my fed-fearing uncles would be caught dead at the place. Without any business to transact, Daddy was all mine, which was great. He seemed at home here, even more than he did at Dinty Moore's. Because of his love of American history, he was right in his element. I learned a lot more from him on his weekend tutorials than I did at Calhoun.

We had Cokes on the hotel's Thomas Jefferson patio and watched a cotillion at the George Washington ballroom. Daddy reminded me of my dancing lessons that I had dropped in favor of riding and teased me about what I would do if one of the handsome cadets in their gray uniforms asked me for a waltz. I was actually nervous one of them would. Wishful thinking. I was dressed in a skirt and sweater and white bucks, hardly waltz material. Daddy rarely teased me, but he did here. I think West Point made him relax. He showed me plaques honoring some of the Thayer's many famous guests. Daddy pointed out one for General Sherman, who burned down Atlanta. "Too bad he missed Tennessee," Daddy said, referring to his nemesis, Kefauver.

Daddy showed me a sign on a room where General MacArthur's mother lived while he attended West Point. Daddy didn't say anything, though I couldn't help but wonder why, if Douglas MacArthur's mommy could live at West Point, Paul Lansky's mommy, my mother, couldn't even come for a little visit. During the day we toured the austerely grand Gothic campus. Daddy told me it looked a little like Oxford, in England, though centuries newer. I could see how much he longed to have had a different life, one that would have enabled him to attend schools like this.

Daddy also took me to visit the grave of his Brooklyn friend, Colonel David "Mickey" Marcus. Daddy told me that Marcus had been one of the rare Jewish graduates of West Point and went on to become a lawyer and served as an assistant U.S. attorney. In that position, he had worked with crime-buster Thomas Dewey to send Lucky Luciano to prison. Daddy had hated him for that. It took New York's most famous rabbi and Zionist leader, Stephen Wise, to change Daddy's mind. The anti-Nazi work Daddy had spearheaded before and during the war had brought him into the circles of New York's highest and mightiest. He just didn't brag about it, but he was in the loop. Totally.

A highly decorated World War II hero, Mickey Marcus had left New York and the law for the battlefield, leading Israel's Haganah, or freedom fighters. Rabbi Wise urged Daddy to forget the Luciano past and think of Israel's future and provide backing for Marcus. Daddy put aside his grudge and stepped up to the challenge. Daddy donated a lot of money to the cause of Israeli independence and provided the soldiers there with stores of weapons. Tragically, Colonel Marcus was accidentally killed in Israel by his own sentry in 1948. Kirk Douglas would later star in a movie about him, *Cast a Giant Shadow.* Having learned the Marcus story, I could see how Daddy might have wanted to lead same kind of hero's life, but if he couldn't do it, Paul, he was confident, would do it for him.

I finally saw Paul marching on the parade ground. It was hard to tell him from all the other cadets, and that was a good thing, a wonderful thing. He fit in. No one could have been prouder than my father. Meyer Lansky's son was at West Point. The family was now part of the American ruling class. We weren't "you people" anymore. We were *the* people, the chosen people. We met Paul's roommates. One, Jaime Ortiz, was a handsome boy from Puerto Rico. He reminded me of a very proper version of Lucille Ball's husband, Desi Arnaz, on the *I Love Lucy* show. Paul's other roommate was Eddie Freeman, whose father was the colonel in charge of the Old Soldiers' Home in Washington, D.C.

Colonel Freeman was a real military bigwig and liked Daddy so much that he sent us special VIP invitations to Eisenhower's inauguration in 1953. Daddy refused. He told the colonel he didn't want to do anything to embarrass anyone, but the one he would have embarrassed, just by showing up, was Estes Kefauver. Yet that was Daddy, low-profile, low-key. Never show off, even when you have the advantage.

The boys at West Point all looked handsome. Obviously I was presold, because of Paul, and because of Gordon MacRae in *The West Point Story*. Too bad none of them noticed me. Actually one did. Kind of. I met him in the Thayer gift shop, where he was buying some souvenirs for his parents in Buffalo. His name was Gabby Hartnett and he was two years ahead of Paul, graduating in 1952. He was a star athlete, earning four letters, in football, baseball, skiing, and boxing. The summer of his graduation he was going to the Olympics in Helsinki, Finland, to represent America in the pentathlon.

Was this guy ever fantastic. It was almost as good as meeting Gordon MacRae. I thought about telling Gabby that I knew Champ Segal and Frankie Carbo, the big fight managers, but I was sure a proper West Pointer wouldn't have approved. Then again, maybe he would have. He wanted to know all about me, my school, where I lived, my last name. Naturally I told him. I had nothing to hide. My brother went here. I belonged. Then Daddy walked in and gave me the dirtiest look, *that* look. Gabby seemed to want to meet Daddy, but I didn't dare.

"You have a friend?" Daddy asked.

"I wish," I said.

"Who is he?"

I told him his name, that he was going to be an Olympic champion.

"You believe that?" Daddy was raining on my parade. Daddy didn't believe anything.

"He goes here, Daddy. He's going to graduate."

"You believe that?'

"Look at his uniform. What do you think he is, some kind of spy?"

"You never know."

"Daddy!"

"I never saw him with Paul," Daddy said.

"He's an upperclassman."

"Then why was he talking to you?"

That stung. Why *not* talk to me? I guess Daddy thought this heartthrob was way out of my league. And he was right. Who was I, who

In Havana, age 2, 1939.
(COURTESY OF THE AUTHOR)

Mommy in 1938, shortly after I
was born. (COURTESY OF THE AUTHOR)

From left: Paul, home
from military school;
Buddy, looking elegant;
me; Mommy; Daddy, the
big businessman, New
York, 1941. (COURTESY OF
THE AUTHOR)

Daddy, in his trench coat,
with me in New York, 1940.
(COURTESY OF THE AUTHOR)

At Birch Wathen
School, age 6, 1943.
(COURTESY OF THE AUTHOR)

Mommy and Daddy's West Coast palace, 1933. (COURTESY OF THE AUTHOR)

Ben (Bugsy) Siegel's wife Esther and daughter Millicent in Los Angeles, around 1946. (COURTESY OF THE AUTHOR)

My first friend, Wendy, with me in the Boston Public Garden, 1941. (COURTESY OF THE AUTHOR)

Daddy and I on the hospital grounds of the county jail outside Saratoga, N.Y., 1953. (COURTESY OF THE AUTHOR)

Cutting my sweet sixteen birthday cake with boyfriend Marvin Rapoport at the Copa, 1953. (COURTESY OF THE AUTHOR)

My wedding to Marvin. Top row: Daddy, Marvin, Harry Rapoport. Bottom row: Me, Anna Rapoport, 1954. (COURTESY OF THE AUTHOR)

Riding on Sunday Swing, Madison Square Garden, 1955. (COURTESY OF THE AUTHOR)

At the Diplomat Hotel in
Hollywood, Florida, trying
to look sophisticated for
Dean Martin, 1958.

All dressed up, 1954.

Daddy and his old pal Ben
Siegelbaum in Israel, 1971.

Top row: Me, Daddy, my stepmother Teddy,
Paul. Bottom row: Annette (Buddy's wife),
Buddy, and Grandma Yetta Lansky.
Miami, 1957. (COURTESY OF THE AUTHOR)

Dean Martin and I, 1957.
(COURTESY OF THE AUTHOR)

Daddy and I in Jerusalem, 1971. (COURTESY OF GARY RAPOPORT)

Left: Paul, wife Edna, and Meyer Lansky II. Right: Daddy, me, and Gary Rapoport, 1960. (COURTESY OF THE AUTHOR)

Paul, Daddy, and I, Miami, six months before Daddy's death, 1982. (COURTESY OF THE AUTHOR)

Daddy, Teddy, Gary, and I, Miami, 1973.
(COURTESY OF THE AUTHOR)

Jimmy "Blue Eyes" Alo, Daddy, and Harry "Nig Rosen" Stromberg, Miami, 1982. (COURTESY OF THE AUTHOR)

Vince and I, Miami, 1983. (COURTESY OF THE AUTHOR)

couldn't even get Jimmy C or Curtis, to go after a West Point Olympian? "Just nice, I suppose," I answered Daddy. Father knows best.

"You can't be too careful. Even here." I had absolutely no idea how brilliant and all-knowing Daddy would be. It took six years to find out, when I ran into Gabby Hartnett once again under very different circumstances. Right now, all I had was another foolish crush. I wanted so badly to have a boyfriend, any boyfriend. He didn't have to go to West Point. But it would have been nice.

I would have given anything to be able to show up at Calhoun, at Aldrich, with Gabby Hartnett. So I did the next best thing. At the Thayer gift shop, I bought the most expensive West Point pin I could find. I started wearing it to school. I told everyone I was pinned to one of my brother's fellow West Point cadets. His name was Gabby Hartnett. I just hoped he didn't win the Olympics and get his picture in the papers with his real girlfriend, who, for all I knew, could have been Miss America.

What a lie I was living. I didn't have a boyfriend; I didn't even have a girlfriend. Terry's family moved to California in 1952, and I wasn't seeing that much of Eileen, who had fallen in love. Natalie and I weren't all that close. All the girls at Calhoun were having sweet sixteen parties, big events where they all had beaus. Daddy had been promising me the biggest of all sweet sixteen parties, at the Copacabana, no less, for years. But how could I have a party without a boyfriend? I couldn't pretend Gabby Hartnett was still in Helsinki. I was desperate. I dreaded turning sixteen. December 6, 1953, one day before Pearl Harbor Day, was a day I was sure would also live in infamy, the day Sandi Lansky turned sixteen, with no boyfriend, no nothing. Hoping against hope for a miracle, I didn't tell Daddy that I didn't want the party he was planning.

Buddy had left New York. At the ticket agency, Buddy had picked up a bad gambling habit, betting on all the football games, basketball games, boxing matches. If there was a contest, Buddy would bet on it. To get him out of harm's way, Daddy installed him in the middle of nowhere at a resort in the Florida Keys called Plantation Yacht Harbor that he had bought. Daddy was obsessed about Buddy having a job, if only running the hotel switchboard. He even set up nurses, drivers, and a whole clinic at the resort to care for him. One of the few times I talked to Buddy, he joked that "the only nightlife here is the mosquitoes."

When the city fathers of Broward County caught Kefauver fever and cracked down on the gambling that had made Daddy a fortune, Daddy sold the Colonial Inn to the owner of Minsky's Burlesque, who thought he could make just as much money from naked strippers as Daddy had with roulette wheels and card tables. He made a big mistake. Daddy also closed Club Boheme and concentrated on local real estate like the isolated resort where he parked Buddy. I know Buddy loved the "action" of Times Square, and to take him away from it was like sending a junkie to rehab. I missed him, and I missed his advice. I certainly needed it now, at this low ebb of despair.

I had to do something to change my life. So I did. I campaigned to get a nose job. Mommy, who didn't want me to get my teeth pulled so I could get my braces, would have never let me get my nose fixed, even though Dr. Eagle had gone on record saying that it might help my chronic sinusitis. I was amazed that she had let them take my tonsils out when I was little. Instead, I turned to Daddy, who was distracted with lots of legal problems that the Kefauver hearings had stirred up. The government was constantly harassing him about taxes, licenses, anything. My harassing him about my nose, which I had decided I hated, was easy to deal with. Just say yes.

Daddy told me to go see Uncle Georgie Wood, who would take care of everything. All the actresses that George represented, or dated, had nose jobs. He knew the best plastic surgeons, and he sent me to the best of the best, Dr. Scheer on Park Avenue. Talk about intimidation. I had never seen so many beautiful women in one place, not at the Copa, not at the Stork Club, not at Dinty Moore's, not on the Miss Universe pageant on television. Maybe I would come out like that. I told the doctor that I wanted the same little nose I had when I was a baby. I had brought baby pictures to show him. He said, sure, I can do precisely that. For George Wood, he would have promised me anything.

Before Uncle George could arrange an elaborate ruse for me to get away from Mommy so I could transform myself into a beauty queen, or at least someone who could get a date for her sweet sixteen party, I was once more upended by the cruel reality of Daddy's famous life. My father was going to jail. Jail? Jail was for criminals. Then I realized that that was the point Kefauver had been trying to make two years before. Now the coonskin prophecy was coming true. A funny thing had happened on my way to the nose job.

Saratoga Springs was a few hours' drive north of West Point. Famous for its horses and summer race track since the Civil War era, Saratoga was New York's answer to Hot Springs, Arkansas, and in the 1940s, Daddy came to be to Saratoga what Owney Madden was to that southern resort. Daddy owned two nightclubs there, the Arrowhead Inn and the Piping Rock Club. Both had casino gambling, which was technically illegal but was tolerated for years. In the summer high season, the clubs were packed with celebrities and politicians.

But the Democrat Estes Kefauver, who had major presidential ambitions, had singled out Saratoga Springs as a massive den of iniquity and blamed the New York Republican Party, led by current Governor Tom Dewey, who lost the presidential election by a hair to Harry Truman, for allowing this ungodly corruption. If Kefauver was going to be holier than thou, the Republicans decided they had to be holier than Kefauver. Accordingly, they needed to blame someone. Those someones were Daddy and Uncle Joe Stacher, who were indicted on criminal gambling charges.

Moses Polakoff wanted to fight the charges. He knew how two-faced they were. Daddy had proof of Kefauver's own gambling habits that had been as effective in thwarting the senator during the hearings as showing a cross to Dracula. He had equal proof of the gambling habits at Saratoga of many top Republicans. The problem was too many. Daddy would be going up against the whole Republican establishment. A man who detested publicity, Daddy did not want a trial. To him a trial was all about complain and explain. He preferred to go quietly—and briefly—to jail.

So the Professor bargained out a deal with the authorities. For the first time in his life, Daddy went behind bars. The sentence was for only three months and it wasn't at some brutal prison like Sing Sing, but rather a county jail outside Saratoga in a town called Ballston Spa. There may have been one other prisoner when Daddy went in. However, the idea of Daddy in jail was a terrible *shonda,* a secret word I had picked up from my parents when they didn't want me to know what they were talking about. *Shonda* was Yiddish for shame. Uncle Joe Stacher didn't go to jail. He paid a fine of $10,000 and got a suspended sentence. But the authorities wanted to be able to brag they had caught the Big Fish. Before he went, Daddy sat me down at the 36th Street apartment and, for the first time in his life, tried to educate me a little about the gambling business. This was hardly a confession about a life of crime. As I said, Meyer Lansky didn't explain, even to his daughter. The lesson was more about the politics, as I mentioned above, and government hypocrisy. "When I was young, I had a choice," he said to me, with unusual difficulty for a man who was normally so sure of himself. "I had two roads I could have taken. There was one to the right, and one to the left. This was the road I took. This was my choice." That was all he said.

Daddy, who could be very cryptic and evasive, didn't mention the word "jail." He just said he would be "tied up" for a little while, and that everything would be fine. He didn't say he had made the wrong choice. There were no regrets. But there was this silent undercurrent of shame, the shame of being behind bars, of being in a jail, when, just down the highway, his son was marching on the parade grounds of West Point, preparing for a career on the right side of the law.

I went up to visit Daddy several times while he was at Ballston Spa, which was a funny-sounding place to be in police custody. One of Daddy's errand-men, Billy Blanche, would drive me up there. I couldn't go with my mother. If Mommy wouldn't visit her son at West Point, she surely wasn't going to visit her ex-husband in jail. I'm not certain how much Paul came over, either, as long as Teddy was around. I doubt he wanted his pals at the academy to know where his father was. I stayed with Teddy at a rooming house where she was renting space. She smoked all night. It was like sleeping in an ashtray. The first time I got there, I learned that Daddy wasn't in jail. He was in a local hospital, where he was recovering from a bleeding ulcer. I got very upset, but when I saw him, I was so relieved.

Daddy looked fine, wearing his expensive Sulka silk robe and smoking his cigarettes, eating a big plate of lamb chops and watching a show about the Civil War on television. The only concession to his ulcer was a big glass of milk, which he never normally drank. Buddy later told me that Moses Polakoff got a doctor's note so Daddy could get out of jail. I didn't know much about ulcers, but when I learned they could be caused by the stress of bottling up your emotions, I thought they could have been for real. Eventually Daddy's sentence was reduced for good behavior. He was out of Ballston Spa and back in action in less than two months.

Teddy was never my friend, always my rival, resentful of my re-lationship with Daddy. She could be very tricky. She took me to the stores in Saratoga and encouraged me to get whatever I wanted. Then, trading on the now-famous Lansky name, she'd have the stores send the clothes to my mother. Teddy was an incredible miser, and only lavish with someone else's money. Nevertheless, I saw Teddy could be useful to my beauty scheme. I used my new "relationship" with my stepmother as a cover to get that nose job. Teddy, unlike Mommy, was all for it. As an ex-beautician, she believed in doing whatever it took to look your best, including going under the knife. Now that school was out and Mommy was too depressed to even go to the Lake Mahopac resort this season, I was pretty much on my own. Surgery would be my summer camp this year. Aided by Uncle Georgie Wood, I planned a "cover" visit to Brooklyn to spend some time with Daddy's sister, Esther Chess, who was married to a lawyer there. Mommy didn't really care where I went at this point, as long as she knew I was "safe." Aunt Esther secretly took me for the plastic surgery at St. Clare's Hospital just west of the theatre district in Manhattan.

The surgery was awful. I came out with a swollen face that looked like I had been in the ring with Joe Louis. The bruising was so bad that the doctors gave me radiation treatments to reduce the swelling. That was state-of-the-art in the fifties. God knows what I was exposed to. I spent three days at St. Clare's then went to Brooklyn to recuperate. The swelling finally went down, but Dr. Scheer didn't deliver what he had promised. I did not get back my baby nose. When I went to his fancy office to complain, he assured me that it would get smaller over time, that it had to "settle." The new nose was bad. Mommy was worse.

When I went home after my extended "vacation," during which I had pretended that I had caught a severe cold, Mommy went psychotic. She shrieked when she saw me. "What have they done, what have they done?" she wailed. This was the only real emotion I had seen in my listless mother for the longest time. It was a kind of shock therapy. Too bad it didn't last, or make her better. Luckily, Daddy was away, so she couldn't call him. I gave Mommy a song and dance about health rather than vanity. I did this for Dr. Eagle. I did this for my sinuses. I didn't tell you because I didn't want to worry you. Sure . . .

Things had been going from bad to worse. Mommy's father had passed away, so she had lost that ballast. She never spoke to Esther Siegel anymore, or to Flo Alo. She had no friends, other than the television, which she never turned off. For the last year I could barely do my homework. Mommy insisted on the rooms being so dark, no overhead lighting allowed, so that the only light I had was the sliver of light from the bathroom or the flickering light from the television screen.

I wasn't a very inspired student to begin with. Adding darkness to laziness was not a good formula to prepare me for Vassar, which was near West Point and where so many of the Calhoun girls were planning to go. Aside from the fit she threw over my new nose, Mommy barely spoke to me at all, about my education, or anything else. She spent a lot of time talking to herself, in a mumble I couldn't understand. "What, Mommy?" I'd often ask her, thinking, hoping, she was saying something to me. "What'd you say?"

"Nothing. Nothing . . . " she trailed off. Other times she would say stuff to herself, then burst out laughing. I felt so creepy being around her. You don't want to think of your mother as a crazy person, like the bag ladies who walked up and down Broadway near the Westover, talking, laughing, cursing to themselves. She'd only go to Steinberg's Dairy Restaurant, which had to be the most depressing restaurant in New York

Mommy had greatly reduced her frequent trips to the psychiatrists. I'm sure they wanted to see her, but she had gotten too despondent to keep her appointments. However, she still was hooked on their prescriptions. Her medicine cabinet looked like one big drugstore. I saw a lot of bottles of Lithium. Sometimes she would come to get me at Calhoun looking ragged and unkempt, which was embarrassing. It was bad enough not having a boyfriend. I wanted to disappear. The very worse thing was the day I found my mother in her bedroom arranging something in a cigar box. I walked over to see what it was. I screamed! In the box was a collection of dead cockroaches. She was arranging the bugs in military file, like a marching platoon. "My West Point cadets," Mommy said, without a smile or a change in her flat tone of voice.

I wasn't sure what was scarier, the cockroaches or Mommy. I never told anyone. I was too afraid, too ashamed. My brothers never saw her. Daddy never came up, always dropping me off downstairs. She was my secret. But her brother, Uncle Julie, who lived very close by on Riverside Drive, would come by weekly. He was clearly distressed at his once elegant sister's tragic decline. He didn't tell me to find a way out, but I could see in his eyes that he wanted to try to save me.

Instead Daddy came to the rescue. When he got out of Ballston Spa, I met him at Dinty Moore's to show off my now healed and unswollen nose. He seemed impressed. Then I told him I'd love to live with him and Teddy in Florida, where he was spending more and more time. I told him if I lived there, I could see more of him. He didn't ask me about what Mommy would say. But he asked about my horse, about my school. I told him that school would come first, that I had always liked going to school in Florida during our winters when we were a family, that the horses could wait. So Daddy said yes. He always said yes to me. That was the good part.

The hard part was telling Mommy. The sadness on her face when I told her was different from the shock at my redone nose. She looked crushed, betrayed. She had taken many blows in recent years, losing Daddy, then Buddy, then Paul going away. And now me. This was, as they say, the unkindest cut of all. Yet Mommy was too defeated, too far gone, to try to argue with me. She didn't cry. She just stared into space, like someone in court who just heard a guilty verdict they knew was coming.

Mommy had come to expect everything in her life to go wrong. This was one more awful and final thing. I tried to give her some hope to cling to, saying that this was just an experiment, that I wanted to try a new place, some place where I could finally meet some cute boys. I sensed that she didn't believe me. She knew her daughter, the last life preserver in a life that was sinking fast, had drifted away from her reach. I don't know how I got through that hideously sad farewell.

I started public school in Hollywood, Florida, in August. New York schools started in September, but before widespread air conditioning, Miami schools started in the brutal heat of summer, but finished in the relative coolness of early spring. The luckier kids could then head north for the summer. This lucky New York kid was going in the opposite direction, hoping for the best, or for better than I had

had it. Daddy and Teddy had a new rental in Hollywood. It wasn't much nicer than the first one, but it was better than the Westover. And, aside from the endless smoking, Teddy seemed friendly enough, better than Paul had given her credit for.

Daddy enrolled me in the tenth grade at South Broward High School. My younger cousin Linda Lansky was in seventh grade there. Her parents, Uncle Jack and Aunt Anna, had been living in Florida for years. Jack was Daddy's man in Miami, running his clubs and properties. He lived in a fancy white Spanish mansion, much grander than Daddy's place, but Daddy's rule was don't attract attention. At South Broward I broke the rule right away. I hated the way the teacher made me sit in typing class. It made my back ache really badly. I was also placed in beginning Spanish. At Calhoun I'd taken intermediate French, but they didn't teach French here. I had no idea how valuable that typing would have been—much more useful than the French. I complained to Daddy about the public school, and he immediately, put me in the private Pine Crest, in Fort Lauderdale, where they taught French and not typing.

Typing was for secretaries, the people the Pine Crest girls' husbands would hire, not for the little ladies and pampered housewives-to-be. I made one friend there, Mary Ann Turner. Her father owned the patent on the cellophane that bread was wrapped in. That was the kind of rich girl atttending Pine Crest. Before the bus picked me up every morning at 6:30, Daddy joined me for my breakfast ritual of Rice Krispies and a daily vitamin. I never liked those vitamins, but they were orders from my once-beloved Dr. Eagle, so I followed them.

Before I could figure out whether or not I hated Pine Crest, I discovered that I hated Teddy, far more than Paul ever dreamed of hating her. Living with Teddy, even though I had my own room and was gone most of the day in school, quickly became a strain, a battle for Daddy's attention, a battle that Teddy would never win. As usual Daddy took me everywhere with him, to show me off to his friends, at handball, at card games, at dinners. To Daddy, I became the trophy child. To Teddy I became "the other woman."

If anything went wrong in the house, I would get the blame. One day after school, Teddy was waiting for me, hands cocked on her hips. She led me into the living room and pointed to a pastel portrait of herself hanging in the center of the wall. "Look what you've done!" She glared daggers at me.

I couldn't tell what she was talking about. "Huh?" I asked.

She pointed out smudges on the portrait with her long, blood-red-manicured nail finger. "You did it. You ruined my picture."

"I didn't touch it."

"Don't lie to me! You ruined it."

Suddenly, the live-in black maid rushed into the living room, to my defense. "Oh, no, Miz Lansky. It was me. Don't blame that poor child. It was me. I dusted it. It was dirty. I'm sorry, Miz Lansky."

"Get out!" Teddy screamed. I'm not sure who she was screaming at, me or the maid. I never saw the maid again. But Teddy never apologized to me. I ran out of the house crying and went down the block to see Grandma Yetta, who, after Daddy, became my best friend, my only girlfriend, in my new home. She was in her seventies then, and she spoke with a heavy Old World accent. But I knew she loved me. I stayed with her until dark, when Daddy would be home. When I got there, Teddy was all sweetness, as if nothing had ever happened. I bit my tongue. Never complain.

There was another blow-up a few weeks later. Someone gave Daddy a little poodle that became fond of me. Teddy, who was phobic about animals, confined the dog to the kitchen at night. One school evening I was doing my homework and listening to the radio, which was way better than the homework. They were playing Patti Page's "How Much Is That Doggy in the Window?" Almost as if they were playing his song, the poodle began scratching at my door. He had escaped from the kitchen. Like any normal dog lover, I opened the door and let him in to enjoy Patti Page and Tony Bennett and Perry Como and Frankie Laine, all my "boyfriends." And then I let the dog come to bed with me. No sooner had we fallen asleep than Teddy roared into my room and snatched the poodle from my arms. The poor dog began whimpering. I was even more scared.

"I told you that dirty mutt was never to enter your room, never mind ruining the bed!"

"I didn't do anything wrong!" I cried.

Daddy heard the fracas. He came in and quickly rendered his judgment. "She didn't do anything wrong. Leave Sandra alone, Teddy." Meyer Lansky's judgments were final. Daddy took the trembling dog from Teddy and gave him back to me. Teddy turned on her heel and left the room. Daddy kissed me goodnight, winked at me, and closed the door.

Down the hall, I could hear Teddy yelling at Daddy. It went on and on until I finally fell asleep, dog in my arms. The next afternoon Daddy picked me up at Pine Crest and told me great news. Teddy had left. I hoped it was forever. No such luck. Ten days later she was back. Daddy had to give the poodle back to the people who had given it to them. I tried to stay away from Teddy as much as I could, escaping to Grandma Yetta's or sometime to Flo Alo's. What I did know was that I couldn't live in the same house with Teddy. I wanted to go home to Mommy. Bad as that was, it was better than this.

As a dry run for coming home, I got Daddy to let me fly to New York in early November to go to my favorite annual event, the National Horse Show at Madison Square Garden. This was as big a deal in New York as the World Series. So was seeing Mommy after four months away from her. It was an emotional reunion. She was so happy on the first day, but then she lapsed back to her old sadness and despondency. I didn't know what to do. I couldn't handle Mommy; I couldn't stand Teddy. I was the girl without a country.

And then it happened. I was "saved." On the second night of the Horse Show, a tall, fair, nice-looking boy came up to me at the Garden and introduced himself. Or rather, reintroduced himself. He was

Marvin Rapoport. I had no idea who he was. I didn't remember him, which seemed to deflate him. He reminded me that we knew each other from the Aldrich Stables long ago. Then it hit me. He was the spoiled rich brat who had stolen my horse Bazookie.

"Come on," he pleaded. "I didn't steal him. Only borrowed. He was stunning."

"All right. You're forgiven," I relented. He seemed a lot nicer, and a lot cuter, than I remembered him. Also a lot older. As we talked and talked and talked that evening, I found out he was twenty-three. A grown man. Eight years older than I was. Why was he being so nice to me? Atoning for his theft? No, it had to be something else. Could it be *me*?

Marvin asked if he could buy me a soda, then another. And another. We talked all evening and had a wonderful time. He knew everything about riding, jumping, and breeding, but we had a lot in common besides horses. His brother Raymond was Buddy's age, and the two had been friends in New York. Marvin was from a rich family that owned Rapoport's Dairy Restaurant down on Second Avenue. It was a New York dining landmark, nothing at all like Steinberg's Dairy Restaurant where Mommy took all her meals. Rapoport's, and its chief rival Ratner's, were the Jewish Sardi's and Dinty Moore's. The Yiddish theatres, which had their heyday earlier in the century and whose leading light was Sholem Aleichem, who would inspire *Fiddler on the Roof*, were all close to Rapoport's.

All the actors and playwrights had hung out there. Even when they changed their names and went to Broadway or Hollywood, like Paul Muni or Edward G. Robinson or Lee J. Cobb, they continued to go to Rapoport's and Ratner's. A "dairy restaurant" was a very kosher, rabbi-approved place that did not serve meat or chicken. Today this kind of restaurant would be considered very healthy. Rapoport's was famous for its smoked salmon and sturgeon, its lox and eggs, its blintzes, its soups and onion rolls. Because of my weird diet, I wouldn't eat most of this stuff. I had never been to the restaurant, but I had certainly heard of it. It was as much a part of New York as 21.

Marvin worked at Rapoport's for his family, as a host and manager. Dealing with all the celebrities, he had a lot of charm. He knew just what to say. I remembered Mommy pointing that out years ago when he took Bazookie, then tried to sweet talk his way out of it. Now I liked all the sweet talk. At the end of the evening, he offered to drive me home. He had a fancy black Cadillac convertible with red leather interior. When he stopped at the Westover, I wished I were still living at the Beresford or the St. Moritz so I could invite him up for a snack. I wished Mommy was her old self, so I could show her off as the woman I was going to grow up to be. Now I didn't dare. Marvin asked if we could meet the next day to go to the horse show again. I was thrilled to accept.

We ended up going together for the entire remainder of the show, three magic nights at the old Madison Square Garden on Eighth Avenue. For me, the time was an Arabian Nights fantasy, the horses, the riders, the rich and glamorous patrons, and a man in my life, my own blond Valentino, my sheik of Araby. We never got tired of each other. We talked about his love life, which seemed so sophisticated compared to my adolescent innocence. Marvin had dated showgirls and actresses, he confessed, including Dyan Cannon, who years later would marry Cary Grant. But he hadn't liked any of them.

He said he was looking for someone "pure and special." Me, me, me, I prayed.

Marvin would pick me up at the Westover, downstairs, of course, and take me back. We also went over to the Aldrich Stables, the thing I missed most about New York. Daddy had sold Time Clock when I moved to Florida, so we rented other horses and rode in Central Park. It was wonderful to ride together with Marvin. We were Roy Rogers and Dale Evans, a natural pair.

Marvin was my first real date, and I felt like Cinderella. I hated for it to end. When it did, I popped a very impulsive question. I asked him if he would escort me to my sweet sixteen party. I was trembling, waiting for the answer. Marvin smiled and said he'd be delighted to go. Then he kissed me goodnight, my first kiss since Jimmy C. Amazing! An older man had just kissed me. He was almost as old as Gordon MacRae, and almost as handsome. My life was transformed. I was dancing on air.

If I had been thinking about leaving Florida and staying with Mommy, I gave up those plans. I had to go back to Florida and hold Daddy to his promise of a sweet sixteen party, a party I had wanted to avoid until I met Marvin. Teddy wouldn't bother me now. I had a mission to accomplish. Marvin drove me to the airport. He kissed me goodbye. I was madly in love. Daddy turned out to be easy. He was a man of his word. Marvin called and wrote me letters, almost every day. I wrote back, mostly telling him how excited I was about coming back to New York. I didn't have much to report from dull Florida.

The month passed quickly, and in early December I flew back on Eastern to La Guardia, where Marvin greeted me with a big kiss. So romantic, so grown-up. Daddy didn't come. Instead he called in instructions for the big night, December 13th, where we had two huge tables at the Copacabana on 60th off Fifth Avenue, filled with my friends from Calhoun and the stables, including Eileen, there with her future husband. There were no relatives. I would have liked Daddy there, but he might have had to bring Teddy. It was *my* party, and he knew she would have spoiled it.

I invited Mommy. As expected, she refused. She wouldn't leave the apartment. Nor were there any relatives, from either side of my family. It was the kids' night. Marvin was by far the oldest one there, and I could see how envious all the girls were, with their teenage, pimply dates in badly fitting rented tuxedos. Marvin looked like Cary Grant by comparison. He dressed and danced beautifully. I was the belle of the ball dancing with him, and he was so smooth that he made me look like Ginger Rogers.

The headliners that evening were the Kean Sisters, a comedy duo who also sang. They had a famous number with Ethel Merman from *Gentlemen Prefer Blondes* about three little girls from Little Rock. That night they did it with two girls. Then there were the famous Copa Girls, the stunning chorines with those huge towering headdresses. They were gorgeous, though not topless. For a nightclub, the Copa was pretty much family entertainment, a live version of Ed Sullivan.

The waiters, who treated me like a queen, brought out the biggest birthday cake I'd ever seen. Then the whole restaurant stopped, and every table joined in "Happy Birthday to Sandi." I had a feeling the whole place knew that Meyer Lansky's girl was the guest of honor, and they paid appropriate respect. The only awkward moment was at the end of the party, when the valets couldn't find Marvin's Cadillac convertible. We worried that they had stolen it. One word from the boss, Julie Podell, who took his orders from the *real* boss, Uncle Frank Costello, and it magically reappeared.

Returning to Florida couldn't have been more of an anticlimax to my magic night. There were endless letters and endless flowers from Marvin, but I soon injected some drama in early January by getting appendicitis. They took me to a place called Doctors' Hospital, where Grandma Yetta took charge and grilled the doctors, making sure they did the operation properly. "You better do the right thing! You take out her appendix," she ordered them. "But nothing else!" Then she turned to me and kissed me. "I took care of it," she said confidently. I could see where Daddy got his authority. Between the nose job and now this, I was getting to be an old hand at hospitals. For a second I thought about becoming a nurse.

My room at Doctors' Hospital looked like a botanical garden, there were so many bouquets from Marvin. In one of them, Buddy, who came to see me, found a note, with a big question: "WILL YOU MARRY ME?" in all capitals. Buddy, the gossip king, went into overdrive, showing the card to Daddy. Naturally, even with an IV in my arm, I was ready to say yes, yes, yes, I do, I do. Teddy would have been delighted to let me, just for good riddance. But Daddy, who hadn't yet met Marvin, was typically cautious. He advised me that I was way too young, and that I should at least finish high school before making such major life plans.

Daddy may have controlled the world, but the one thing he could not control was his teenage daughter. I was so willful. I wanted Marvin. Was it love, or was it a way of escaping the twin terrors of Mommy and Teddy? Right now I thought it was love, love, love. When I got out of the hospital, Daddy and I must have had dinner together at every famous restaurant in Miami, a different one every night, the Embers, Joe Sonken's Gold Coast, and Joe's Stone Crab. He tried to ply me with glamor and luxury and convince me that at sixteen, marriage was not the greatest idea, that I should give this relationship some time to develop. His pitch was that of the future Supremes' hit "You Can't Hurry Love." Mine was "Get Me to the Church on Time." To me, love at first sight was what love was all about—head over heels.

Daddy and I were in a Mexican standoff. To break it, he offered to fly to New York to meet Marvin and, more important to him, Marvin's parents. I hadn't met them, either, which shows how blindly I wanted this to work. If they agreed, he would agree. My father, who thought he could out-negotiate anyone, was sure he could talk the Rapoports out of what he considered to be sheer madness. The appendectomy gave me the excuse to drop out of school for a while. Once out, I wanted to stay out. School seemed so trivial for this newly adult bride-to-be.

In early February Daddy and I flew back to New York. I was turning into a real jet-setter, five years before the first jets started flying. Marvin picked us up in his Cadillac and drove us to his parents' home in Long Beach, Long Island. Marvin, at five foot ten, towered over Daddy. I normally could never read Daddy, but when he first laid eyes on Marvin, he gave him *that look* of his. He covered it up quickly; that look had me worried. I sat in the back seat. Daddy and Marvin talked, mostly about Rapoport's. Daddy knew more about restaurants than anybody in the world. He loved to eat, and he loved to talk about the business. That was a good sign, because Marvin talked with great authority and experience.

Marvin gave us a tour of Long Beach, which, he told us, used to be known as the "Riviera of the East." He showed us the French and Spanish-style mansions where some famous residents lived or used to live, Valentino, Humphrey Bogart, James Cagney, John Barrymore, Florenz Ziegfeld, all also patrons of Rapoport's, Marvin proudly noted. His parents' large house was near the ocean, though it was so cold the Atlantic looked frozen. Anna Rapoport was the boss of the family, glamorously dressed and just as assertive as Grandma Yetta. Anna was from Hungary, and she seemed as if she wanted to be as glamorous as fellow Hungarian Zsa Zsa Gabor. She was the front woman at the restaurant. Daddy Harry, a reserved, quiet man, did the books. But Harry was anything but back office. Harry Rapoport, after all, *was* Rapoport's. He had his own charm, and a dry wit, and the customers loved him.

We were sitting in the living room by a roaring fire. We had barely begun talking when Marvin stood up and presented me with a three-carat diamond engagement ring. I had never before seen Daddy at a loss for words. He was speechless. This was supposed to be a discussion, not a *fait accompli*. Awkwardly, the parents suggested Marvin and I go driving somewhere so they could talk to Daddy. They talked for hours and hours. In the end, I got my way. Mrs. Rapoport, I was told, had promised to treat me like a daughter, her daughter, to be the mother I currently lacked. She said, with two of her three sons all grown (the third was close to my age), she welcomed the chance to be a real mother again, and to have a girl in the family she could fuss over the way she never could with her boys. This somehow broke down Daddy's resistance.

Marvin drove Daddy and me back to the Warwick Hotel on 54th Street and Sixth Avenue. With Miami now his main base, Daddy had given up the 36th Street apartment. The Kefauver hearings had made him too famous in celebrity-mad New York. In Miami he could still be anonymous. I could barely contain my joy that the marriage was moving ahead. I didn't want to rub it in, because I knew I had beaten Daddy in this negotiation, and Daddy never wanted to be beaten. The next day I surprised Mommy by visiting her with my wedding ring on. That was my own *fait accompli*. Now she was the one who thought I was the crazy one. The tables had turned. I hadn't told her about Marvin before, just as I had not told her about the appendectomy. That nose job was enough of a trauma for her. The marriage, she declared, was absurd, ridiculous. Just meet Marvin, I begged her. You'll see. "I've *already* met Marvin," she reminded me, fully alert and in control for the first time in a long time. "I have met him and I have seen." Suffice it to say, I did not get her blessing. I returned to the War-wick; Marvin and I decided that the wedding should take place right away. If we weren't going to wait, why wait at all?

We planned a big ceremony for a few days off. Then Marvin and I went downtown to the courthouse to get a marriage license. Problem! As a minor, I needed both parents' written permission. Daddy was on board; Mommy was dead set against it. So Daddy, who obviously couldn't talk to Mommy, had to address himself to the one person who could—Paul. Paul, in his final year at West Point, thought the mar-riage was ridiculous as well, but Daddy made his request, and Paul relented. Paul would never refuse Daddy, even for something crazy like this. He took a train down to New York that night and somehow convinced Mommy to sign the paper. I still don't know how or why he did it. Maybe just to get rid of me.

Now it was all systems go. Two days to the wedding and I re-alized I had no trousseau, nothing to wear. Daddy took care of the money part. But I had no idea how to be a wife, or dress like one. Marvin came to the rescue. He said he knew everything about beauty and fashion. First came the clothes. Marvin loved to shop more than Mommy ever did in her happy days. Daddy had given me enough money for Saks or Bonwit Teller or both of them combined. Marvin took the cash and said why pay retail. He had connections.

So we drove to Seventh Avenue to some dingy showroom in what looked like a warehouse. I tried on a lot of ugly dresses that Marvin dismissed because he said I was "too hippy." It was over a decade before hippie meant something cool. Marvin meant I was too fat, which hurt my feelings. I was willing to starve to please him. Finally, he settled on a red dress with white polka dots that I thought belonged in a circus, and a bunch more, for our upcoming honeymoon in Mexico and Las Vegas. What did I know? He was the fashion plate, the man of the world. I bought what he told me.

The morning of our wedding, Marvin picked me up and drove me to Brooklyn. A hairdresser friend of his worked in a beauty shop there. I didn't realize Brooklyn even had beauty shops. From Mommy's high-fashion days, I thought all salons were on 57th Street. When they finished with me, I might have been right.

Marvin's friend, who was very theatrical and flamboyant, decided to make me a blonde, a real blonde, not the natural dirty blonde I already was. To begin, the friend stripped my hair to a bright ghastly orange. "My God, I look like a carrot," I gasped. Then he completely waxed off my eyebrows. Marvin himself penciled new ones in. He loved this stuff. He and his friend applied makeup and eye shadow, supposedly in the style of Zsa Zsa Gabor, but more like that of Marvin's mother. This so-called beautician was better suited to doing special effects for monster movies. They oohed and aahed, but I felt like a freak. I walked into that beauty shop a sixteen-year-old and walked out a silver-haired, overly made-up matron, the spitting image of my mother-in-law to be.

There was no time for vanity. Marvin then drove me to the Westover, where I had to pick up a lot of things for our honeymoon, and where I had decided to put on my wedding dress. Mommy was even more horrified than she was by my nose job. "I warned you, I warned you," she cried, cursing herself for signing the consent form for Paul. "You look like your Grandmother," she said, referring to her mother, who was anything but a beauty. "Please, darling, please. I beg you with all my heart. It's not too late to stop this. It's all wrong! Stay with me. Don't do it."

I left her in tears. If Marvin had come up, she might have killed him. In my clown dress and old lady hairdo, I rode with Marvin down to an old synagogue on the Lower East Side that had served as a congregation for members of the Yiddish theatre. This was my second synagogue. The first was on a Calhoun field trip to the enormous and ornate Temple Emanu-el on Fifth Avenue. This place was very run down, though Marvin called it "historic." Daddy was there waiting, as were Uncle Jack Lansky and his wife. Daddy and his brother looked funny to me in their skullcaps, which I had never seen them wear before. I know I looked even funnier to them. Poor Daddy. When he saw my hair and dress, tears came to his eyes, and they were not tears of joy. I had no one else there, no Citrons, no Paul, no Buddy, no Grandma Yetta.

There were tons of Rapoports. This was much more their party than ours. Marvin's normally sedate father was very excited to see me, so much so that he kept pinching my behind. I guess it was a gesture of affection. Maybe he was excited because I looked just like his wife.

A rabbi performed the ceremony. I had no idea what he was saying or what the ceremony meant, with the tent and the business with stepping on the glass. To me it was all foreign mumbo-jumbo. I just said yes and basked in the chorus of *mazel tovs*. I kept reminding myself that all of this was better than going back to live with Teddy.

After the ceremony, we drove up to the Versailles at 151 East 50th Street, for the wedding reception. That day we had driven out to Brooklyn, up to the Upper West Side, then down to the Lower East Side, and now back up to midtown. I hoped our highway to eternal happiness would not follow such an erratic course. The Versailles was a famous supper club that featured French singers like Edith Piaf and Maurice Chevalier. The Versailles was Daddy's show, and Daddy's treat. The father of the bride had the great Edith Piaf there to serenade Marvin and me with French *chansons d'amour*. Between her big showstoppers, like "La Vie en Rose," an American combo sang "An Old Fashioned Wedding" and "Almost Like Being in Love." I didn't think about the "almost" until some time later.

The Versailles was decorated like an over-the-top French chateau, the kind of décor that got Marie Antoinette beheaded, tons of crystal and silver and unicorn tapestries and fake copies of Renoirs and Cézannes. There was a French menu with foie gras and caviar and steaks with béarnaise sauce and rack of lamb, all the stuff they didn't serve at Rapoport's Dairy Restaurant. The waiters kept saying not to worry, that everything was kosher. There were toasts and dancing and endless photos and a fortune teller who seemed shocked that I was the bride. "You? You're a baby," she marvelled. She read my palm and said, "You will have a long life." She didn't say a "long and happy life."

I wasn't looking for omens. I was worried about our wedding night. I had as little an idea about what to do then as I had about how to look for the wedding. All I could hope for was that the night would go better than what had come before. Our honeymoon hotel was Marvin's bachelor apartment at 360 East 56th Street, right off Sutton Place, one of the nicest neighborhoods in the city. I had not seen Marvin's place before, just as I had not met his parents. And following Mommy's Jimmy C orders, I hadn't gone any further with Marvin than a lot of kissing, nothing more.

Now was the moment of truth. I knew *something* big was supposed to happen. Actually I was hoping it wouldn't, that we could somehow put it off until we got to Mexico. My appendix surgery was barely a month before. I still had scars and pains. Moreover, I had never been naked in front of a man before, except Dr. Eagle and that didn't count. I hadn't even had a drink at the party. I was too young, and the Versailles wouldn't serve me for fear of losing their liquor license. Because Meyer Lansky was there, the whole world, and the cops, were watching like hawks. I had nothing to calm my anxiety.

I went into Marvin's bathroom and changed into my new flannel nightgown. There was nothing sexy about it. Marvin had picked it out. Maybe his mother had one, too. I was taken totally by surprise when I came out of the bathroom and found Marvin lying in bed, completely naked. Aside from the accident with Daddy in the shower, I had never seen a grown-up naked man. And I had never, ever seen one with an erection. Gee!

Marvin gently pulled me down on the bed beside him. He started kissing me and tried to take off the nightgown. I was worried about messing up my awful hairdo and looking even worse the next morning on our flight to Mexico City. In those days travel was dressy and glamorous. You had to look your best. Marvin took charge and calmed me down. He seemed to know what he was doing. Whatever it was was quick and didn't hurt nearly as much as I thought it would.

Marvin did what he had to do, then rolled over and went to sleep. There wasn't any cuddling or a lot of mushy declarations of love and passion. Those were embarrassing. That didn't bother me, but the next morning I saw that the sheets were covered with blood. "That's for Maddie," he told me. Maddie? I was confused. Maddie was his maid. She would clean things up. I was worried that the blood was caused by my incision opening up. Marvin assured me that was not the case, and gave me a brief lecture on the birds and bees. "Got that, Mrs. Rapoport?" he asked. He could be cute and witty. I finally felt that I belonged somewhere, to someone. Meanwhile we had a plane to catch and a real honeymoon to go on. Honeymoons were where babies were made, and, as I would soon find out, nobody wanted to be a father more or faster than my new husband. Why he was in such a tear would be the new story of my life.

CHAPTER SEVEN

THE HONEYMOONERS

"Don't drink the water!" That was the only travel advice the revelers at the Versailles kept giving us for our honeymoon to Mexico. They didn't tell us about museums or cathedrals or pyramids or volcanos or other things that I had seen in the travel brochures Marvin had collected. Just the water. The idea was that we were at risk of getting terribly sick, so we had to be extremely careful. Why go there? Why? Because it was a *deal*. Marvin's mother had worked out a swap for catering office parties with a travel company called Perillo Tours, a kind of blintzes-for-tacos trade, and our honeymoon would not cost a penny. That, to Mrs. Rapoport, was worth the dysentery risk. "Deals," whether for clothes or travel or restaurants or whatever, were very important to Marvin's family, who liked to trade their dairy delicacies for anything and everything. That was business.

Daddy would have been delighted to send us to Europe, probably in the $2,600 Regal Suite on the *Italia* that had attracted so much notoriety. However, the Rapoports made such a big show of taking care of everything that Daddy felt it would have been rude to try to override them. Besides, he was so shell-shocked by the blitzkrieg-shotgun nature of our marriage that he didn't have time to think about the arrangements. Whatever, I was excited to be leaving the country and seeing the world. What was adventure without risk?

The trip to Mexico City was smooth. We left a bitter snowy February in New York and landed in Mexico's perfect eternal springtime. I only drank Cokes, Marvin only drank tequila, no ice, and we didn't get sick. The main thing I remember was the sex. I had no idea you were supposed to do it every night, before bedtime, like saying your prayers, which I never did. I secretly fretted that I would have to do this for the rest of my life. At first I tried to be flattered that Marvin was so wildly attracted to me. Yet the sex wasn't wild at all. He'd lie in bed in his boxer shorts, wait for me to come out of the bathroom, get on with the job, then roll over and go to sleep. It was like a duty, a chore, and before the end of the honeymoon, I found out exactly what the job was.

"Are you pregnant yet?" Marvin began asking me. That was before I had a chance to miss my first period. I barely understood that was the first sign of pregnancy. There were other signs, Marvin told me. He had clearly read some pregnancy manual and had become an expert on the matter, an amateur gynecologist. I had never been to a real one. Maybe this was another Rapoport way to save money. He kept asking me if I was nauseous so much that he made me want to throw up. Did I go to the bathroom more often? Were my breasts tender? Did I feel tired? Of course I did, trudging up the steep hills of Taxco all day to silver shops. Why was he in such a hurry? Couldn't we just take our time? It took nine months to make a baby. Couldn't we at least enjoy a few weeks? I tried my best to make the most of it and feel sophisticated and grown-up. After all, I was a "married woman" now.

The two main things Marvin loved were the shopping and the bullfights. Paying the bills with the huge wad of cash Daddy had given him for the honeymoon, Marvin sent his family a ton of Mexican curios, *tchotchkes*, as my new mother-in-law might say. Maybe he had plans to transform Rapoport's into a kosher Mexican restaurant serving lox enchiladas. I hated the bullfights. I couldn't stand watching a beautiful animal get stabbed to death. Marvin was obsessed less with the bulls than the matadors. He kept going on and on about how cool and handsome they were. He even found a costume shop that made *traje de luces*, or traditional matador suits, and wasted a whole afternoon trying them on. Somehow I was able to talk him out of it. Where in New York could he wear one, other than on Halloween?

By the time we survived a very turbulent flight to Acapulco on a flimsy prop plane, I was so shopped out that all I wanted to do was lie by the pool. I was still under doctor's orders not to swim, because of the appendectomy. I wished I could get a note excusing me from the ritual baby-making attempts. I was so sore. After Acapulco, we had another white-knuckle flight through the volcanoes back to Mexico City, took a big plane to Los Angeles, then a small one to Las Vegas. In 1954 Las Vegas was still a tiny town, a small oasis of gambling and a touch of Hollywood glamor in the middle of a very barren desert. Was this what Uncle Benny died for, was my first impression.

If I couldn't see the future, I could sense the allure of the present. It was nighttime and the February air was warm and scented with flowers. The glow of neon from the hotel signs lit up the desert night. It wasn't Times Square, but Times Square was 20 degrees. This was 70. And you couldn't gamble in Times Square. Daddy was there at the adobe shed of an airport, dressed in a fancy suit and tie, which stood out among the cowboy types in ten-gallon hats. Even in the Wild West, Daddy was pure New York. I thanked my lucky stars Marvin hadn't arrived wearing that bullfighter suit. Daddy might have had him shot on sight.

We didn't stay at Uncle Benny's (now Daddy's) Flamingo. Instead, Daddy put us in the Thunderbird, his sprawling hotel with the giant neon head of an Aztec god at the entrance. Maybe Daddy's idea was to continue the Mexican theme of our honeymoon, though I doubt it. Daddy wasn't "artistic" the way Marvin seemed to be. We had our own cottage, a honeymoon suite they called a "lanai," with a big private patio that had direct access to the Olympic-size swimming pool.

The headliners, announced on a hotel's marquee, were Kathryn Grayson, whom I had just seen in the film hit *Kiss Me Kate,* and the Irving Fields Trio, playing in the Pow Wow Room. Daddy later introduced us to them and whoever else was performing during our ten-day stay. One of the stars we met was Nat King Cole, who was there on business and stayed in his own gleaming airstream trailer on the grounds of the Thunderbird. Later we learned that black people, even a star like Nat King Cole, weren't allowed to stay in the Vegas resorts, only in servants' quarters on the poor side of town. Daddy's management team had bought this special trailer so Mr. Cole could stay at the hotel without actually staying inside of it and triggering a nasty incident. The West, it seemed, was more like Estes Kefauver's Old South than New York.

I spent my days lying around in the sun by the pool, getting my fair skin slowly suntanned, watching Marvin swim and wishing I could dive in. But I had to follow doctor's orders to protect my healing incision. Marvin was instantly hooked on gambling. Since his father-in-law owned the house, Marvin thought he could bet the house. I was too young to enter the casinos, but Marvin dressed up and assumed the role of a high roller. The minute he lost his first hundred dollars, Daddy was notified. Meyer Lansky quickly cut off his son-in-law's credit and gave Marvin a cordial lecture: "Don't bet more than you have." What he didn't say but was understood was, "Don't play with other people's money."

"Sure, Dad. Gotcha, Dad. Whatever you say, Dad." Marvin dared not disagree with my father. However, the "Dad" word seemed to grate on Daddy's nerves. He suppressed a slight cringe every time he heard it. Still, he remained polite and was always the perfect gentleman to my new husband.

I would have loved to go horseback riding in the desert. After all, this was the West, cowboy country. There were horses everywhere. Because I was still recuperating, Daddy refused. If Daddy had known the workout I was getting every night, he might have changed his mind. That, or kill the guy who was doing this to his one and only baby girl. Marvin and I spent most of our time out of the lanai making the rounds of the assorted resort hotels, meeting the Las Vegas uncles who owned them and collecting "tribute" for our marriage.

We had an endless round of lunches and dinners, at the El Cortez with Dave Berman from Minneapolis, at the Desert Inn with Moe Dalitz from Cleveland, with Dandy Phil Kastel from New Orleans, who was also at the Thunderbird and just starting to build the Tropicana. We dined with Daddy's investment partners at the Flamingo, Moey Sedway and Morris Rosen. Another partner, Gus Greenbaum, drove up from Phoenix to meet us and pay his respects. They toasted us, and Daddy toasted Morris's son Jackie, and his wife, Benny Siegel's daughter Millicent, who would soon have a child with the crazy name of Cinderella. They called her Cindy.

At these celebrations, all of Daddy's associates would raise endless rounds of drinks to me and Marvin. I was still stuck with ginger ale; Daddy didn't want to lose his liquor license serving minors, even in a state where gambling and prostitution were legal. The finale would be to make a big show of presenting me with a fat envelope. As soon as we returned to the lanai, Marvin would tear it open and marvel at the loot. "I'm the banker!" he insisted. The envelopes invariably contained dozens of hundred dollar bills. We must have left Vegas with tens of thousands of dollars, enough to keep Marvin in horses and matador suits, if he wanted them, for a lifetime.

Our honeymoon seemed to go on forever. No sooner had we flown to New York, loaded down with our vast bank haul, than we had to make another honeymoon trip to Miami with Marvin's parents. We drove down in Marvin's Cadillac. In Henderson, North Carolina, we were caught in a speed trap and a redneck officer who'd been hiding behind a billboard that said "Jesus Loves You" pulled us over. The officer had a cornpone accent that made Estes Kefauver sound like a Shakespearean actor. "Ya'll Yankees," he called us. "Where's the fire, folks? Ya'll Yankees gotta learn to slow down and smell the barbecue." He examined Marvin's driver's license. "Rap-o-port," he read the syllables, way slower than molasses but not sweet at all. "We ain't got no names like that down here. That a Jew name?" he asked Marvin.

"It's a German name," Marvin offered.

The policeman shined his flashlight over all of our faces. "What part of Germany ya'll from? You from Berrr-lin?"

"German a long time ago," Marvin stuttered. "We're from New York."

"Do I look stupid, boy?"

"No, sir," Marvin said, fearfully.

"You people don't look like no Germans to me."

He took us down to the station, following the Cadillac on his motorcycle, his large gun reflecting Dixie moonlight. Marvin's father always travelled with his own pillow. Resigned to spending the night in jail, he brought his pillow in with him. Fortunately, there was a justice of the peace at the station who was there all night to hear such kangaroo proceedings. We paid a big fine and went on our way. It was my second encounter with southern justice, the first being the Kefauver hearings. High and low, they both seemed equally rigged.

It took five days to drive to Miami, stopping to tour the antebellum landmarks in Charleston and Savannah en route. The very best part of the family holiday was getting a reprieve from the endless sex. Marvin couldn't, or wouldn't, perform his husbandly chores with his mother in the adjoining motel room. That might have been sacrilegious. However, Mr. Rapoport continued to proclaim how thrilled he was to have me as his daughter-in-law, punctuating every declaration of joy with an exuberant pinch or squeeze of my poor bottom.

When we got to Florida, we stayed for two weeks at another Rapoport place called the Seagull Kosher Hotel. It was hardly the Roney Plaza. Then again, Teddy wasn't there, which was a huge positive. With Daddy still out west, this was a Rapoport holiday more than a Lansky one, though we did get to see Buddy and introduce my new family to Grandma Yetta, who whispered something to herself under her breath that sounded like an exasperated "*Gott in Himmel*," or "God in Heaven." Mrs. Rapoport was very nice to me. I couldn't understand, though, why she kept taking me aside and begging me to "make Marvin change his friends." I hadn't really met any of his friends other than the awful beautician and the guys in the Seventh Avenue showroom. Sure, I promised her, not knowing what I was in for.

Back in New York, after I hand-wrote the thank you notes that Marvin carefully dictated to me to my uncles in Las Vegas, my next task was to try to master the art, or science, of being a housewife. Since I had never even learned to take care of myself, taking care of a husband was, at the outset, a major challenge. For my first breakfast, Marvin asked me for "three-minute eggs." Clueless, I took three eggs from the fridge and laid them on the counter to unchill for three minutes. When Marvin cracked the shell, raw yolk exploded all over him. I had no idea I was supposed to boil them.

Another night, Marvin asked me to try to make him tongue, a Jewish specialty. How could I cook a tongue when I could barely cut my own meat? Well, he asked for it, and he got it. Lighting the gas stove, the oven exploded, singeing what was left of my eyebrows. When Daddy learned that the maid Maddie only came in two days a week to clean, he volunteered to pay for her to come in seven days a week to cook as well as clean. In addition to our maid, Daddy also bought us two new horses. One was called Rex Lee Fashion, which sounded like the name of the showroom Marvin took me to buy my trousseau. The other horse was Moonbeam's Golden Genius. We stabled the horses at a farm in the New Jersey hunt country and went out every weekend to ride. Marvin preferred New Jersey to Central Park. There was a lot more of it, and the air was better.

In the city, I finally got to see the friends of my husband who had caused his mother such consternation. After working at Rapoport's all day, he'd come uptown and take me out to dinner, never to the big, high-profile places like Dinty Moore's or the Colony or Lindy's or Luchow's, but to cozy candlelit restaurants in Greenwich Village or on the Upper East Side. The weird part was that I seemed to be the only woman at most of these places. The tables were filled with men, young men, old men, sometimes famous men. I remember seeing the actor James Mason one night with a young man who was just as handsome as he was. They were holding hands. I had never seen that before. I figured movie stars could be eccentric. Then I noticed a lot of the other male couples were doing the same, or getting even closer.

When I pointed this out to Marvin, wide-eyed, he just laughed and told me how sheltered I had been, that I had no idea how "sophisticated" the city could be. I'm not sure if any of these men were the friends his mother had wanted me to try to get him away from. There was always someone in these places to whom he nodded hello, though he never would introduce me. Maybe he thought I wasn't ready to move in such fast company. If not, I had a worldly mentor to bring me up and out. The idea was that my husband would teach me to be sophisticated, too. And what girl in Manhattan didn't want to be sophisticated? As a sixteen-year-old, I realized I was a babe in the woods, with a lot to learn.

One of the highlights of 1954, aside from my marriage, was my brother's graduation from West Point. I don't remember why, but Marvin didn't come. I think he had to work at the restaurant. Sadly neither Mommy nor Buddy attended, either. I sat with Grandma Yetta, while Daddy and Teddy sat, seemingly miles away from us. That was the first and only time Teddy had come to West Point. The graduating cadets all hurling their caps in the air was a spectacle I'll never forget. In a touching moment, Paul gave my father his graduation ring. Daddy gave Paul a new car, a Ford sedan, which Daddy ended up having to sell, because Paul was going off to pilot training school and wouldn't need it. Marvin couldn't understand why the great Meyer Lansky hadn't given his son something fancier, if not a Cadillac, at least a convertible. Marvin's style wasn't Daddy's style. The training school was in Washington State. It was far away, but I had long ago gotten used to Paul being out of my life.

After months of never-ending sex and the never-ending query "Are you pregnant yet?" I finally gave Marvin the answer he had been waiting for. The lucky day was, of all days, Labor Day, September 3, 1954. We were up in Syracuse to attend the horse show at the state fair there. Marvin was the happiest I had ever seen him. I learned months later that he celebrated by buying himself a new horse with money from a bank account Daddy had set up for me that Marvin figured out how to access. He kept the horse at a separate farm, and with a different trainer, from our other horses.

When I discovered Marvin's little caper, I was too busy planning my maternity to be angry with the father of our child. Whatever was mine was his, I supposed. As soon as they learned I was pregnant, Marvin's family took over. His oldest brother Raymond's wife, Evelyn, took me to her gynecologist in Queens. Why go all the way out there? I complained, but Marvin insisted. I think they got a deal on that, too, as the doctor always had a menu from Rapaport's open on his desk. In the end, Daddy would pick up all the medical bills.

While Marvin was away all day at work, I tried to acquire some homemaking skills. Going to camp had already made me an expert on making beds and creating hospital corners, and Mommy, when she still cared about things, had taught me how to dust. I tried to learn to iron, but when Marvin got mad at me for burning his silky nylon undershorts, I gave up and sent them to the cleaners. I also learned to shop at Bloomingdales for linens and crystal and cooking gadgets that I then had to figure out how to use.

Sometimes I'd give up on the homemaking and just buy clothes for myself, or cashmere sweaters and English shirts and other gifts for Marvin. Interestingly, the minute Marvin found out I was pregnant, our sex life immediately stopped. At first I thought he was protecting the baby from needless trauma. Then I realized that he wasn't interested in sex for sex's sake. Sex was a means to the end of parenthood. Whatever, I wasn't insulted. I was relieved.

In December, I finally realized how real my pregnancy was when I passed out while Christmas shopping at Saks Fifth Avenue. The salesgirl who came to my rescue went through my pocketbook to see who I was and whom to call. As I came to, I watched her nearly faint when she saw how much cash was jammed into my purse, maybe thousands of dollars. She told me she had never seen so much money. I'm not sure she saw my name or figured out who my father was. That might have knocked her out as well.

Unable to go riding anymore until the baby arrived, I had to escape our small apartment and go for a walk. Greta Garbo lived a few blocks away, on the cul de sac of 52nd Street overlooking the East River. I'd see her wandering around in a slouch hat and dark glasses, looking as lost in her life as I was. Eventually Marvin bought me a dog, a little poodle named Nappy, for Napoleon, for whom Marvin later bought a companion, named Maria, for Napoleon's Austrian wife Maria Luisa. The poodles would become my best friends and walking companions. Some days I'd take a cab up to Calhoun to meet my old classmates on their lunch break and go to a soda shop. I would alternate between feeling very grown up and feeling like a dropout loser.

On one hand, the girls were so impressed that I had become the very first of them to get married and get pregnant. On the other, I felt that something was terribly wrong with me and my family. Buddy didn't finish high school. Now I was following in his sad and crippled footsteps, without his excuse of being crippled. Mommy's mental problems haunted me as well. Would I end up the way she did? And what about Daddy, constantly being mentioned in the news, sounding like Public Enemy Number One. I tried to banish those fears from my mind, as well as the constant nausea that began to plague me, by watching a lot of television quiz shows and listening to a lot of music on the radio.

My tastes ran to Doris Day, Nat King Cole, the Four Aces, and the Ames Brothers, Hit Parade stuff from people who would appear in Daddy's nightclubs. Elvis and the rock 'n' roll explosion were almost two years away. Whenever I didn't feel too sick to get out of the apartment, I went to the movies—*From Here to Eternity* and *A Star Is Born*. Marvin went with me to the latter. He was a major Judy Garland fan, playing her records endlessly. I wasn't sure why he loved her so. In real life, as I learned from the movie magazines, she seemed more depressed than Mommy.

I didn't have to wear the maternity clothes I had bought until I was seven months' pregnant. At five foot four, I normally weighed 115 pounds, which made me tall for a Lansky and skinny for the time. I weighed 130 at the peak. The Queens doctor and his nurses had led me to believe that I was having a girl. Accordingly I spent a fortune at Saks on girls' baby clothes and picked out the name Wendy, after my first friend in Boston, as well as my first doll.

Was I ever surprised when on June 3, 1955, a beautiful bouncing baby boy came into the world in the Queens hospital where the Rapoport doctor was affiliated. I had had no idea what going into labor was. It started at the Devon Horse Show in Pennsylvania, and it was so bad that I had to beg Marvin to take me home. The amateur gynecologist had no idea that the baby was coming. He and I both thought that what I had was a belly ache. Back in New York I tried to heal myself with Alka-Seltzer, until Maddie figured it out and called the ambulance. The doctors called the slow process "lazy labor."

Marvin named our blessing Gary Van Rapoport. When Daddy, who flew up from Florida, heard the name, he made one of his rare attempts at humor by asking why we were calling his grandson a *truck*. Uncle Abe Zwillman and a lot of other uncles came to see Daddy and me at the hospital. I don't remember who else, I was so out of it. Teddy was not there. Daddy didn't want to upset me at this tender moment. All I do recall was that my room seemed like a flower shop. I don't know where Marvin got the name Van, whether from the actors Van Johnson or Van Heflin, or maybe from the grandest of the old New York Hudson Valley Dutch families, the Van Rensselaers. Maybe Marvin was acquiring snooty airs from all the riding. Maybe my new married name would be Sandra Van Rapoport. Maybe we would start spending summers in Newport, Rhode Island, with the rest of the socialites.

We weren't on Fifth Avenue yet. Instead, we were back on the Upper West Side, in a big apartment Daddy rented for us at 451 West End Avenue at 82nd Street, to accommodate the baby and the live-in help Daddy would be providing. We were very nearby to Mommy, who perked up and bought us the entire layette from the same saleswoman at Saks who had waited on her when Buddy and Paul and I were born. We were equally near to Mommy's brother Uncle Julie Citron, who could be counted on in times of trouble.

Ten days after Gary arrived, the Rapoports hosted the circumcision, or *bris*, at the new apartment. It was a big event, with over sixty guests, with lots of friends and relatives bearing lots of gifts, many big and expensive. For example, Evelyn's husband, Raymond, arrived with a very fancy baby carriage from Best & Co. I wasn't allowed to see the *bris*, not that I could have stood to watch. One funny detail was that for the event I dressed Gary in a girl's christening dress I had bought at Saks, when I thought he was going to be she. I was still pretty ignorant about Jewish rituals and didn't have my own religious identity.

Marvin had been thinking less about our new apartment and our first child and more about a second honeymoon. He was dying to go to Europe. His mother had a new deal with Perillo Tours and had found us a baby nurse to stay with Gary while we went away for a month. This nurse, who looked like a stevedore and had a thick German accent, could have been a prison camp guard. I didn't want to leave my baby at all, much less with this Nazi-like hausfrau.

But the Rapoports shamed me into going, insisting their Marvin needed a holiday, all the expenses of which, aside from the free airfare and hotels, Daddy would be paying, with an emphasis on clothes and furniture for our new place. Because Gary was being bottle-fed, not breast-fed, the Rapoports assured me that my presence was not essential. In early July, barely a month after Gary arrived, Marvin and I flew on Sabena to Brussels. My Calhoun French was nowhere as good as I thought. Nobody understood a word I said, so I gave up and stuck to English. Because we were on a tour, the trip was very much Europe's greatest hits: "If it's Tuesday, this must be Belgium." We visited the Grande Place in Brussels, then were herded onto a train to Paris, where we checked off Notre Dame, the Eiffel Tower, the flea market, the Moulin Rouge.

Marvin skipped most of the sightseeing and went on a mad shopping spree, buying half the men's clothes on the Rue St.-Honoré. Who did he think he was going to be, Maurice Chevalier? Despite this supposedly being our second honeymoon, there was nothing at all romantic about it, no cozy hand-holding dinners, no gypsy violinists, no strolling on the banks of the Seine, no sex. None whatsoever. I concluded we were going to be a one-child family. What if I wanted a companion for Gary? Don't think about it. After dinners with the tour group, Marvin would disappear into the Paris night, or the Venice night, or the night of wherever we were. Maybe he wanted to see the Paris churches and the Venice canals by moonlight. I was tired and glad to go to sleep.

After Rome, with the Coliseum, the Forum, the catacombs and more wardrobe building on the Via Condotti, Marvin arranged a week-long extension to the itinerary so we could go to Naples, Pompeii, and Capri. What he was really after, I soon learned, was not culture but connections, Daddy's connections. The biggest of them all was Charles "Lucky" Luciano, whom Marvin had managed to track down in Naples and arrange a "family reunion" with me, the honeymooning daughter of his dearest American friend. Did Daddy know about this? I pressed Marvin, who admitted he did not. "It'll be a great big surprise," he insisted. If I knew anything it was that Daddy did not like surprises. What could I do? Luciano had invited us to lunch. It was an offer we couldn't refuse.

The meeting was at a fancy restaurant overlooking the sea in the port area of Santa Lucia. The name of the restaurant was the California, just in case we were homesick. But there was nothing American about the place, no hamburgers or anything like that. Vesuvius, the volcano that had buried Pompeii centuries ago, loomed menacingly across the bay. This wasn't just the Old World; this was the ancient world, the world where all the myths came from. Now we were going to meet a modern one, Lucky Luciano, the emperor of the underworld. The California, which in fact was owned by Luciano, was the best restaurant in Naples, with a vast antipasto table that filled one whole room, and packed with elegant gentlemen eating lobster and crabs and other delicacies that the local fisherman delivered to the restaurant straight from their boats outside.

When the regal maître d' led us to the prime banquette where Luciano was waiting for us, my first thought was that Daddy had played a brilliant trick and had flown over to surprise us. That was how much Luciano and Lansky looked like each other. The same size, the same face, the same custom suit. When we got closer, I saw that it was no joke. It was the real thing—the man who was supposed to be the ultimate "godfather," the man the mob-busters said controlled the crime of America, through my father, even though he was an ocean and a continent away.

Lucky Luciano leapt up from the table and gave me a bigger, warmer hug and kiss than I had ever gotten from anyone in my family, or Marvin's, either. He gave Marvin a kiss and hug as well. That, I pre-sumed, was the Italian style. Marvin must have been used to it, from the restaurant world. This guy was family, for sure. I instantly began calling him Uncle Charlie. He liked that. Up close, he looked a little older, late fifties, and a lot rougher than Daddy. His skin was badly pockmarked. One of his eyes drooped, giving him a permanently sad appearance, even when he was laughing. (The pockmarks had come from smallpox, the droopy eye from a murder attempt. This man was a survivor.) Sitting at Luciano's feet was his beloved and well-behaved miniature Doberman. The dog's name was Bambi, after the Disney film. Uncle Charlie still had an accent, less the florid Italianized En-glish we had been hearing in our hotels but more like something from Little Italy, an immigrant's English that had never gotten fancied up even when his suits did.

We must have had a dozen courses. He ordered lots of bite-size things, ravioli, rigatoni, fried vegetables, little clams and mussels and shrimp. Marvin was impressed with the California. When he told Charlie how New York had nothing like it, the big boss got wistful and homesick. He said he'd do anything for a big plate of linguini at Angelo's on Mulberry Street.

Over the long meal, Uncle Charlie loved reminiscing about the good old days with Daddy, insisting, over and over, that he'd known *everybody* and Meyer Lansky was the bravest and finest man he'd ever known. He was so effusive about Daddy that he made me blush. While Daddy, true to form, had never told me anything about Uncle Charlie, Uncle Charlie delighted in telling me everything (well, not quite everything) about the "tough little Jew" who had "surprised the hell outta me" by standing up to his tough street gang that used to beat up the Jewish kids and force them to pay "protection" money of a penny a day so they wouldn't get beaten up anymore. "We couldn't beat 'em, so we had to join 'em," he said of Daddy and Uncle Benny Siegel.

Luciano's other best friend was Uncle Frank Costello, and the two Italians and the two Jews became the four musketeers of Prohibition, making their first fortune in bootlegging and later, larger fortunes in gambling, bookmaking, nightclubs, construction, trucking, even restaurants. He amazed Marvin by knowing his family and all about Rapoport's and Ratner's. I guess it proved you didn't have to be Jewish to love blintzes. He didn't talk about the circumstances that had led to his being here, and not back home in New York where he clearly wanted to be. However, he was confident he'd see us back in New York "one day soon." He told us how he and Daddy were cooking up "big things in Cuba, big, big things. Maybe we'll all meet up in Havana," Uncle Charlie suggested. I liked the idea.

This was turning into one of the greatest days I'd ever had, and then, over cannolis and the sweetest gelato I ever tasted, Marvin had to go and ruin it. He told Charles Lucky Luciano that we were out of money, that we had spent too much, and that we couldn't afford to get home. "As a favor to Meyer," as Marvin so sleazily put it, could he be so kind and help us out so we wouldn't be stranded in Naples and have to start sending cables home from American Express.

He lied further by saying we didn't have return tickets and that it was a terrible misbudgeting on our part. He had gotten "carried away buying Sandi clothes so she could look her most beautiful." I wanted to take a knife and stab him at the table, right in front of the mob boss to end all mob bosses. I was sure Uncle Charlie would've been proud of me, if he'd known. Without batting an eyelash, Uncle Charlie called a waiter over and asked for a big envelope. He then reached into his coat pocket and peeled off a huge wad of Italian lira, put it in the envelope and handed it to Marvin, with a handshake. "Enjoy your honeymoon, kids," he said. "You're only young once." He had his driver, in a big black Lancia, drive us back to the hotel. I gave him a kiss goodbye. It was like kissing Daddy. Petting Bambi farewell, I desperately wanted to apologize for my horrible greedy, uncouth husband. Then

I remembered Daddy's credo. Never complain or explain. I swallowed my shame.

Back at the hotel, I let Marvin have it. How could he have done such a thing? "He's rich!" Marvin said, "He's one of the richest men in the world." Besides, Marvin said, and here was the kicker, he had counted out the money, and, by the time it was converted into American currency, all he had given us was $50. "What a tightwad!" Marvin complained. One of the richest men in the world was also one of the cheapest, an Italian Uncle Scrooge. He had made a big show of generosity to his best friend's daughter, and it was one big con. Then again, what would you expect of a gangster?

That was Marvin's excuse, and I didn't believe a word of it. Let me count the money, I demanded, and he refused, claiming it was locked in the hotel safe downstairs, that I was a minor who needed Marvin's adult status in red-tape-choked Italy to access the safe, and a million other dubious excuses.

We sailed back to New York from Naples a couple of days later, and I refused to speak to Marvin for the entire crossing. Not that he seemed to care. He was too busy doing sports on deck and hanging around all the ship's bars, drinking top-label Scotch and champagne and giving lavish tips (surely with Uncle Charlie's money) to the dashing young stewards. Fittingly, the ship was the *Andrea Doria,* the *Titanic* of the 1950s, which would sink the next year in a tragic collision off Nantucket. But my second honeymoon with Marvin was already the voyage of the damned.

Back in New York, our excitement over our new son brought Marvin and me back together. Not that Marvin spent that much time with Gary. Now he had a new mission. He wanted Daddy to set him up in his own restaurant. Having given Meyer Lansky a grandson, the least that Marvin, Mister Entitlement, felt that Daddy could do for him was to set him up in his own business. The better to support Gary, that was the idea, though everyone knew the support all came from Daddy.

Wanting the marriage to work, Daddy found Marvin the situation he wanted. The restaurant was called Spindletop, a luxury steak house at 254 West 47th Street, in the heart of the theatre district. The name came from the rich east Texas oilfields near Beaumont that started the whole Texas boom. The typical New York steak houses, like Gallagher's or Christ Cella, were austere, sawdust-on-floors affairs, but Spindletop was a New York fantasy of Texas excess: giant steaks, giant cocktails, a red plush bordello atmosphere, and waitresses in low-cut costumes and black net stockings that prefigured the Bunnies of the Playboy Clubs. At Spindletop, Texas was the thing.

Spindletop was owned by an old acquaintance of Daddy's named Joe Marsh, who had been a captain at the Riviera nightclub/casino on the Jersey Palisades. Joe was coarse, a bit of a tough-guy street thug, though he always made a big fuss over me. "I used to take you to the toilet," he'd never cease to remind me. Joe, who was handsome in a brutal way, had a stunning showgirl wife named Joan who was a Texan herself. One of her former boyfriends was a Texas oilman who had never gotten her out of his system. To keep her in it, he put up the seed money for Spindletop. Now Joe wanted to cash out. He approached Daddy, who bought a half-interest in the place for Marvin, but insisted that Joe stay on to teach Marvin the world of steak. After all, Marvin's whole life had been spent in a meat-free dairy restaurant. Spindletop would be a brave new red-blooded world for him, and, hopefully, for Gary and me, a wildly successful one.

Marvin came into Spindletop in the fall of 1955. He was a fast learner. This kosher dairy man got an education in beef and soon became known for serving some of the best and biggest he-man sirloins in the ultimate steak town, the home of the New York Strip. Under him, the restaurant continued to thrive. I wish I could have said the same for our marriage. We had less time to ourselves than ever, and when we did go out, it was to those same all-boy boites, mostly on the Upper East Side. "Why am I the only woman here?" I exasperatedly asked Marvin one night.

Marvin immediately went on the defensive. He was deeply insulted and ceased speaking directly to me. We only spoke through
Maddie, the maid. We had dismissed the German storm trooper baby
nurse when we returned from Europe. Marvin stopped taking me out,
spending most of his spare time with his two best friends, whom I had
finally met, Jay, a decorator, and Cary, a sales manager at the I. Miller
shoe salon. They were two of the handsomest men I had ever seen, the
kind of men girls would die for.

In time I figured out that girls would have died before these men
would notice them. Marvin, I finally came to realize, was, at best, bi-
sexual. His mother already knew. That's why she hoped, against hope,
that our marriage might "reform" him. That's why she begged me to
make him change his friends. Fat chance. The reason Marvin wanted
a wife and child was to have cover for his secret life, the life after hours
in Paris and Venice, the life in the little clubs with the pretty boys.

In the fifties "gay" meant happy. I had no idea what a homosex-
ual was. I had no idea what being in the closet meant, other than you
liked to shop. To have a gay husband was the cruelest blow to self-
esteem any wife could have. To an innocent child bride it was even
more devastating. But not only was Marvin a closeted gay man, he was
an unabashed fortune hunter. He had married me, this silly little kid,
not only for the cover of a marriage and a family, but also for the cover
of my wealth and the big future that Meyer Lansky could buy him.

To be married to a gay fortune hunter was about as bad as it could
get, I thought. Then it got worse. On Daddy's birthday, July 4, 1957,
when Gary was just one year old, the gay fortune hunter walked out
on me and moved in with a new boyfriend. Now I had not only been
used, but abused and abandoned. My only consolation was that Marvin had left me for a man and not another woman. That would have
been worse, more of a failure on my part. How, though, could Daddy,
who knew the ways of the world better than anyone, have not spotted
what Marvin was all about? Maybe he had. Maybe he felt I was a lost
cause and accepted the situation.

Shortly after Marvin departed, I had a dinner with Daddy and his friend Tony Salerno at Dinty Moore's. Uncle Tony and I shared a love of horses. He had a big horse farm in Rhinebeck, New York, and often invited me up to ride. He was also considered New York's "numbers king" and was the sponsor of all the biggest heavyweight championship boxing matches. Uncle Tony seemed far more upset about my being left as a single mother than my father was. "Something oughta be done," he said, over and over, in a soft voice that belied his intense anger and determination. "Let me take care of him, Meyer."

This was the first time in my life that I actually became aware of the role of violence in my father's world. The ability "to teach Marvin a lesson" was a heady power to have at my disposal. Nevertheless, I could not bring myself to invoke it. Before Daddy could answer, I broke in, pleading for Marvin's safety, if not his life. I couldn't bear for anything to befall the father of my child, no matter how awful he had been to me.

One benefit of losing my husband was that I sort of got my mother back. Mommy seemed to thrive in crises, in helping me. She pulled herself together and began spending lots of time in my apartment, looking after and loving her new grandson. That made me happy when everything else made me sad. Uncle Julie's wife, Ruth, came over almost every day, and Daddy chipped in with new full-time maids. He didn't trust Maddie. She belonged to Marvin; she could be a spy. In a way, I was having my baby without having to do it myself. When people asked me how I managed as a young child bride, I told them the truth: "I had help."

Aunt Esther's lawyer husband drew up our divorce papers. Despite his greed for what I had, there was no way Marvin was going to cross Daddy by demanding anything he shouldn't. Daddy was willing to give him Spindletop. That was enough of a going-away present. He would have limited visitation rights. I would have custody of the baby. Saying that I was better able to care for Gary than Marvin was damning with faint praise. Again, I thanked my lucky stars for my family's help.

Although I was now a mother and a soon to be divorcee, I was anything but grown up. Daddy knew this, and it bothered him. He sat me down for a heart-to-heart talk, one of our few. "You have two choices," he told me rather sternly. "You can go to school or go to work. But you have to do *something*." To me it felt like a choice between measles and mumps. I couldn't bear to go back to school. I had never been much of a student, and now that I had tasted freedom, I couldn't go back to the prison of a classroom. Besides, I would be older than my new classmates, so I would feel terribly self-conscious, a scarlet woman who had been held back. School was out.

The other choice was work, an equally alien concept. I had never worked a day in my life. What could I do? Not cook, that was for sure. Not type. I didn't want to answer phones. "What do you *like* to do?" Daddy asked.

I liked horses, but I didn't think I was good enough to be a riding instructor. What else? "Shop," I came up with.

"Done," Daddy said. "That's it. You'll go to work at Saks. You like Saks, right?"

Did I ever. Daddy had a friend, Connie Noonan, who was the big boss of the docks in New Jersey. Maybe because many of Saks's imported goods came through the ports there, Connie Noonan was "connected" high up at the luxury store. One call and I had my first job. I was about to embark on the odyssey of becoming a grown-up. I was about to become a working girl. However, because of the glamour and temptations of being the daughter of one of the kings of New York, I was about to become a playgirl as well. Working girl and playgirl were at odds with each other, not to mention with being a good mother. But I was a big girl now, wasn't I? About to turn eighteen, I was all ready to take a flying leap into maturity. But I would land in a three-ring circus of my own.

CHAPTER EIGHT

THAT'S AMORE

I wasn't the only poor little rich girl walking the perfumed floors at Saks Fifth Avenue. A few days after I started, in September 1956, I ran into Maria Doto, the gorgeous daughter of Joe Adonis, doing the same jobs. Connie Noonan had also gotten Maria into Saks. We were called "floaters," working umbrellas one day, women's lingerie another, men's socks the third. There were many heiresses, debutantes, girls from top families, doing exactly what we were doing, some to have something to do, some to meet men, some to get the employee discounts so they could dress better than the customers they were selling to. Working at Saks was to fashion what working in the William Morris mailroom was to entertainment. You had to be connected at the top to get in at the bottom.

I got to know the young comic Jackie Mason, in men's pajamas. I sold Loretta Young a scarf. I was surprised that she was wearing braces on her teeth, years after being a big star. I guessed being beautiful was a never-ending effort. I met Ed Sullivan browsing in the Stag Shop. He recognized me from my name tag and made a huge fuss over me, declaring what a great man my father was. In terms of the bottom line, Saks was a losing proposition for me. I spent everything I made, and a whole lot more, buying Gary clothes in the children's department, the best in the city, and the one where Mommy had spent so much money on me when I was little. I sent all my purchases at Saks C.O.D. to Mommy, who graciously covered the bills, as ever. I was too embarrassed by my extravagances to send them to Daddy. One day when I was walking home from work, I was hit by a cab. My leg was injured, not enough to go to the hospital, but enough that I couldn't walk to work. Taking cabs back and forth would eat up my salary.

I used the injury as an excuse to quit. My next job was modeling. Modeling? Me? Well, in those days, you didn't have to be as tall as a giraffe to be a model. The top models of the era, Suzy Parker and her sister Dorian Leigh, were only about five foot seven. That was just three inches taller than I was. Daddy may have been tiny for a man, but I was close to normal for a girl. Plus I was skinny for the time, 110 pounds, having shed my pregnancy weight and then some. It all started when I met a woman named Lillian Birnbaum at Saks. Lillian sold luxury clothes wholesale and below, at her apartment near mine on West End Avenue. A coat that would be $350 at Saks would be $75 at Lillian's. Some people suggested she was selling stolen merchandise. I didn't ask. A deal was a deal.

Lillian invited me to shop at her place, which was full of rich girls looking for bargains. Then she asked me to model for her. She told me I reminded her of the new French actress Brigitte Bardot, who had become the talk of the world by running down the beach in St. Tropez close to naked in *And God Created Woman*. Several of Lillian's customers told me the same thing. I guess we were both petite and blonde and had bosoms, though I was too embarrassed to show off mine, certainly not like Bardot. I suspect Lillian, who was a master of flattery, told me of the resemblance and hired me as a model so I would spend even more money on her clothes and recommend her to the wives of Daddy's powerful circle.

Whatever, I was totally lacking in self-awareness and totally in need of self-esteem. So I took the flattery to heart, so much so that

I decided, skinny as I was, that to be a model I needed to be even skinnier. The only real model I had ever met was Tippi Hedren, the future Hitchcock star, who used to ride at the Aldrich Stables, whose name had been changed to the Manhattan Riding Club. Hedren was even thinner than I was. She was also professionally beautiful, which I was not. But being in dire need of illusions that may have been delusions, I took the modeling goal seriously. To that unhealthy end, I found a fancy diet doctor on Central Park South who prescribed amphetamines, or diet pills, to suppress what little appetite I managed to have. These were part of the pill culture Jacqueline Susann would write about in her 1966 best-seller *Valley of the Dolls,* her "dolls" being the downers, or barbiturates, that her characters knocked themselves out with. My pills were taking my slender body and ego on a soaring trip. I had been down so long, up wasn't a bad way to go. For a while.

I made my drug and other connections at my new beauty parlor, the Larry Mathews Salon, on West 57th Street in the slightly seedy Great Northern Hotel. Larry Mathews was to Elizabeth Arden what the Carnegie Deli was to Dinty Moore's, nothing fancy but wild and, oh, what a crowd. When Marvin ran my beauty program, he had turned me into an aging frump. Now, with him gone, I felt entitled to a walk on the wild side. Larry Mathews was as wild as beauty got. The place was open around the clock, like an all-night diner. The clientele was pure show business. Marilyn Monroe was said to go there, though I never saw her. I didn't see the Sardi's opening night crowd, but rather burlesque strippers from 42nd Street, chorus girls from the Copacabana, struggling actresses from Stella Adler and the Actor's Studio, and lots and lots of pretty women without day jobs who turned out to be fancy call girls. This was a long, long way from Birch Wathen and Calhoun.

I heard about Mathews through the Copacabana grapevine. Other customers, who earned their living from the neck down, went for elaborate hair removal and coiffure of the nether regions, an art pioneered by Mathews, an ex-GI and head shot photographer who had a talent for getting his customers more camera ready than they thought they were. A lot of the strippers would want to dye their private areas the most exotic colors, and the salon accepted all challenges. Suffice it to say, it was an education.

At Mathews, I became friends with a pretty blonde girl from Queens named Joy, who was the girlfriend of Murray Kaufman, a song plugger who had made a hit of *How Much Is That Doggie in the Window?* He would soon become the famous disc jockey Murray the K. Murray was married, though that didn't seem to bother Joy, who went out with lots of married men, as long as they "took care" of her. Joy had the bright idea of fixing me up on a date with Murray's friend George DeWitt, the handsome and famous host of *Name That Tune,* one of the biggest game shows on television. Two contestants would face off, and an orchestra would begin to play. Then, as soon as they could recognize the song, the contestants would race each other across the stage to ring a big bell and "name that tune." The winner would get money and the chance to keep racing and ringing. What innocent times we were in, though Joy was anything but innocent.

At first I was too intimidated to go out with George, who was not only a huge celebrity but was married. Not that I was looking for a new boyfriend. I was too shell-shocked by Marvin for that. Joy insisted I needed an adventure, so I gave in. Murray sent me over to the studio, where I watched them shoot *Name That Tune* live. I was so impressed at George's charisma. He was a real TV star! I hoped I wouldn't be boring to him. After the show, George took me to a very dark restaurant called Roma di Notte, where the seating was in grottos. I supposed that since George was both famous and married, he wanted to lay low. I wasn't insulted.

But I was overwhelmed. George, in his late thirties, was so good looking, with the thickest, most amazing dark hair I had ever seen. He was also charming and funny. He had been a fighter pilot in the war, so Paul's being in flight school gave us something in common.

The fact George knew my father seemed to make him a little nervous at first. "I don't want to get rubbed out if you don't like me," he joked. That put us on a more equal footing, and we both relaxed.

George, an Italian whose real last name was Florentine, had gotten his start as a singing waiter in Atlantic City, where he grew up. His dad had been a policeman. In addition to starring with Frank Sinatra at Daddy's friend Skinny d'Amato's 500 Club in Atlantic City, George had been a mime, specializing in impersonations of black stars like Jack Benny's valet, Eddie "Rochester" Anderson. Today he might have been boycotted by the NAACP. Those were the days of *Amos 'n' Andy,* and that was the humor then. He also had been a regular at the Riviera on the Palisades. In a way, we were almost family.

Then came the moment of truth. George invited me back to his apartment on Central Park South, in the very same building as George Wood, when Daddy was living with him. Uncle Georgie would have been the last person I wanted to run into. The risk of exposure did add to the thrill of it all, but we made it into the apartment unobserved. The view of the park was very romantic. George had the fanciest record player I had ever seen. He put on the number one hit of the week, Dean Martin's *Memories Are Made of This.* George had a big bar in the apartment. Having just turned eighteen last December, I had finally started drinking, sweet things that tasted more like soda than alcohol. George concocted something for me. We held hands, kissed. At a certain point, George began to lead me into the bedroom. I stopped in his bathroom to prepare for the main event. I wasn't prepared for what I saw there: two head molds with toupees on top. All that great hair was a fake. I wanted to flee. But how could I be rude, and to a star?

Adding irony to injury, when I emerged from the bathroom, another big hit of the moment, Frankie Laine's *The Great Pretender* was blaring away. In bed all I could think about was the hair. I was nervous to touch it, but too curious not to. It didn't move. Not a hair. And it had looked so *real.* I can't even remember the sex. I think it was better than with Marvin. I'm not sure. When I was leaving, George seemed awkward. It had nothing to do with the toupee. "I'd love to give you . . . something," he stammered. "But I know you, of all people, don't need the money." Because Murray Kaufman gave Joy money, George may have thought I was moonlighting as a call girl as well. Until he found out who my father was. What a joke! I almost wanted to accept it, for fun, but I was too much of a lady to be a lady of the evening.

George called me again a few times. I always found excuses. Then I found another star to go out with. This one was like hitting the celebrity jackpot, and way, way, way over my teenage head. My next beau was Dean Martin, one of the hottest stars in the country in the fall of 1956. I met Dean through a new friend, a singer named Micki Marlo. I had met Micki when she was a guest on the radio show of Bea, one of the first female disc jockeys in New York and an early and prominent talk show hostess. My mother and Bea's mother had been good friends, and Bea had invited me to sit in and watch her spin the platters and patter on her broadcast from the International Club, next door to the Latin Quarter. I was bored and idle, so why not? Micki looked just like Elizabeth Taylor. Her real name was Moskowitz. She was married to one of the Mayo Brothers, a white dancing act that had enough rhythm to play the Apollo Theatre in Harlem. Micki's husband, Bobby, was a great friend of Dean, who was depressed and at loose ends after breaking up with Jerry Lewis that year after a decade of remarkable success. They thought I might cheer Dean up. Talk about the blind leading the blind.

Not knowing that I would ever meet Dean, much less date him that summer, weeks after Marvin left me I had gone to see the last Martin and Lewis show at the Copacabana with Barbara Lastfogel and another girlfriend. Barbara was the niece of the head of William Morris. I had met her in the agency offices when she was waiting to see Uncle Abe Lastfogel and I was there to see Uncle George Wood. Abe

Lastfogel may have been one of the most powerful agents in the business. He was surely the smallest, the Napoleon of Broadway.

Barbara was, on the other hand, tall and beautiful. Her mother may have been a showgirl. All eyes were upon her. She was a great girl to go out with, as she was catnip to men, and there was always an overflow for me. At the Copa, we saw Jackie Gleason rush on stage and beg the guys not to break up the act. Martin and Lewis were crying. The Copa girls were crying. All the girls in the audience were crying. I might have been crying, too. What a silly reason to get upset, I had thought, over two comedians. Gordon MacRae, maybe. But Martin and Lewis?

All I knew was that I preferred Dean to Jerry. Jerry, who was the bigger star at this point, was too corny and goofy for me. Dean felt more like my uncles. That wasn't far from the mark. Dean had grown up in Ohio, with Italian as his first language. He had been a boxer, a rum runner, a blackjack dealer, and, finally, a struggling singer at clubs run by Daddy's partners in the Midwest. Now he was struggling with how to get out from under Jerry Lewis's long shadow.

Dean called me and asked me to meet him for drinks at Bemelmans Bar in the Carlyle Hotel with its murals of surreal animals frolicking in Central Park. I rode horses at the stables, now the fancy "riding club," with Barbara Bemelmans, the painter's daughter. I felt pretty surreal listening to this famous star lamenting that his career might be over. Stars weren't supposed to lament. They weren't supposed to have anything to be sad about. Dean had just gotten back from Rome, where he was shooting his first film without Jerry, a sex farce called *Ten Thousand Bedrooms*. In it Dean played a rich hotel tycoon, like Conrad Hilton, or Meyer Lansky for that matter, who goes to the Eternal City on a real estate deal and gets in romantic trouble, stuff that I doubted would have happened to Daddy. Dean said the movie, still not finished, was a lost cause, a guaranteed bomb. He was looking for serious dramatic stuff to do next, "if anyone'll have me." Poor Dean.

If he was looking for sympathy, he more than got it from me. We didn't stay long at the bar. We walked out into a lobby and into a service entrance, where Dean led me up some back stairs to a suite on the second floor that overlooked an airshaft. Why would you stay at the Carlyle, which had some of the best views in the city, and look at an air shaft, I asked him, without trying to be rude. "Because I'm afraid of heights, baby," he admitted. He also told me his buddy Frank Sinatra was over at the Waldorf. He would take me over to see him were it not for Frank being forty stories up in the Waldorf Towers, a trip Dean simply could not take. Dean began kissing me so I would shut up and not dwell on his phobia, one that put him on lots of trains and boats, and on a sea of booze when there was no other way to go but to fly.

Dean's acrophobia did nothing to diminish his masculinity. I had never seen anything like it. We made love six times in a night that wouldn't stop. I counted. He wasn't a big man, just about five foot nine, but he was strong, a boxer from a steel town, and he made me feel that he was ravenously grateful for a woman's softness after being locked in the blast furnaces all day. He had wonderful wavy hair, sort of like George DeWitt's hair, but Dean's was real. His image as a heavy drinker was for the press. With me he wanted to be fully conscious and savor every moment. Between rounds of lust, we'd split a Coke.

That one night with Dean compensated for two years with Marvin. I didn't expect that I would ever hear from him again. I was just doing this to satisfy my bobby-soxer, groupie fantasy. I had expected nothing but sex, and I had gotten exactly that. We didn't talk about our personal lives at all. It was a one-night stand, or what Erica Jong, in *Fear of Flying,* would celebrate as a "zipless fuck," no strings, no guilt, no tomorrow. How surprised I was when tomorrow did indeed arrive. The next day Dean called me at home and told me what a wonderful night he had and how he couldn't wait to see me again.

In January 1957 I went to Florida for six months to fulfill the residency requirement for my divorce. Dean was going to be doing a series of shows at the Diplomat over the Christmas holidays. Could I come early and meet him? What an offer. The only problem was that Paul had caught everyone by surprise by planning to get married in Tacoma, Washington, of all places, at the very same time. While he was at flight school out there Paul had fallen for a pretty blonde, a very gentile Unitarian divorcee six years older than he was. Her name was Edna Shook, and she was from Tacoma. By comparing the situation to mine with Marvin Daddy was able to find a lot of reasons to celebrate the match. And celebrate it he planned to do, reserving a whole floor at Tacoma's one old-guard hotel, the Winthrop, and preparing to spare no expense. How could I refuse to attend?

Nothing worked out as planned. Buddy was ailing; it became too hard to fly him out. Mommy was acting better, for Gary and me, but she couldn't handle a long trip either, not even for her son. Uncle Jack and his family had some excuse. There were no uncles in the Pacific Northwest to join the party, so the party shrunk to three—Daddy, Teddy, and me. I didn't feel anybody there cared whether I was there or not. The big fuss was being made over Edna, as it should have been. She was already pregnant. Their son, Meyer Lansky II, would be born in August. Paul was flouting Jewish tradition in naming his firstborn after Daddy, and with a "II" on top of it. To hell with tradition; honor was the word. For my father it must have been the thrill of a lifetime.

I was a nobody in Tacoma. However, in Miami I knew there was one lonely star who cared whether I was there or not. Two days before the wedding, I had a big argument with Teddy, which became my excuse to check out of the Winthrop and fly back to Florida. The airport in Tacoma was fogged in, but I wouldn't go back to the wedding party for anything. Instead, I took a bus for hours and hours to Portland, Oregon, where I was able to get a plane to Miami. Paul was hurt, but gentleman that he was, he turned the other cheek. Only later, when my behavior got totally out of control, did he give up on me.

Dean had had no idea I was actually going to make it. The huge smile on his face when I appeared in the front row of his last show on

opening night at the Diplomat made the wrath of my family worth
enduring. Dean wasn't concerned about the wrath of his family, either.
About a week before we saw each other, his wife, Jeannie, gave birth
to their daughter Gina. I read about it in the fan magazines. I didn't
mention it, and neither did Dean. That was our unspoken pact: no
families, no strings.

Giving a twenty dollar bill to the captain to let me backstage, I
sat with Dean for about forty minutes after the show, as he accepted
the well-wishes of a long line of fans rich or connected enough to get
to his dressing room. When everyone was gone, he sat back, thanked
me for the "miracle" of my coming and told me how great I looked.
I was wearing a black chiffon dress and high heels. I'd come a long
way from the tomboy at the stables and the matron at my wedding.
We exited the hotel's nightclub and went through the fragrant gardens to Dean's second-floor room. All the fancy suites were higher up.
Dean didn't care. He'd leave all the "Come Fly with Me" business to
his buddy Sinatra. Dean's pleasures—and mine—were strictly on the
ground.

I didn't dare let Daddy know of my affair. Dean asked me to travel
with him to Chicago, New Orleans, and San Francisco, to go with him
on the road, to be his girl. But not his wife. That would have been the
rub for Daddy. I never thought of him as vindictive, but he was overprotective. He would have felt Dean was using me. That I was using
Dean would not have occurred to old-fashioned Daddy. Where misbe-
havior was concerned, Daddy had a policy of zero tolerance.

Daddy had recently caught Buddy running up a tab of $25,000 in
losses gambling on sports. Daddy warned the leading local bookmakers he would shut them all down if they took another of Buddy's bets.
Daddy had the power to end Dean's minus-Jerry career before it ever
got started. Whether he would have done that, I will never know, as I
was pretty good at keeping secrets and keeping my mouth shut. After
all, I had learned discretion from the master.

The Lansky compound in Miami, where I would spend the divorce waiting period, was a plain, efficiency motel Daddy had bought, not far from the Diplomat in Hollywood. It was called the Tuscany, but there was nothing Italian about it. The man who controlled the grandest hotels in Las Vegas and was spending his time building the grandest new hotel in Havana housed himself and his family in a very unprepossessing motor court far from the glitter of Miami's gold coast. Daddy was spending most of his time in Cuba now anyway. He didn't need the Fontainebleau or the Eden Roc, the new twin towers of Miami Beach hospitality, which were the closest things to what he owned elsewhere. His attitude was the opposite of that espoused by Zero Mostel in *The Producers*: "If you've got it, *flaunt* it!" Meyer Lansky's was: "If you've got it, *hide* it." The masterpiece, the jewel in the Lansky crown, which Daddy was building in Havana, was to be called the Riviera, like the club in the Palisades. But this place would be a skyscraper hotel, a temple of pleasure, of legal gambling, of superstars entertaining the super-rich, doing everything legally that puritan America forbade.

In 1952 Fulgencio Batista, who had been living in exile in Florida, returned to power in a coup d'état. He was a big fan, and a big pal, of my father's, who had run the casinos at the racetrack for him when I was a little girl. Now Batista was back and the casinos were roaring. Daddy and Batista went way back to the Prohibition era, when Daddy had a huge operation smuggling Cuban cane sugar into the States to make bootleg whiskey. Ever since then, Daddy also had interests in Cuban casinos. He knew how much Americans loved to gamble, and nearby Cuba was an ideal place for Yanks to bet their lives without breaking the law. Nobody knew gambling better than Daddy, and Batista knew it. To make sure the visiting Americans weren't being fleeced at the tables in this exotic foreign environment, Batista, back in power, appointed Meyer Lansky as his "gambling czar." In America my father was being hounded as a criminal; now in Cuba he was set up as the law unto himself. The reversal of fortune just ninety miles offshore must have felt like sweet vindication to Daddy. He would never gloat.

Then Daddy was in charge of the new casino in Havana's grandest hotel, the Nacional, and set up Uncle Jack there as his man in Havana. The hotel was now being managed by Pan Am's Intercontinental chain. That this most establishment of American companies turned to Daddy to run the hotel's moneymaker was testimony to the respect that he deserved and was getting, albeit not at home. Soon he put together backing for the Riviera, which would not only be grander than the Nacional, but would be the biggest gambling hotel on earth, outside of Las Vegas.

Twenty-one stories, nearly five hundred rooms all with ocean views, central air-conditioning (the first ever in the Caribbean), a nightclub called the Copa Room that was an exact replica of the site of my sweet sixteen party. The Riviera was scheduled to break ground the next month, January 1957, and open to the world in December, a year after my hibiscus-scented Miami night with Dean. Meyer Lansky's Riviera would be a destination unto itself. Conrad Hilton, make room for Daddy.

The dumpy Tuscany was not in the same universe as the fantasy Riviera. But the Tuscany was my reality, and the means to the necessary end of getting Marvin Rapoport legally out of my life. In New York Daddy had set me up with a wonderful and beautiful nanny for Gary named Frances Roe. She looked just like Lena Horne and was from Kentucky, with a black mother and a white father who had abandoned them. I took her to Florida with me, along with Gary and the two poodles, Nappy and Maria. Florida was not the best place for Frances, who hated the sun. She wore huge hats to protect her fair white skin.

Frances had only one downside. She was a bit of a Robin Hood, taking from the rich, giving to herself. Since good help was hard to find, I solved the problem by buying two of everything for Gary, knowing we'd invariably end up with one. The Tuscany was something of a family reunion for me. Buddy was living there now, running the switchboard, which was a natural occupation for him; he was practically a human switchboard. Whatever was happening in Miami, he knew about it. Grandma Yetta Lansky lived at the Tuscany as well. Although Daddy and Teddy had an apartment at the Tuscany, luckily for me, Teddy preferred Cuba, where she was decorating another, fancier apartment for them to move into when the Riviera was complete. Daddy taught me how to drive well enough to pass my driving test and rented me the cheapest Chevrolet. Such was the no-frills life of the crown princess of casinos.

To pass the time, I started hanging out at the Hollywood Dog Track. I not only loved the greyhounds, but I also developed a fondness for the son of the recently deceased founder, a charming but married young Irishman named Billy Syms. Daddy and Billy's father went way back. They owned a dog track in New Jersey in the thirties, another in Iowa in the forties, and I'm sure Daddy owned part of this dog track in Florida as well. While Billy and I were like family, that didn't stop him from jumping on me. His aphrodisiac was giving me money to bet on the races with. I discovered that I loved to gamble, but I hated to lose, even with other people's money. I was a sore loser.

Although Billy's wife was pregnant, he was the one who looked like he was carrying the child. He had a big stomach that kept getting bigger. Billy would get a bottle of brandy, and we'd go out to his car in the dark parking lot and make out like teenagers. Of course, I was still a teenager, so the style had a touch of logic to it. The thing about the Hollywood Dog Track that stayed in my mind was not Billy Syms, but the statue of a naked woman in the middle of the field. The model for that statue had been Jeannie Biegger, the former Orange Bowl Queen who was currently the wife of my "lover" Dean Martin.

My other lover that winter of divorce was the comedian Dick Shawn. Dick was one more married star for me. I met him when he was headlining at the La Ronde room of the Fontainebleau. I had become friends with the two maître d's of the showrooms of the two rival hotels, Andre at the Fontainebleau and Jacques at the Eden Roc. Jacques had been a captain at the Riviera in New Jersey, working with Marvin's Spindletop partner Joe Marsh. The two maître d's fought for my patronage. Having Meyer Lansky's daughter in the house was apparently, and surprisingly to me, something to brag about. Andre was the one who set me up with Dick, taking me backstage, after which Dick took me upstairs. He was a cheapskate, unwilling to pay my cab fare home, which detracted from his otherwise witty allure and huge athletic build.

For all my flings, I had to behave a bit like Superman, wearing very casual clothes to go out, pretending I was going shopping, and then stopping at a gas station to change into something fancy to wear to the nightclubs, and then stopping at the gas station on the way home in the early morning and change back again. When Daddy was in town, he would always do an "inspection," knocking at my door between seven and eight in the morning to make sure I was safely in bed, alone. Cuba was keeping Daddy so busy that he didn't have very much time to distrust me.

The divorce came through in June 1957. Marvin didn't even show. Daddy's powerful criminal lawyer Joe Varon handled things, in a case of overkill. I had two witnesses, Flo Alo and a bookmaker pal of Daddy's named Joe "Niggy" Flax, so called again because of his dark tan. Niggy ran the cabanas and all the concessions on Hollywood Beach. No wonder he was so dark; he spent his whole day in the sun. At night he took bets. Marvin was assessed lots of child support, which he never paid, and was ordered to pay Daddy a small fortune he had borrowed, which he never did.

My disastrous marriage had no deterrent effect on my brothers. Six months after Paul married Edna Shook in Tacoma, Buddy tied the knot in Miami at a big party at a restaurant called The House of Prime Ribs. That may have sounded like a roast beef emporium. It was actually a Chinese restaurant that was renowned for its barbe-cued spareribs. The House of Prime Ribs was a classic part of Miami kitsch. So was the place where Buddy met his bride, Wolfie Cohen's Rascal House, reputedly the greatest Jewish delicatessen in the world, including the Stage and the Carnegie. My future sister-in-law, Annette, was a tall and very pretty hostess at the Rascal House. She always moved Buddy to the front of the endless lines and gave him the prime red leatherette banquette. Divorced, she was raising a young son. Like Buddy, she was in her mid-twenties. And Jewish. Which mattered to no one except Grandma Yetta.

Buddy had wanted to marry Annette when they first met in 1955. Because Daddy didn't trust anything Buddy did, he had made him wait for nearly two years before he gave them his blessing. Daddy re-alized that Buddy would always need someone to look after him. Even if Annette was a fortune hunter, she probably was a better deal than all the nurses and drivers Daddy had hired over the years. Because she was a hard worker, there was a chance she could be the good influ-ence Buddy had yet to find. Although, as usual, no Citrons showed up for the wedding, a lot of Lanskys did. Micki Marlo flew down to sing for the party. Grandma Yetta had the time of her life, gorging on pork spareribs that we told her were lamb, kosher lamb. Some Old World habits died hard.

By late summer 1957, I was back in New York with Gary and Frances, Nappy and Maria. I was now an officially unmarried woman. I was ready to start a new life. Too bad I had absolutely no idea what kind of life I wanted. I was back to the same dilemma I faced when Marvin left me. Daddy had given me the choice of school or work. My answer turned out to be none of the above. Then what? Diet pills, al-cohol, cigarettes, and sex with celebrities may have made me feel more "adult" but they didn't lead me to any insights.

The only consolation I had was that I was not alone in my con-fusion and lack of direction. With Frances, Mommy, Aunt Ruth, and other maids taking care of little Gary, I had lots of time on my hands. I became something of a barfly. One day at the cocktail lounge of the Essex House Hotel, near the St. Moritz on Central Park South, I met a very blonde young man who was literally crying in his cups. He looked like the quintessential California golden god, a forerunner of the Beach Boys. When he introduced himself, I saw I had made the right call. He was Gary Crosby, son of Bing. If I was gangland royalty, Gary Crosby was Hollywood aristocracy of the highest order.

Who was a harder act to follow, Bing Crosby or Meyer Lansky? The difference between my brothers and me and Gary was that we knew not to try. Hollywood was the most powerful siren in America. Nobody there seemed to have a more charmed life and an inside track than Gary. A Stanford graduate who costarred in a movie with Bing when he was nine, Gary recorded a double-sided gold record with his father when he was sixteen and had appeared on *The Jack Benny Show*. After that, he had minor parts in a string of B-movies that no one ever saw. Worst of all, his beloved father, the Oscar-winning priest in *Going My Way,* had just stolen, and married, the love of Gary's life, Kathy Grant, an ambitious Texas beauty over thirty years Bing's junior. Daddy marrying Teddy was bad taste. What Bing Crosby had done to his son was damage, serious damage.

Gary and I became drinking buddies but never lovers. He was too traumatized to try anything with another woman at this point. I was still holding a futile torch for Dean. We saw each other for another six months or so, but the sex-and-only-sex, fun and good as the sex was, lost its novel allure over time. I would have liked someone more soulful, like Gary, but he was coping with more pain than I could begin to handle, probably even more pain than Buddy, who at least had seemingly found a path to happiness.

The best thing about Gary Crosby was his horror stories somehow made me feel much better about myself. Nothing I could tell him about Marvin could compare to what Bing had put him through. And compared to Bing Crosby, Daddy was a saint. For example, Gary had had a lifelong weight problem. The skinny, aquiline Bing would taunt Gary as "Bucket Butt," then pull Gary's pants down and whip him until he bled badly. His recurring fantasy was to kill Bing. I was glad he didn't carry a gun, for fear he would use it on himself.

In 1957 Daddy was fifty-five. He wasn't a kid anymore. He was considered the elder statesman of American crime, a dubious distinction. But his imminent transformation of Havana into the Monte Carlo of the Western Hemisphere promised to give him the global respect and honor that he had long deserved, if not craved. Little did any of us know that a reversal of fortune was in the wings that would make my father the most hunted and haunted senior citizen in American history.

CHAPTER NINE

GIRL GONE WILD

"My-ah, I had no i-de-ah you had such a splendid daw-tah." The tall, peppy but elder Bostonian looked me up and down, with a keen regard that reminded me of a judge evaluating thoroughbreds at a horse show.

"That's why they made him ambassador," Daddy said to me. "He says nice things." Daddy was unused to flattery. He didn't want me to get a swelled head.

"It's a pleasure to meet you, Mister Ambassador," I said. I had never met an ambassador before. I hoped I was calling him the right thing.

"The ple-zhah, my de-ah, is all my-an. And you must call me Joe." He kept looking me up and down, with a twinkle behind those round horn-rimmed glasses. I kept noticing him as well, with his florid face and fancy glasses and clothes that were even nicer than Daddy's. Aside from Uncle Abe Zwillman, I'd never seen a man so perfectly tailored. Ambassadors, I assumed, had to dress the part. Still, those looks were leers, and, if the ambassador weren't clearly very important and a very old friend, Daddy might have well given him the bum's rush as a dirty old man.

It was early fall, 1958. Daddy was up in New York from Havana, where his Riviera was a roaring success. Out on a shopping spree, I had dropped by his suite at the Warwick, unannounced, not expecting to find him in. But there he was, with the man he introduced to me as Ambassador Joseph Kennedy. Introductions and compliments aside, I could see that I had interrupted some serious business. I quickly took my leave, made a long tour of Saks and Best's and Bonwit's, then returned to find Daddy alone.

"He wants his son to be president," Daddy told me about the reason for the ambassador's visit. Daddy explained that although Joseph Kennedy may have stepped down as ambassador to England nearly two decades ago, just at the outset of World War II, once an ambassador, always an ambassador. Daddy didn't say much, never did. He did tell me that he and the ambassador had both been in the liquor business "way back" and that Kennedy had owned a film studio, RKO. Now Daddy called him a "banker," which might have been what Daddy may have called himself, if pressed.

That dirty old man, though I didn't dare say that, was now around seventy and had led a great life, Daddy said. Most of his dreams had come true, and his biggest dream was to see his son Jack, a war hero in the Pacific and now a senator from Massachusetts, succeed President Eisenhower in the White House. I was sure Daddy would have liked to see Paul in the White House someday, too, though Paul seemed to have his head in the clouds with his passion for flying. Besides, Daddy's career and his life with my uncles had put a ceiling on Paul's ambitions. Getting into West Point was amazing enough. Paul was so idealistic. Politics, to him, would have seemed too much like business, Daddy's business.

And he would have been right. Here was one of the richest, most powerful men in America, a Harvard man, I found out, and former chairman of the SEC, coming to Daddy for help. These were early days, but presidential campaigns had to be planned long in advance. And here was Daddy, being asked to be on the ground floor. What on earth, I wondered aloud, could Daddy do for him?

"I know a few people," was all Daddy would say. I knew he was dissembling, as usual. This sharp-eyed, predatory Joseph Kennedy wouldn't have been at the Warwick unless Daddy could call some key shots for him.

"What would they do in return?" I asked my father.

"He's an old friend," Daddy said.

There didn't have to be a deal. Daddy went on to tell me how the ambassador had lost his oldest son in a plane crash during the war. He had never gotten over that. Daddy liked doing favors. However, I would have loved to see Daddy get some respect in his life. Maybe if Jack Kennedy ran and won with Daddy's help, he could make Daddy an ambassador himself. Ambassador to Cuba! That would have been perfect. That would have shown Estes Kefauver, who had run for vice president and lost very badly. "Come on, Daddy, won't they do something for you?"

"Yeah. Leave me alone." That was his fondest wish. It would never come true.

The Riviera opened, on schedule, in December 1957 and quickly become one of the hottest tourist destinations in the whole world. Ginger Rogers was the first headliner at the Copa Room, but Daddy said she stunk. She could dance, but, in his opinion, she couldn't sing a note. Daddy was an armchair talent scout. Whenever we'd watch Ed Sullivan together, he was the fiercest, cruelest critic. I guess his clubs had hired enough talent that he of all people would know good from bad. Ginger Rogers may have been bad, but she was a legend, and her presence helped put the Riviera on the map.

After Ginger, Dad had brought down people like Vic Damone, Steve Allen, Abbott and Costello, and Cantinflas, David Niven's costar in *Around the World in 80 Days*. Daddy hired the Mexican comic to attract the rich Mexican gamblers who were the biggest tourist group in Cuba after the Americans. Lots of stars, people like Ava Gardner and William Holden, flew in from New York and Hollywood to gamble and to play and to mambo the night away. Why wasn't *I* there? Because Daddy was, and Teddy was, and they would have been watching me like hawks. Besides, I was having too much fun, out of sight in New York City.

I had found my first post-Marvin boyfriend, a real boyfriend and not a married fling. His name was Wynne Lassner, but everyone called him "Brownie." I don't know why. In his early forties, he was a theatrical manager who handled a lot of black talent, like Duke Ellington. That may have been the origin of his nickname. People had no idea how racist they would sound today. Brownie had offices in the Brill Building in Tin Pan Alley, which was the Tower of Babel of the music business. He had just gotten a divorce from the singer Eileen Barton, who'd had the biggest hit in the country in 1950 with *If I Knew You Were Coming I'd Have Baked a Cake*. She never followed that up, and the marriage dissolved.

Barbara Lastfogel had fixed me up with Brownie. She was dating his roommate, the actor Paul Burke, after his divorce. We all went out together. What a foursome. Burke, a dashing New Orleanian whose father had been Jack Dempsey's sparring partner, was the star of the NBC series *Noah's Ark,* in which he played a veterinarian. The next year he was a detective on the hit ABC show *The Naked City*. Brownie Lassner was a real heartthrob. He looked like a young Robert Taylor, as pretty as a boy could be, and he dressed like Fred Astaire, often in black tie.

We went to all the greatest clubs and restaurants in the city as a group, always getting the best table, Le Pavilion, the Colony, 21, Toots Shor's, the Stork Club, El Morocco, with sunrise breakfasts at the Brasserie in the Seagram's Building. The only places I tried to skip were Dinty Moore's and the Copa, where the word of my presence was most likely to get back to Daddy. Then again, I had nothing to hide. Brownie may have been an older man, but he was unattached and certainly eligible.

Not that I was looking for anything different from what I had gotten with Dean Martin and the others. The apartment Brownie and

Paul were sharing overlooked the East River and was furnished like a set in a Fred and Ginger movie. I had what must have been good sex, in that I looked forward to having more of it. Brownie's hair was luxuriant and, unlike George DeWitt's, real. So was his enthusiasm. My affair ended when Walter Winchell wrote in his column, "Congrats to Meyer Lansky on the engagement of his daughter to Wynne Lassner." Daddy hit the roof. He had overdosed on weddings—mine, Paul's, Buddy's. He wasn't ready for another, and he didn't think I was, either. This was one of the rare times when Walter Winchell published a retraction, and a deep apology. The biggest columnist in the world didn't dare cross Daddy. Brownie Lassner made a graceful exit.

Barbara Lastfogel remained my partner in crime. She was a celebrity magnet. One night we picked up Mr. Magoo himself, Jim Backus, at P. J. Clarke's, the location of a famous scene in the alcohol addiction film *The Lost Weekend*. Jim lured us into a potential ménage à trois at his East Side apartment by pretending he was ill at the bar and needed our help to get home. Jim was a wild and crazy guy who regaled us with stories like the one where he was expelled from military school for riding a horse through the mess hall. When we tucked him into bed, alone, we went out into the night and couldn't find a cab. A big fire truck finally came along. We lifted up our skirts and the firemen stopped very short and picked us up. We rode home at dawn swinging from a ladder. Walter Winchell would have paid a fortune for that tip.

I quickly got over Brownie. I had no shortage of handsome dates and glamorous nights on the town. Although I had given up the charade of wanting to model, I had not given up the obsession with being skinny and the equation of weight and beauty. I got deeper and deeper into diet pills. My "drugs of choice" were Dexedrine, the original diet pill, and Biphetamine, a stronger formulation that became known as the Black Beauty.

Both were basically speed. I had no idea that, as the antidrug slogan a decade later went, speed could kill. I loved the speedy feeling. I loved staying up all night dining and dancing and having sex, and still being able to be a great and caring mom to Gary. And be as skinny as a rail, or as Tippi Hedren. The size I wanted to be was zero, and so was my self-awareness. Museums, concerts, galleries, those were all out. It was all fancy food, handsome men, hot sex. My only culture was the culture of narcissism.

Remarkably, in spite of our divorce and the humiliating way he left me, Marvin and I were able to kiss and, if not make up, at least remain cordial. That was far better for Gary, who needed a man in his life, even a man like Marvin. On the surface, he was man enough. His big successful steak house and his high roller clientele and the gorgeous actresses he dated were better for business than going public about the gorgeous actors he went home with. One of his girlfriends at the time was Dyan Cannon, who would go on to marry Cary Grant.

I would bring Gary, now three, to Spindletop. The waitresses would make the biggest fuss over him. Sometimes I would see Daddy's friends there, with women who were not their wives. They looked so embarrassed, "outed" as it were, caught in the act. I'd just smile, and spare them the embarrassment of introducing Gary to them. He was the restaurant's mascot, its pride and joy. Marvin was a very doting, beaming father. He'd show Gary off to everyone. Once he introduced him to Liberace, who was so nice that he took Gary to the circus and gave him a pet turtle. The first movie I took Gary to was *The Sun Also Rises,* the Hemingway bullfight film with Tyrone Power and Ava Gardner. When Gary saw the bulls enter the ring he yelled out, "Look, Mommy, cows!" and the audience cracked up.

Speaking of Daddy's friends, J. Edgar Hoover's FBI and the Eisenhower Republicans were giving the Unclehood such a terrible time that I was certain Daddy would be doing everything in his power to get Joe Kennedy's son elected. Then he would have a friend in the White House who could call off these dogs, these crime hounds. Unfortunately, the dogs weren't imagining things. There was something to sniff, something that smelled awful. Starting in the middle of 1957, the blood started flowing in Daddy's world and the bodies began to pile up.

If I had once enjoyed a Pollyanna-ish rationalization that Daddy's "entertainment" business was just another all-American road to riches, that illusion was permanently shattered. Ben Siegel's unsolved murder, then a few years later Willie Moretti's, had led to tremors shaking my worldview that Meyer Lansky was a high financier, a Wall Street guy working a different street. Now the tremors became an earthquake that was off the Richter scale. First was the May 1957 assassination attempt on Uncle Frank Costello right in the lobby of the Majestic, where my parents used to live.

Uncle Frank was coming home from a night out at the glamorous French restaurant L'Aiglon, next to the St. Regis, then nightcaps across the street at Monsignore, a romantic Italian boîte with strolling musicians. His large entourage included Gene Pope, Jr., who owned the *National Enquirer,* and John Miller, the paper's top gossip columnist, who had become my friend as well, from the nightclub circuit we all rode together. At the Majestic, a man stepped out of a limo, broke through the doormen, shot Uncle Frank in the head, and then fled into the getaway car on Central Park West.

This was my turf, now running with blood. The assassin was bold, but was a bad shot. Uncle Frank only had a grazing head wound. The police quickly arrested a man named Vinnie "the Chin" Gigante, a muscleman who worked for Vito Genovese, a jealous would-be usurper of Uncle Frank's throne as "Prime Minister." Like Daddy, Uncle Frank despised publicity. He had never forgotten how badly he had been hurt by the Kefauver circus. Accordingly, he refused to accuse Gigante. Glad to be alive, he dismissed the violence as an isolated incident. Wishful thinking.

A few months later the bullets flew again, hitting their target. This was the brutal rubout of Albert Anastasia in the barbershop of the Park Sheraton Hotel on Seventh Avenue and 56th Street. I had been there many times with George Wood, who got his hair cut there and loved to be pampered by the staff, with manicures, steams, shaves, the whole spa treatment. George wanted Daddy to go there, too, but Daddy was loyal to the Waldorf. Besides, he had no time for all the pampering that George loved. In late October, Anastasia was in the midst of his own beauty regimen. He needed it. I had met him a number of times with George and Daddy. A former dock worker who had worked his way up to be Uncle Frank Costello's right hand on the Brooklyn waterfront, Anastasia was an early version of the "Teflon Don," a crime boss accused of many murders, convicted of none.

Today the justice came outside of court. Two men with scarves covering their faces ran in, threw the barber aside, and fired a round of bullets at Anastasia, blowing him out of the barber chair and his riddled body onto every front page and television screen in the world. In basically every article, Daddy was mentioned as well, in high profile. This was the same hotel where Daddy's predecessor as the Jewish brains of organized crime, Arnold Rothstein, who supposedly fixed the 1919 World Series, was shot to death in 1928. The press said Daddy was the "new Rothstein." The comparison, and its terminal implications, made me very anxious for Daddy's safety.

The anxiety became a cold sweat when the coolest of all my uncles, Abe Zwillman, was said to have lost that cool and hanged himself with a rope in the basement of his West Orange mansion in February 1959. A new Kefauver-like crime commission, the McClellan Committee, had been formed in 1957 to investigate racketeering in the big labor unions, and they went hard after Uncle Abe. The chief lawyer for the Senate Committee was Robert Kennedy, the brother of the man Daddy was supposed to help put in the White House. Wasn't he feeding the hand that could bite him, I wondered?

"He's just a rich kid," I had heard Daddy tell one of his friends. "Just playing cops and robbers." Daddy was certain the ambassador would exercise a fatherly restraint if need be. No such luck. When it came to the battle between labor and management, Daddy was naturally on the side of labor. No matter what excesses people like Jimmy Hoffa may have committed, those were small infractions compared to the felonious exploitation, as Daddy saw it, of the workers, poor immigrant people like the Lanskys, by the fat-cat capitalist owners, the establishment that would never let him in. If he couldn't join it, he had to beat it. Sure, it was easier for a millionaire Harvard brat like this Robert Kennedy to take on the labor leaders than to face the truth that his own father got to the top in league with Daddy, Uncle Abe, and other of McClellan's prime targets.

The government was one relentless crime machine. They had just driven Uncle Joe Adonis out of the country, harassing him so badly that he self-deported to Italy, where he lived in splendor with Uncle Charlie Luciano. But it was a homesick splendor, and it wasn't his choice. I doubted that hanging himself was Uncle Abe's choice, either. In addition to the McClellan investigators, the IRS had also targeted the King of Jersey. Yet no one had seemed more mellow, more fearless, than Abe Zwillman. What were a few agents compared to the likes of Al Capone and Dutch Schultz? Buddy, our family crime reporter, insisted that he had been strangled, then strung up.

Uncle Abe had done a lot for the people of New Jersey, and they knew it. Over two thousand people stood outside the Newark funeral home where his body lay to pay respects. Daddy did not attend the funeral, just as he had not attended that of Uncle Abe's partner Willie Moretti. Too much publicity, guilt by association. Anyhow, in early 1959, Daddy was stuck in Cuba. Havana, and Daddy's vast success there, the success that was intended to make him the legitimate world leader in legal gambling, had proved too good to be true. Overnight, on New Year's Eve, 1958, Batista surprised Daddy and the world by fleeing, with his family and his money—money Daddy had made for him—to Florida. In his place was the triumphant underdog rebel leader, the one no one, including Daddy, took very seriously, Fidel Castro.

Daddy's bet on the continued strength of the Cuban strongman Batista had turned out to be the worst gamble in a lifetime of taking risks. He had invested over $20 million in the Riviera, a lot of it his own money. Today that would be over $200 million. Now he could lose it all, because nothing was more of a red flag to Castro's Communist philosophy than a lavish gambling casino. Even worse was a casino run by American fat-cat capitalist mobsters for other foreign fat-cat hedonists, all exploiting the poor local peasants, who got none of the spoils. In fact on the first day of 1959, when Castro declared all the casinos closed, a mob of Cuban farmers stormed the Riviera, bringing their pigs, goats, and sheep into its marble halls before Daddy's security forces ejected them. There were stories on the news of Teddy, armed with a mop and a giant bottle of Spic 'n' Span, on her knees scrubbing the floors after them. They made for great copy, but struck me as pure tabloid invention. Teddy was too lazy, too used to the maids Daddy paid for, to clean up after herself, much less a herd of Cuban pigs.

The casinos soon reopened. As much as Castro hated American capitalism, he liked the jobs that those capitalist pigs had created for his people. Money talked, even to Fidel. Yet it was just a matter of time, Daddy feared, before the money from Moscow would start talking louder than the money from New York. If the Communists had their way, the casinos would be closed for good. And there was the new public relations nightmare of getting American high rollers to come back to play in a country that had gone from playground to Cold War battleground in a split second. The threat to Daddy's fortune, his future, his life, was as real as Castro himself.

Before that fateful New Year's Eve, the only Castro I had heard of was the Times Square sofa bed store, Castro Convertibles. Now the name took on a menacing air. The new liberator, or dictator, depending on how you saw him, was capable of converting my privileged life into a peasant pigsty. The danger was physical as well as financial. In May, Castro's police arrested Uncle Jack and threw him in prison, along with one of his top managers. Daddy was able to bail them out and send them back to Miami, where he went himself. He was so desperate for his own situation that he actually took long meetings with FBI agents there, describing the imminent Communist threat and warning America about the potential of "Russians Next Door." No one would listen. In October 1960, Castro took over the Riviera, as well as all other American properties in Cuba, from Woolworth's to Westinghouse.

Daddy, who had the soul of a revolutionary, ended up betting on the dictator Batista over the populist Castro. He was betting against himself. But he, like most of the world, had seen Castro as a million-to-one long shot, not worth thinking about. Now Castro closed the tables and had Meyer Lansky's millions. The stress of the revolution had also stolen Daddy's health. In addition to his digestive ailments, his bleeding ulcers, Daddy developed pericarditis, a deadly heart lining infection. He was at Memorial Hospital, in Hollywood, Florida, in intensive care, for over a month.

Close to sixty, Daddy seemed to be facing the end. Paul flew in across country. I flew down. Picking me up at the airport, Uncle Jack gave me his grim summary of the situation. "Your father is broke. Your father is dying. You're getting nothing." Such were the charms of Jacob Lansky. As serious as Daddy was, he was a stand-up comic compared to his younger brother. The usually dour Uncle Jack was as dull as dishwater, the last guy you would expect to run a casino. With his thick hair and bushy eyebrows, he looked like the head of the mineworkers' union, John L. Lewis, but minus the fire. He had no drive, no dynamism. Fortunately Daddy had enough for two, and took care of his baby brother, installing him as his front man. But Daddy made all the decisions; he didn't trust Jack's judgment.

Jack's wife, Aunt Anna (so many Anns and Annas in my family) had come from a poor family on the Lower East Side. She was forever whining to Jack, "You shoulda stayed a furrier," which was Jack's career until Daddy put him in the fast lane. Anna was convinced Daddy had lured poor Jack into trouble, and that their now-lavish lives could be snatched away from them at any minute, that she and Jack would be snared in any government dragnet that was after Daddy. In short, though Daddy had *made* their lives, he had also *ruined* them. With Cuba gone, Uncle Jack was all dressed up in the white tux he wore at the Riviera, all dressed up with no place to go.

Jack had the ultimate Depression mentality. Every glass wasn't half empty. It was completely empty. He expected the worst: misery, poverty, and death. Daddy's illness was a long and tense siege. I quickly ended up in a fistfight with Teddy over Daddy's care. Blaming me for Daddy's illness, she leapt upon me and tried to strangle me. Uncle Jack, stronger than I had ever given him credit for, had to pull her off. In his oxygen tent, Daddy didn't look like the king of crime, or the king of anything. Gasping for breath, he looked like a sick little old man, hanging to life by a thread. There was no power there, just loneliness. And if that life ended, what did he have to show for it? A pile of subpoenas from J. Edgar Hoover? Two wives, one on the edge of insanity, the other terminally superficial and greedy? Me? A disgrace. Buddy, another disgrace? A foreclosed high-rise gambling den in a banana republic? A bunch of craps tables in the Nevada desert? Paul was the one and only point of honor. All I could do was pray for Daddy to extend his life so he could leave it at a later day on more dignified terms than these.

Miraculously, Daddy survived the heart infection. But no more handball. Maybe golf, if he were lucky. The days of vitality were behind him. But he was still here, still standing. Thanks a lot, Uncle Jack, thanks for the confidence. In some ways, Daddy was a man without a country, that country being Cuba. But he still had Las Vegas. If one dream turned into a nightmare, he would roll over and dream again. However, life did not begin at sixty, especially with Washington, D.C., breathing down your back.

A new administration and a friend on Pennsylvania Avenue seemed to be Daddy's best insurance policy, so he threw himself into his promise to get Ambassador Kennedy's son elected that November

1960. Working with him was the big boss of Chicago, Sam Giancana. "Mooney" (Italian American slang for "crazy") Giancana was more father than godfather to Frank Sinatra, who happened to be Jack Kennedy's very best friend. Maybe, maybe, the power tables would turn in Daddy's favor.

While Daddy rode bravely through his valley of fear, I continued to sleepwalk through my own valley of the dolls. Mine was the Oz of amphetamines. I was becoming a total drug addict. When Daddy was sick in Florida, I needed all the pharmaceutical help I could get to make it through those months of fearing I would lose my own Galahad, the only man on earth who could protect me. I could not face the possibility that all my comforts and security and money could suddenly vanish, like Uncle Jack had warned me that they were about to.

Uncle Jack was wrong. But it could happen. I wasn't prepared for such a cataclysm. I refused to think about it. I didn't have time to go to diet doctors. Instead I went directly to the source and began cozying up to and bribing pharmacists. My big connection was the drug store at the Fontainebleau, where I sweet-talked and high-tipped the druggist into giving me whatever I wanted, pills not by the dozens, but by the hundreds. A doctor may have told me to take them twice a day, at most. I popped them at all hours, whenever I felt I needed them, which was all the time. Once at the Fontainebleau pharmacy on a drug run, I ran into Joe DiMaggio, who sent profuse regards to Daddy. I had met Joe with Daddy many times, often at Toots Shor's. I couldn't have been more ashamed at what I was doing. Alas, I wasn't ashamed enough to stop.

Meanwhile, I was still living the glamorous life of the madcap Manhattan heiress/gay divorcee. I would still see Dean Martin from time to time, meeting him for a secret rendezvous in Chicago or Boston. Dick Shawn would call when he was in the city. There were plenty of other stars: Jeff Chandler, David Janssen, Hugh O' Brien— Wyatt Earp himself. I met a lot of these men at Danny's Hide-Away, a riotous steak house on East 45th Street near Grand Central Station owned by Danny Stradella, a tiny jockey-size impresario who loved introducing famous men to pretty girls. That was probably why this smallest restaurateur in New York had the biggest celebrity clientele. I was also a regular at 21, where the famous and charismatic manager Chuck Anderson would never let me pick up a check. Ditto Edwin Perona at El Morocco. Ditto Ed Wynne at the Harwyn Club. In fact, I don't think I ever paid a check in any New York nightclub either when I was by myself or with some girlfriends. Instead of charging it to the Diners Club, my Meyer Lansky plan was far better—there were no monthly statements. How, I puzzled, could a man so revered in New York be so reviled in Washington? With all my craziness, I was lucky never to be robbed or kidnapped. One rich guy, whose father owned the Kinney Parking lots, did slip me a Mickey Finn at The Living Room, across from the United Nations. I woke up the next morning somewhere in Westchester County, a farmhouse. I didn't want to think what had gone on. I took a cab back to New York. The driver loved the fare.

I kept avoiding the Copacabana. That was Frank Costello's club, and master gossip John Miller was guaranteed to convey my every excess to Daddy. But one of the captains there had borrowed $700 from me, and months later, he still hadn't paid me back. I was profligate, but welching on debts in my family was considered bad form. So one night I arranged to meet Uncle Augie Carfano at the club, to get him to use his charms on the captain to collect the marker.

I got to the Copa fifteen minutes later than our scheduled appointment only to find him gone. I was upset that I had been stood up. What's fifteen minutes when a girl like me could be hours late? I was even more upset the next morning when they found the bodies of Uncle Augie and his date that night, ex–beauty queen Janice Drake, shot to death in his Cadillac in Queens. Janice was the wife of comedian Allan Drake, whose faltering nightclub career Augie had bolstered the way Uncle Willie Moretti had bolstered that of Frank Sinatra. Drake may have traded his wife to Augie as a career move. Those things were known to happen. And so were murders, in the long mean season of bloodshed that had kicked off with the failed Frank Costello hit. Outsiders, and even insiders like me, may have thought the Copa the most glamorous club in America. These clubs were fun, for sure, but they weren't worth dying for.

Another of my main hangouts, one where there was never a body count, was the Carlyle Hotel, where I had met Dean at Bemelmans Bar. Because of my stablemate Barbara Bemelmans, I always thought of horses at the Carlyle. After the split with Marvin, I lost what had been our only shared passion—for horses. I thought about riding again, but instead I'd pop another Black Beauty and stop thinking. At the Carlyle I met a really older man, someone nearly as old as Daddy. Maybe with Daddy's health in the balance, I was looking for a father substitute. This one would have been close. Charles Revson, the nail polish king, the creator of Fire and Ice, was what Daddy might have become had he played it straight and taken an interest in beauty products.

Revson was near sixty, close to Daddy's age and just about his size. We had a lot in common, starting that we had both been born in Boston. His family was even poorer than Daddy's. His father worked as a cigar roller. Charlie had a huge chip on his shoulder, a drive to succeed like Daddy's. He was an even bigger control freak. When his company Revlon sponsored *The $64,000 Question,* he insisted on fixing the show, making it more suspenseful, so that the audience would grow and he could sell more cosmetics. In doing this, he provoked the quiz show scandals of the fifties. But the government didn't dare come after Charlie. He was Teflon, too.

Charlie had an apartment in the Waldorf Towers that had belonged to Herbert Hoover. He must have had a staff of ten, liveried butlers, uniformed maids, French chefs, though all he'd ever eat for lunch were Geisha brand tuna sandwiches, alternating with sawdust-lean corned beef sandwiches with very old dill pickles. God help it if he detected a note of sweetness. He'd throw as big a fit as Daddy would if he was served a hamburger with an onion on the side. Picky, picky, picky. His was the coldest apartment I'd ever been in. Charlie was an air-conditioning freak. The apartment was like the North Pole. He bought me a mink coat to keep me warm in bed.

Charlie knew that the way to a woman's heart was through cosmetics. He'd take me on tours of his factory in the Bronx that were amazing turn-ons. He'd send me yellow roses every day, but I preferred lipstick. So I got huge care packages of every Revlon product, every color, every fragrance. Once when I was in Florida, he fouled up. I asked him for a case of bubble bath. He sent me a case of talcum powder by mistake. We broke up soon after that. I don't recall if the events were related. I was too drugged out.

What was I thinking? I wasn't thinking. I even went to bed with Marvin again one night on the eve of his flight to Greece for a very gay holiday with his new boyfriend on Mykonos. He had not improved with age. What drugs and alcohol could do! And then the craziest thing happened. I got pregnant again. Not that I had taken any precautions. I had no idea what birth control was. I had been lucky it hadn't happened before. Also, I was so skinny that I was missing periods left and right. I wasn't keeping track. I also had an eighteen-inch waist and wore cinch belts. I didn't figure it out until two weeks before I went into labor on January 23, 1961.

My water broke. The only person I could turn to was the janitor in my building on West End Avenue. There was a blizzard outside. Driving like a race driver in the Monte Carlo rally, he made it through the icy, snow-drifted streets out to Long Island Jewish Hospital, to the same OB-GYN who delivered Gary. My new baby was three months' premature. It was a boy. He weighed a pound and a half. They immediately put him in an incubator. I was too out of it to recognize the tragedy, the pathos of the situation, the fragility of his tiny life. All I could think about was how to keep Daddy from finding out.

That wasn't easy. Buddy happened to have called for some reason to speak to me. Frances the maid told him I had gone to the hospital.

She didn't say why. She didn't know the whole story, and she knew better than to blab even if she had, but Buddy couldn't help from blabbing. Just the word to Daddy that I was in the hospital had him on the first plane to New York. He found me in the maternity ward. Why, he asked, are you here? Thank God the doctor was away. I had pledged my nurse to secrecy. I gave her a hundred dollar bill. That helped.

"Female trouble," I lied to Daddy as fast as I could. "There was no room in the regular ward. The whole city has the flu. The place is full."

I think Daddy was so sick of hospitals after his recent siege that he wanted to get out of there in short order. That's why he fell for my story. He got me out of there, too. The baby, whom I didn't even name, remained in the hospital, in the incubator from January until May, while Daddy brought me down to Miami to recuperate. He put me up at the Aristocrat Hotel on the beach. I called the hospital every day to check on my child. He was still very fragile. I had no idea what to do. I couldn't tell anyone except my hairdresser, who was the only friend I had at that point. I was in no shape to raise another child. Without Frances, I couldn't have handled Gary. My plan, if I had one, was to come back to New York and give the child to my hairdresser's mother, who lived in Hell's Kitchen. She lovingly volunteered to raise the baby for me.

In May I came back to New York and brought my still-tiny little baby home to organize giving him away. Mommy, who was there caring for Gary, saw him, and saw something that totally transformed her. "That baby is sick," she said. "We have to take care of him. We can't let him go." I had assumed Mommy was too lethargic to even notice. Instead she was galvanized by the sight of the child clinging to life. "We," she kept saying. "We." I figured out that in my baby she saw her own baby, my brother Buddy. Mommy somehow took charge, organizing appointments with some of the doctors she had taken Buddy to, thirty years before. Some were dead, some were old men. But some were there.

The diagnosis was grim. The baby, my baby, had severe birth defects, far worse than what Buddy had. There was no way I could give him to my hairdresser's struggling mother. This child had special needs she couldn't begin to deal with. Amazingly, it was the two unlikeliest partners, Mommy and Marvin, who teamed up to take command. First, the poor child needed a name. Marvin agreed to take paternal responsibility, and Mommy came up with David Jay Rapoport, naming him after the early Supreme Court Justice John Jay. For all the legal troubles we had had, Mommy thought we could use a lawyer in the family. D.J., as we began calling him, needed the best medical care money could buy. That meant we had to turn to the money. That meant telling all to Daddy.

For Mommy, D.J. was a second chance at motherhood, someone to love, to nurture, to rescue. To Daddy, on the other hand, D.J. was one more slap in the face, another exhibit of failure, proof that he lacked what it took to achieve the American dream. The way Daddy looked at me made me feel as if it were all my fault. All the drugs, the drink, the tight dresses. Did I cause D.J. to enter the world this way? Had I ruined his life before it began? My guilt was overwhelming. But so was my joy. D.J. had brought Mommy fully back to life, and back to my life.

When Daddy came to my apartment to have a summit conference, there were my two parents, together again. They hadn't seen each other, hadn't spoken, for over a decade. Both seemed shocked by how old the other looked. We were all speechless. Then Mommy broke the ice by dropping D.J. into Daddy's lap. "Our grandson, Meyer," she announced. Daddy had no comeback. He just embraced D.J. For that one brief moment, we were a family once again. Now it was up to me to rise to the occasion, as she had, and make my own life worth living. Given my own addictions and misdirection and a lifetime of spoiling, stepping up to the challenge was going to be a tall order indeed.

CHAPTER TEN

NOTORIOUS

Unlike my mother, I didn't need a psychiatrist to turn me into a drug addict. I did it all by myself, first with the diet pill doctors, then with the drugstores, then with friends who helped me buy what I wanted on the street. I had occasionally gone with Mommy to her shrinks. I always suspected that they were exploiting her, a suspicion confirmed by the fact that the challenge of looking after Gary and then D.J. was the one thing that made her act like her old self. She had at least as many pills as I did: Milltown, Librium, Lithium. Pill-curious, I tried them all, but they really made me sick. Mommy needed to go down. I needed to go up. I never went to a psychiatrist for my own problems. What problems? My only problem was getting enough Biphetamines to make me feel anywhere from secure to omnipotent. An unexamined life was the only life I could continue living.

And then I met someone who forced me to take a good hard look at myself. For the first time in my life, aside from Gordon MacRae and a brief delusion with Marvin, I thought I was falling in love, madly in love. It happened at the Harwyn Club, a converted carriage house on East 52nd Street off Lexington. The owner, Ed Wynne, was as handsome as any movie star. A former manager of the Stork Club, this six-foot-tall blond Irishman reversed the usual formula for nightclub success. Instead of using pretty girls as the lure to attract a male clientele, he somehow attracted the city's handsomest men, whom the pretty girls would all follow.

Before entering the nightclub business, Ed had been a baseball umpire, of all things. That was very fortuitous, because his former life in the sport enabled him to bring in the most famous Yankees, Mickey Mantle, Whitey Ford, Don Larsen, Billy Martin, Yogi Berra, to drink at the Harwyn. The place also became A-list when Grace Kelley used the Harwyn, her favorite New York hangout, to announce her engagement to Prince Rainier of Monaco. Where the Yankees went, all New York followed, particularly the hard-driving, baseball-obsessed Madison Avenue types. It was one of these striking "Mad Men" who knocked me off my barstool one fateful night in 1962.

He was tall, athletic, dapper. They all were at the Harwyn, but there was something extra about this one. I racked my brain. Did I know him? Had we had a fling? If so, had I done something shameful? My nights were an endless blur of handsome men, of wild times. Did I dare say, "Have me met?" He was too good-looking for me to risk blowing it. So I kept staring, out of the corner of my eye. I didn't want to seem desperate. There was something about the way the guy carried himself that seemed less Madison Avenue than West Point. There was a military correctness, a confidence that reminded me of Paul.

Ah, that was it. Just as I was about to grasp the wisp of memory, the Mad Man saved me the trouble. "Sandi," he said with a billion-dollar smile, crossing the crowded barroom to meet me. "Sandi, right? I know you . . . Gabby Hartnett."

"The gift shop at West Point," I recalled.

"Absolutely." He shook hands, very properly, very officer-and-gentlemanly. He had the firm handshake of someone in command, with all the self-confidence that I had completely lacked.

"What a memory," I said. "I was just a kid."

Gabby looked me up and down. "You're not anymore," he replied and insisted we sit down and he buy me a drink.

I ordered a J&B on the rocks. That was a man's drink, a Mad Man's drink. Gabby, whose real name was Edward, filled me in on what he had done since graduating from the academy in 1951. He had indeed gone to the Helsinki Olympics. He didn't win any medals there, but he did in Korea, where he commanded a howitzer battery and rose to become a captain. Back in New York in 1954, he had just graduated from law school at Fordham by going to night school for five years while working in an advertising agency. He had not gotten married. He was too busy. I was so impressed with his motivation, the opposite of mine.

Rather than tell Gabby my torrid, sordid history since he last saw me in my white bucks and bobby sox, I focused on what Paul had been doing. I told him about flight school, and now about the army's sending Paul to get a master's degree in industrial engineering at the University of Michigan. Paul was so outraged by the whole D.J. episode, that it was the last straw for him regarding my decadent behavior. He stopped speaking to me and would keep a stony silence for years. But I still loved him and kept up with his adventures through Daddy and Buddy. Paul was soon heading over to Vietnam, to advise the Kennedy administration on the escalating war over there. How exotic Saigon sounded. How boring, I laughed to myself, compared to all the action at the Harwyn Club. Why leave New York? Everything on earth was right here.

"But what about *you*?" Gabby pressed. "I want to hear about yourself."

I was embarrassed enough about my crazy marriage. I was convinced my child, make that two children, would be a deal breaker. Daddy had paid a small fortune to send D.J. up to Boston to the Crippled Children's Hospital, to try to do everything for his grandson that he had done for his son. Hopefully, D.J. would turn out better than

Buddy, who, despite his marriage, was constantly getting into gambling trouble and other hot water. Annette wasn't as good an influence as everyone had hoped.

I didn't tell Gabby about D.J., or about Buddy, or even about Gary. He was single. He didn't want someone else's kids or their baggage. He'd want to start his own family. The less said the better if I wanted a chance with this guy. He seemed like the first normal man I had ever met. He could be my hero, my new Galahad, to take the place of Daddy, whose vulnerability haunted me in my thoughts and in my nightmares. So I hid behind Paul's normalcy, behind their old school tie, even if they had never met. The West Point connection gave me dignity, gave me cover. How bad could I be?

Not too bad. I gave Gabby my number, shook hands goodnight. Two weeks later he called me up and asked me to dinner. It was nothing fancy, not the Brownie Lassner celebrity circuit. Instead we went down to Chinatown, to Bo-Bo, an authentic Cantonese restaurant where the highlight was Gabby ordering in Chinese. He had learned the language in Korea, liberating the Chinese Communist prisoner-of-war camps. Gabby tried to teach me how to use chopsticks. I had barely mastered the knife and fork, but when he took my hand in his to guide me about the proper chopstick placement, I swooned. I blamed my giddiness on the MSG.

It was the first meal I had had in New York in years without a drink and cigarettes. We sipped tea. Aside from my diet pills, I was on my best behavior. Gabby picked me up at West End Avenue, downstairs, and took me back there. We shook hands good night. That hadn't happened to me for a long time. He was a devout Catholic, a former altar boy. Husband material.

We had a number of dates, altar boy dates, that always ended with a handshake. No smoking, the rare cocktail or glass of wine. We went to French bistros where Gabby spoke French, sukiyaki parlors where he spoke Japanese, and paella places in the Village where he spoke Spanish. Gabby could have been a diplomat, I told him. He said he did a lot of work with foreign accounts. We went up to the Cloisters for art and to Yankees games for sports. I took him riding, renting horses at the stables, now the Riding Club. All the people there remembered me. They were so impressed.

I took a crazy chance and told Gabby about Gary, though not about D.J. That was too dark. Gary was six. He went to school right across the street from our apartment. I was like Mommy had been with me, taking him to school, home to lunch, back to school, home again. It wasn't much of a commute. Gary was following in my "democratic" footsteps, gravitating to the poor kids. His best friend was the son of the Puerto Rican handyman. His name was Jesus, an adorable kid straight out of *West Side Story*.

Jesus used to take Gary home and to church. One day they skipped school together. The school said they were missing. I found them at the church. Jesus had brought Gary to meet his priest. He wanted the priest to convert Gary. I had thought Jesus was a little gang kid in the making, a junior Shark or Jet. Instead he was a missionary. One night Gary was playing outside with Jesus, when Gabby was picking me up. I introduced them. He lifted up both boys and swung them over his head. What a great dad he would make.

At another authentic meal in Chinatown the conversation turned to communism and then to communism in Cuba. It was right after the Bay of Pigs invasion fiasco, after which Castro felt justified in closing the casinos, once and for all, ending Daddy's hopes of ever getting his investment back. At the same time, Castro formally embraced communism and Nikita Khrushchev. Daddy had been 100 percent right about Castro, that he would fall for the Russians. Somehow this led to a discussion about Daddy, who never, ever wanted me to talk about him, and his business, to anyone.

Gabby didn't seem like anyone. He was special. He listened so sympathetically. He made me feel smart, like I knew something. He would understand. So I started talking, saying what little I knew, about how unfair Castro and Washington had been to Daddy. Even crueler than Cuba had been the Kennedys' betrayal. Daddy had helped put John Kennedy in office. All he had wanted in return was to be "left alone." For a while President Kennedy kept his father's promise.

Then, in late December 1961, Joseph Kennedy suffered a debilitating stroke, from which he would never recover. Suddenly Daddy became fair game. John Kennedy couldn't control his rabid brother, who immediately ended John's friendship with Frank Sinatra. Then he went after the two underworld figures who may have done the most to put the Kennedys in power: Sam Giancana and Daddy. I felt so safe with Gabby, I'm sure I went on and on too much about all this. After all, how could I not trust him? I was equating chastity with respect, maybe even love. Sex was easy. Restraint was hard. The man hadn't even tried to kiss me. He was, I assumed, saving me for something special.

Indeed he was. While I was seeing Gabby in 1962, another big Lansky wedding came on the horizon. Uncle Jack's daughter, my cousin Linda, was getting married. How I would have loved to invite Gabby down to Miami for the big event, to show to my family that I, too, could get a West Point man. How I wanted to rub it into Paul, one academy man to another. I knew Daddy would be proudest of all, that his crazy little girl had finally settled down and come through with flying colors, a war hero, a lawyer, a star. Instead, Uncle Jack and his wife didn't even invite me to the wedding. They thought I was a bad girl, a bad person, a mess, that I would spoil their big party.

I'm sure I ran my mouth about my misgivings about Uncle Jack and his family, how he owed Daddy everything, what an ingrate he was. I didn't hear from Gabby for a couple of weeks. Maybe he was turned off by my family, although I hadn't even scratched the surface with him. He had been born in Colorado, brought up in Buffalo. They probably didn't have people like the Lanskys there. I wanted to call and apologize for dumping my family garbage in his lap. I didn't.

Nice girls didn't call guys, and I was trying my damnedest to be the nicest girl I could be. Then one afternoon, while Gary was in school and Mommy was at her place, the doorman rang and said Gabby was downstairs. With another man. Could they come up? Sure. Any friend of Gabby had to be a friend of mine.

If Gabby looked like Gary Cooper, his friend looked like Wally Cox. I don't remember his name. He was short, with glasses and a cheap suit. Today the word is "nerd." He had a sweaty handshake. If he'd been on *What's My Line?* I'd have bet that he was an accountant. The last thing I would have guessed was FBI agent. I invited them in and offered them instant coffee, the only kind I knew how to make. "Beautiful apartment," Gabby offered, a little nervously. This was the first time I had ever seen him nervous. This was the first time he'd ever been in my apartment. I offered to bring out some appetizers. "No, Sandi, thanks," Gabby said. "We need to talk business." That's when the nerd flashed his badge. Reluctantly, Gabby pulled out his. "I'm so sorry," he apologized. "Procedure."

I came far closer to fainting than I had when Gabby held my hand to teach me how to use chopsticks. "Sandi," Gabby said, trying to be familiar and formal at the same time. "Are you okay?"

"No. Okay? Are you kidding?" I was flabbergasted. "I thought you were . . . my . . . " I couldn't get out the phrase.

"We'd like you to help us," Gabby said "We'd like you to help your country."

"*Your* country," I wanted to snap back, but I was way too frightened. I had never had a run-in with the law before. The closest I had come was getting a speeding ticket in Miami, coming home at dawn very drunk the previous winter. I should have lost my license, on the spot. When the cop asked for my license and saw my name, he tore the ticket up. We ended up having a pancake breakfast together. He asked me out, but I was leaving too soon. No such luck this time. These guys meant business.

Gabby laid out what they were there for. The FBI, together with the IRS, was conducting an investigation into "skimming" in the Las Vegas casinos, whereby a huge amount of the take was not accounted for but "skimmed" off in cash, like the cream on top of milk, and never declared. That skim was where organized crime made its fortune, tax free. "I haven't been to Las Vegas since my honeymoon in 1954," I said, recalling but never mentioning the endless fat envelopes Marvin and I collected from my uncles. I guess that was the "skim."

"It's not you. It's your father," Gabby came right to the point.

"I don't think Daddy goes to Las Vegas anymore. He's been in Miami, Havana . . . "

"He doesn't have to *be* there," Gabby said. "Your father is a brilliant man."

Gee. Thanks for the compliment. "Daddy has been sick," I almost pleaded with them. "He almost died. He's been in and out of hospitals."

"We're not after your father, Miss Lansky," the nerd interrupted me with what surely was one of the biggest lies I had ever heard. We're looking into his associates, who *do* go to Las Vegas, whom you may know." The accountant pulled a thick notebook out of his briefcase and began reading names. "Benjamin Sigelbaum, Edward Levinson, Irving Devine, Jack Entratter, Vincent Alo, Jacob Lansky . . . " Ah, Uncle Jack. Was that what they were up to? Gabby knew I was on the outs with Jack and Anna over the wedding. Did they think a social slight would cause me to rat out my family?

Gabby broke in. "Sandi. I know these are your family, friends of your family. But do you really think they care that much about you? That they have your interests in mind? Just look at the facts . . . " I guess they did expect me to rat them out. People must have turned informants for less. "If your dad is innocent, if he's not involved, you can help him . . . " By informing on everyone else, I thought to myself. Nice girl. Family girl.

I thought about the names on the list. Of course I knew them. With so many of Daddy's old friends and allies either murdered, dying, or deported, this was the new Lansky generation. Bennie Sigelbaum, a Miami hardware magnate, was no Bennie Siegel in looks. But he had a huge personality, was a great storyteller, and Daddy liked him. Eddie Levinson, who ran the Fremont casino hotel in downtown Las Vegas, had worked for Daddy in Havana. Irving Devine, another "Niggy" because of his tan, had a huge meat company that supplied all Daddy's hotels. Niggy's wife, Ida, was supposedly the successor to Virginia Hill, the mob moll who carried fortunes in the linings of her many mink coats. The tall, courtly, cigar-smoking Jack Entratter was like a godfather to me. He used to run the Copa; now he had been sent to Las Vegas to run the Sands, which he had put on the map as the home of the Rat Pack. Dean Martin loved him.

All of these people had been kind to me. All had amazing stories, "true crime" stories that may have appealed to Buddy. But I hadn't had the slightest interest. Were they skimming? What difference did it make to me, or to anyone except these creeps from the FBI? Who were they hurting? J. Edgar Hoover, whom Daddy had told me was one the biggest gamblers of them all? I had my own true crime stories, my drugs and how to get them. That was the only crime I was obsessed with. "I've heard of them," was all I would give Gabby.

"You don't know them?" he looked at me skeptically.

"Maybe. Maybe I met them. I've met so many . . . I don't remember."

All I was willing to give these guys was coffee. After an hour or so, they decided to leave. I knew they'd be back. I had never been so hurt. Gabby could see it. He let his partner go ahead. He said he'd meet him downstairs in a minute.

"I thought we were . . . friends," I told him. Tears came to my eyes. I had tried to be strong. I couldn't hold it anymore.

"We are," Gabby said.

"This was all a trick, a set-up. Those meals, the times we had . . . "

Suddenly he took my hands. He squeezed them as if he meant it. "Believe me. I do care about you. This is my job."

"You're a spy. An undercover spy. How could you?" I cried.

"I liked you the minute I saw you at the Thayer. I liked you the minute I saw you at the Harwyn. I like you every time I see you. I like you now."

"I hate you. Get out of here!" I opened the door to the hallway. He let go of my hand, worried that someone might see him. He had used me, yet something about him remained conflicted. I sensed there was some altar boy left within him.

I was a wreck. I couldn't tell anyone what happened. I thought about telling Daddy, but I was scared. He would have blamed me. Why did you get involved with this spy to begin with? I couldn't explain. There would have been no use trying. A week later, Gabby surprised me with a call. I worried the phone was tapped. He asked me to meet him, just to talk, and not for the FBI, not for the record, but about us. I had liked him so much, I couldn't let it go, a moth to his very dangerous flame.

I had Gabby meet me at Gitlitz, a decrepit deli on Broadway around the corner from me. Gitlitz was to meat what Steinberg's was to dairy, somewhere all-American people like Edward Patrick Hartnett would never, ever go. Gitlitz was very fluorescent, the least flattering light in New York, filled, like Steinberg's, with aging European émigrés and Holocaust survivors. In lesser clothes, Daddy could have fit right in. I wanted to take Gabby out of his element, make him look at these poor people, who the Lanskys and my uncles would have been just like if they hadn't been successful, and make him feel guilty for picking on the old and infirm.

Without his partner, Gabby was a different person, the person before, the person I was falling in love with. With no idea what to order in this alien environment, he had nothing but a cup of tea. He was all remorse, totally conflicted. He told me how he had grown up dirt poor, how he was in debt to the FBI, who had sent him to language school, to law school. West Point was a free ride as well. He genuinely loved his country for giving him a chance to make something of himself.

"My father loves his country, too. As much as you do," I said, proudly enumerating how he had attacked the Brownshirts in Yorkville, how he had saved the docks from the Nazis during the war.

Gabby knew all that. He knew more about my family than I did, a lot more, though he had never met anyone but me and had only seen Paul. However, he had been drilled in J. Edgar Hoover's party line, that Daddy was the wizard of American crime. "Is that the right way to thank your country?" Gabby asked.

"Who did he hurt?" I asked "Who?"

"Bugsy Siegel, Willie Moretti, Albert Anastasia, Longy Zwillman, Augie Pisano," Gabby reeled off the names in a way that left me reeling as well.

"These were his best friends. You're crazy. Where do you get this?"

"There but for the grace of God," Gabby said, looking around at the old Jewish men shuffling in and out, eating their pastrami sandwiches as if they might be their last supper. Gabby cited chapter and verse on how Daddy may have been involved in the hits on my uncles. He didn't pull the trigger, but he may have given the nod, if only to stay alive himself, to keep his power. Like a thoughtful teacher, like Daddy could be when he had the time, Gabby outlined a pitched battle going on in the "LCN," La Cosa Nostra, which was the official name the FBI was giving to what the public was calling the Mafia. Daddy was right in the middle of it, between Frank Costello on one side and Vito Genovese on the other. The winner was a sly fox named Carlo Gambino, who got Costello to retire and sent Genovese to prison for life. Meyer Lansky, a brilliant logical Jew caught between two crazy mobs of Italians, had to do what he had to do in order to survive, even if that meant that his dearest friends did not survive.

"*Sauve qui peut.*" Gabby summed it all up in the French expression that he may have learned in law school, but that I had never learned at Calhoun. "Every man for himself." All he was doing, he said, was accepting the hard reality of Daddy's life. "It doesn't have to be *your* reality," he told me. I didn't believe him anymore than I believed those awful books during the Kefauver Hearings or the vicious broadcasts of Robert Montgomery. But he made the case not like a rabble-rousing demagogue but rather like a calm lawyer—facts, facts, facts.

"What do you really have against my father?" I tried to get to the heart of the matter.

"Nothing personal," Gabby said. "He works for bad people."

"So do lawyers," I defended my father. "You're a lawyer. If lawyers can give bad people their day in court, why can't my father give them their day at the bank?"

"This is more of a conspiracy, but . . . okay . . . fair question," the lawyer conceded.

"If you knew something about your father, something . . . something bad," I asked Gabby. "Would you tell it . . . to someone . . . like yourself? Would you?"

He thought for a long time. "Probably not." He turned his eyes downward, as if in shame.

"So what do you want me to do?" I asked him.

"Forgive me. See me again."

I left Gabby and Gitlitz more mixed up than ever. I wandered in a daze up Broadway. I staggered past the happy crowds coming out of Zabar's, their shopping bags bursting with delicacies. My appetite was gone forever. I could see how conflicted Gabby was, which made me all the more conflicted. I think he did like me, but how in the world could the daughter of a crime lord fall in love with the figurative son of J. Edgar Hoover? It was crazier than Romeo and Juliet.

The whole situation reminded me of the old Hitchcock thriller *Notorious,* which I liked to watch when it came on the late show. In the movie Ingrid Bergman plays a girl with a wild past and an addiction to alcohol and men. I could relate. Her father has just been convicted of being a Nazi spy and has committed suicide in prison. Cary Grant plays an undercover American agent who seduces Bergman and convinces her to go to Rio and seduce and marry a powerful Nazi, played by Claude Rains, in order to infiltrate the Nazi cell for Cary Grant, and for America. Does Grant love her or is he using her? With those stars, you know how it ends. Still, the parallels to me were obvious, though in the movie, Bergman has a hot affair with Cary Grant, as opposed to my innocent hand holding with Gabby.

A year or so later there was a hit song on the radio called "Mixed-Up, Shook-Up Girl." Was that ever me right now. I had no choice. Blood was thicker than the gin at the Harwyn Club. If I had one real friend in the world, it was Daddy. Father knows best. So I convinced myself to let Daddy go crazy. It was like turbulence on a plane ride. It would eventually end. I knew that, no matter what, Daddy would forgive me.

I just had to find him in New York, which was less and less likely. I couldn't call. He had given up his suite at the Warwick when he found that it had been bugged. We could go for a walk, but I wanted to be in a public space, like a restaurant, for when he hit the roof at the mess I had gotten us into. He could only get so mad in a restaurant. Dinty Moore's, the old reliable, would be the place. So I waited until he came to the city, after one of his increasingly frequent visits to Boston to see his famous gastroenterologist, Seymour Gray.

I was so nervous, I can't really recall how I broke the news to him, whether it was over the gefilte fish or the lamb chops, or at the end, with the apple pie. "Daddy. I've been seeing somebody."

"Really? Is he nice? Is he a regular guy?" That was code for "unlike Marvin."

"He went to West Point."

Daddy perked up. "Paul introduced you to someone?"

"Are you kidding?"

"You should make up." He suggested without real hope.

"I met him all by myself."

"Is he in the service?"

"So to speak," I hedged. "The secret service." Daddy gave me a puzzled look. "Daddy, I didn't know it, but he turned out to be in the FBI."

Daddy held his fork in midair as if he had been hit by lightning. For a second, I thought he had had a heart attack. But Daddy was as understanding as he was tough. To begin with, he refused to believe that any West Point man could be all bad. What a loyal alumnus he would have made! That got me off the hook for falling for Gabby. Second, my resourceful father, the master of playing all the angles, came up with his usual brainstorm. "Let's turn a negative into a positive. We've got a man inside. Let's use him."

The plan was to feed Gabby and the FBI disinformation to send them on wild goose chases. He gave me a list of names to drop, names and places, I can't remember today and could barely remember then. The idea was to tantalize the FBI with the notion of laundered gambling money, in Switzerland, in Singapore, in Brazil, in the Bahamas, in the Cayman Islands. Those names of questionable bankers and questionable banks (Daddy was an encyclopedia of world banking) would give the FBI and the IRS enough false leads "to keep them off my back until I rest in peace."

The idea of Daddy's mortality, even in slight jest, chilled me, when combined with how old he seemed to have gotten. However, his spirit and his "you can't touch me" defiance was as young as ever. And what about all the awful things, the blood on his hands, the triggers pulled by others, that Gabby had implied? Daddy simply shook his head. For the last twenty years he had been a target for the FBI and the IRS, tapped, bugged, photographed, spied on, audited, reaudited, arrested, prosecuted, nearly deported, and, aside from the little plea bargain in

Ballston Spa over the card games that politicians play, Daddy was as clean as a West Point honor guard.

"If I had done something, darling, they would've gotten me, long, long ago," he said, almost bored by the endless pursuit. "Flat feet," he sighed, using his old Lower East Side slang for a lowly beat cop to dismiss everyone from Gabby to Kefauver to Hoover to the Supreme Court, none of whom had been able to "get" him. By the time Daddy and I left Dinty Moore's to a ballet of bows and scrapes reserved for the true bosses of the town, I knew where I had to plight my troth. My heart belonged to Daddy. The difference between *Notorious* and real life was that Claude Rains was an evil Nazi; Meyer Lansky was a courageous Jew. The Cary Grant in my story turned out not to be Edward Patrick Hartnett, but my own father.

CHAPTER ELEVEN

I Married a Gangster

My romance with Gabby Hartnett never got back on track, if it had ever been on track to begin with. We had a few more dinners, and numerous meetings that included his "accountant" as well as other FBI agents. Coached by my father, I shared vague recollections of hotel and casino operators and assorted fellow travellers that may have made them think they had struck some sort of mother lode. The bigger the names I dropped, names like Howard Hughes in Las Vegas, the producer Ray Stark in Hollywood, the banker Charles Allen in New York, the political boss Stafford Sands in the Bahamas, the more the FBI ears would prick up, like bulldogs to a scent.

All I would say, basically, was that I had heard these names mentioned, or that there were supposed to be meetings, or there were phone messages. It was easy for me to play dumb, because I didn't really know anything anyway. However, the FBI assumed, that as the daughter of the mastermind, I was leading them into a vast global conspiracy. Was its purpose world domination, or merely tax evasion? I had no idea. Their paydirt was fool's gold.

Gabby remained the all-American boy that a normal girl should have married. I was not a normal girl. Besides, I could never really trust him, and I loved my father too much. Meanwhile, I met and fell for a guy who to Daddy may have been even worse for me than an FBI undercover agent—a real gangster. My father had wanted his children to have a different, better, safer life than his own. Paul had done it. Buddy had not, nor had I. I seemed to come close, but no cigar. First I married a rich handsome guy. He turned out to be gay. Then I had found a West Point guy, but he was a secret Fed. Now I found a nice guy, but he was from a major Mafia family. Poor Daddy. He couldn't win.

I first met Vince Lombardo on a blind date, but not with him. My date was a handsome aspiring actor named Nick, who actually was something of a gigolo. He had been the kept man of the actress-dancer Eleanor Powell, who had lit up the screen with Fred Astaire in *Broadway Melody of 1940*. She had married the actor Glenn Ford, but she had a thing for young studs, and Nick was that. Nick had worked as a bouncer at the Copa, as had Vince, who had "graduated" to managing a restaurant in Greenwich Village, a gay hangout called the Tropical Bar, on Eighth Street. Because Nick was always flat broke, he charmed his buddy Vince to "comp" his date meal with me.

Expecting someplace romantic, I had gotten all glamored up in a fancy new silk dress. I was ready for El Morocco. What I got was El Homo. The front was all fairies. The back was all lesbians. I was highly insulted. After Marvin, I had developed a knee-jerk reaction to gay dives, and this was a prime one. I left Nick at the table and holed up in the phone booth, calling friends to find something else to do. Vince came to the booth, knocked on the glass door. He was holding a sizzling platter of steak. He was also very handsome, with deep blue eyes and sandy hair. He could have doubled for Paul Newman as the boxer Rocky Graziano in *Somebody Up There Likes Me*. "You're gonna miss the best steaks in New York," he said with a mesmerizing smile.

"You and your gay boyfriend eat them!" I snarled, as I ran out to get a cab. It was a monsoon. There were no cabs. Eating humble pie and nothing else, I walked back in and asked Vince to call me a cab. A total gentleman, he got drenched hailing me a cab, came back in, found an umbrella and kept me dry until I was safe inside. Two days later, he called me up to ask me out. "I don't date gays," I snarled. I only married them.

"Don't worry about me," he said with a laugh. Then he told me the story about how the night I left, Nick got his comeuppance. He hadn't even seemed to care what happened to me. He had run into two Broadway producers at the bar whom he thought he could hustle for a part. Instead they tried to hustle him into bed. Nick, Vince said, had given him permission to call me up.

"If you're not gay, are you married?" was my follow-up question.

"Separated," he admitted.

Again, I almost hung up. But he hung in, convincing me his marriage was a lost cause. He had married a nice Italian girl, but when he moved with her and their young son to Greenwich Village, she had become a beatnik Frankenstein, spending all her time at peace marches and protest rallies. I felt his pain and agreed to a date. But I had such low expectations that I didn't feel as if it would be worth the trouble to dress up. Instead, I invited him to my apartment for a TV dinner with Gary and Mommy. Maybe I just wanted to scare him away and get it over with.

Vince showed up with a box of cookies from a great old Italian bakery. Somehow he was instantly right at home with my crazy family. Gary shook his hand, then ignored him completely in favor of the television. Mommy gave him the fish eye for about ten minutes, then warmed up. They spent the rest of the evening talking about old times on the Lower East Side, where she and Aunt Esther had sowed their wild oats with Daddy and Uncle Benny. Vince had grown up in the same neighborhood, right near the Henry Street Settlement House, with all its concerts and cultural events. I hadn't seen Mommy so animated since her happy days at the Beresford.

Vince told us how his father spoke his native Sicilian dialect, from where he had immigrated, and English and Yiddish as well. Vince's dad had been a clothes presser in the garment industry, like Grandpa Lansky. We had more in common than I would have guessed. Like my parents, Vince's father was a poor immigrant, his mother a rich one. In Sicily, her family, the Tranchinas, had hired the Lombardos as their bodyguards, or private police force, for generations, to protect them from kidnapping and other medieval savagery.

In America, while Vince's dad wasn't particularly ambitious, happy pressing coats and doing magic tricks in his spare time, his Uncle Anthony had been a crime chieftain in Chicago, very close to Al Capone, and a power in the *Unione Siciliana*. His New York Uncle Rocco had risen to become a rich and powerful bigwig in the Mafia. Uncle Rocco Lombardo's front was a plumbing supply business, which eventually enabled him to live as a gentleman farmer in Connecticut, somewhat like the Citrons in New Jersey.

"I love him!" Mommy exulted when he left. Then her face turned glum. "But Italians never get divorced." That was it. I wouldn't go out with Vince again. He called and called, but I held the line. I couldn't face putting myself out and then getting hurt. Six months later, while taking a walk with Gary, I ran into Vince on Broadway. He held my arm and stared straight into my eyes with his beautiful blue ones. "Sandi. I'm divorced. If you don't believe me, I'll show you the papers." And that was the start of something great.

My romance with Vince broke the mold of glamorous café society New York that I had previously known. Our first date was at Manganaro's, a grocery store near the Lincoln Tunnel with rickety tables in back. And amazing grandma-style, long-cooked Italian food. It was a perfect place for Vince to share his childhood memories with me.

Things didn't seem to have changed that much on the Lower East Side from Daddy's generation to Vince's. Vince's Catholic elementary school sounded like *Blackboard Jungle*. Like Daddy he had constantly been bullied, in his case by the tough Irish majority, endlessly taunted as *wop, guinea bastard, greaseball.*

One day when an Irish tough whacked him one time too many in the back of his head with a ruler, Vince turned around and stabbed a lead pencil in the kid's eye. The nuns called an ambulance. Vince was taken to the office of the Mother Superior, sure to be on his way to re-form school. Irish cops arrived to take him to the station, where they locked him in holding cell and gave him the "dirty wop" tirade. Then Uncle Rocco and some big, scary guys showed up, winked at him, and got him out. Back at school, no one messed with him. He had a reputation as a homicidal maniac. That's what made you a big man on campus on those mean streets.

Vince admitted that as a boy he felt about the Jews the same way his Irish tormentors felt about the Italians. His father set him straight. "Why do you hate the Jews?" he asked Vince. "Because they killed Jesus," was Vince's stock answer. His father slapped him hard across the face. "Who the hell do you think Jesus is?" his father asked him angrily. "An Italian God," Vince had said. His father slapped him again. "No, you idiot. He was Jewish. And if it wasn't for my Jewish friends, we'd be in the street." Afterward Vince preached the gospel of tolerance to his onetime Irish enemies, who now feared him on the playgrounds. They still thought he was out of his mind, but they didn't dare cross him.

Like Daddy's sister Rose, Vincent's father died of walking pneumonia, in 1943. That was the big immigrant disease. Vince was eight. Aided by his rich gangster Uncle Rocco, Vince's mother moved the family to the relative countryside of Brooklyn, to an area called Gravesend Neck Road. She got a job in the ILGWU, the International Ladies' Garment Workers' Union. You see, you didn't have to be Jewish to be in the rag trade. You did pretty much have to be Italian, though, to belong to the Avenue X Gang, the toughest gang in South Brooklyn. With his reputation for insane bravery, Vince was welcomed as a member.

A lot of Vince's gang became members of Carlo Gambino's crime family. He guessed that 75 percent of his pals had already died bloody deaths. Most of the ones who survived were in jail. The two successes he could cite were a cop and an undertaker. Vince got the opportunity himself when, after the war, his mother remarried another Sicilian immigrant named Pete Mazzarino, who also worked in the garment district. During World War I, Pete's job in the Italian army had been to execute soldiers who didn't obey orders. He bragged that he had shot over 150 of them. No wonder he chose to immigrate.

Pete put Vince in a special Boy Scout troop that was a feeder for the Gambinos. He introduced Vince to the feared Carlo at his Catholic Church, and when Vince was fifteen, he gave him the offer of a lifetime: to join Gambino. But he had to know that the Mafia comes before everything else, "before your country and your God," as Vince recalled Pete's pitch. "If I tell you to kill your mother, your brother, what would you do?"

"I wouldn't kill them. No way," Vince told his stepfather.

"Then it's not for you," Pete concluded. However, to avoid squandering Vince's fighting skills, Pete decided to turn him, if not into a hit man, then into a prizefighter. He signed him up with the Police Athletic League. In Lincoln High School, where he was also a champion cross-country runner, Vince fought as a semi-pro. He had seventeen wins and one loss. The resemblance to Paul Newman as Rocky Graziano was more than coincidental. Through his stepfather, via Carlo Gambino, right to the owner Frank Costello, Vince got a job as a bouncer at the Copacabana. He might have been at my sweet sixteen party, though he was surely too busy making money on the side. He supplemented, or rather multiplied, his salary by being a one-man bank, or loan shark, to waiters and busboys. He was also in the numbers business.

Vince claimed never to have heard of my father. I thought I had caught him in the one big lie. Maybe he wanted to play dumb so I wouldn't think he was a fortune hunter. How could he work at the Copa when one of Daddy's closest friends was Frank Costello? "What does he do?" Vince asked me.

"Don't you read the papers, Vince?"

"No."

"Do you watch the news on television?"

"No. Just Ed Sullivan and Sid Caesar."

"How about the radio?"

"Cousin Bruce. Murray the K."

"Jesus, Vince. Did you ever hear of Frank Costello?"

"My boss."

"And *his* boss, Charlie Luciano?"

"Hey. What is this? *$64,000 Question?*"

"Vince, where have you been? Under a rock? Those are my father's partners."

"How can that be? You're father's supposed to be Jewish. What does he do? Keep their books for them?"

At that point I gave up and realized Vince genuinely did not know. And did not care. Vince was oblivious to money. He was also, for all his tolerance, oblivious to Jews. He was of the old Moustache Pete school that didn't believe that non-Italians could be in the Mafia. To him Jews weren't mob material. I had to admit to myself that Daddy's world of crime, whatever it was, seemed so different from Vince's. The difference was between a banker and a gangster. Daddy's world was distant, clean, business-y, straight out of Wall Street. Vince's was straight out of Hollywood, earthy, bloody, dangerous, in your face. That made it romantic.

Eventually Vince got married, had a son, and decided to settle down, trading in the Copa loan sharking for becoming a private eye for a Mafia lawyer, with whom he branched out into the home improvement business. Always enterprising, he ran an after-hours club on 56th and Second. Although he wasn't *in* the Mafia, or LCN, or whatever you wanted to call it, he was perilously close. After dating exclusively for two years, Vince took me and Gary to dinner at his parents' home in Coney Island, within earshot of the Wild Mouse roller coaster. His stepfather, Pete, was Old World, quiet, and scary as hell. Gilda was warm as Mount Vesuvius. They'd made enough food to feed the Italian Army, even after Pete had gotten through with the deserters. During the meal, Vince turned to Gilda and asked her, "Mama. Do you like Sandi?"

"Yes. Very much. Nice girl." She waved at Gary. "Nice boy, too."

"Good, Mama," Vince said. "'Cause this is the girl I'm gonna marry."

News to me! He had never mentioned marriage before. "Vince, is this the way Sicilians propose to a girl?"

"Well?" He smiled at me, waiting, waiting.

"Yes."

Gilda broke out a bottle of Asti Spumante.

Daddy had no idea about Vince until he got a letter from him in Miami (Vince had begged me for the address) asking for my hand. He called me. "Who is Vince Lombardo?" he asked.

"The man I love. The man I want to marry."

"How long have you known him?"

"Two years." He didn't ask anything about him, and I didn't volunteer. Never explain. Besides, I'm sure Daddy had already checked him out.

"Give me his number."

Daddy came to New York to meet Vince, alone. They made a deal. Daddy would let us marry if Vince promised to get out, if he were in, and stay out, under any circumstances, of the Mafia for the rest of his life with me. Vince made the deal. And no one broke a deal with Meyer Lansky. Vince would make his way, and maybe his fortune, in home improvements. We were married on September 12, 1964, in Revere Beach, Massachusetts, back in my birth state. Hy and Elizabeth Abrams hosted the ceremony at their seaside mansion. Hy was one of Daddy's oldest friends, a partner way back at the North Shore dog tracks, a partner now in the Flamingo and the Sands in Las Vegas. I asked Elizabeth to be my witness instead of Teddy. Tough. It was my wedding, and I could pick whom I wanted to.

It was almost exactly ten years after my marriage to Marvin. What a difference a decade makes. A justice of the peace performed the ceremony. Gary was the ring bearer. The best man was Vince's friend Tony Salerno, who was the nephew of Fat Tony Salerno, the big boss who "owned" Harlem. You could keep the boy out of the Mafia, but you couldn't keep the Mafia away from the boy. They were everywhere, although not at Joseph's, the very snooty restaurant, the haunt of Cabots and Lodges, where we had the big dinner. We were staying at the Copley Plaza. Before we drove out to Revere for the wedding, Vince and Tony managed to lock themselves in their room, and hotel maintenance couldn't open the door. Gary figured out how to spring them. He had a future with Vince in the construction business.

Uncle Jack and his wife were there. I had turned the other cheek. So they snubbed me from Linda's wedding; I was too happy to let that bother me now. Because Teddy was there, Mommy, who loved Vince, stayed home. But she was happy, too. Also there was Daddy's chief Boston doctor, Seymour Gray, the great Harvard Medical School professor whose patients included the Saudi royal family. Dr. Gray had kept Daddy alive and well to see this amazing day. I kept looking at Daddy's face. Was he happy? I hoped so.

Daddy was impossible to read. I didn't see the unalloyed pride I remembered from the day Paul graduated from West Point. How could I compare the two days? Daddy was older now, sadder. His life was winding down. There was a lot more to look forward to back then. There was more hope. The hope was gone now. I looked at Vince and his friend Tony. I had married a gangster. That wasn't Daddy's dream for me, but it was too late in the game for dreaming. The best we could do was survive. I hoped we all would. If only little D.J. could have been there. But he was stuck at the Joseph Kennedy, Jr., Crippled Children's Hospital in Boston. His admission there had been arranged by Cardinal Cushing, who had remained friends since we lived in Boston. Despite Doctor Gray's overseeing his care, and the loving nuns who ran the hospital, D. J. was not getting better.

I did my best to put D.J.'s tragic condition out of my mind. That lasted until the next day. Then I started worrying again, and the guilt flooded in. Vince and I had no honeymoon. He wanted to go to work. He also refused, proud manly man that he was, to take a cent from Daddy, or let me take any, either. For the first time in my life, I was no longer the poor little rich girl. I was the poor housewife in Queens, where we moved from West End Avenue to live within our straitened budget. I had no conception of how hard that would be. Mommy had to move back to her place on the West Side. Queens might as well have been Queensland. It was too far for her to come, too far for me to go. She had lost the purpose I had given her when she took care of Gary. Meanwhile, I lost my mind.

I had made an almost full disclosure to Vince. But not total. What I had withheld from him was my continuing addiction to diet pills, which I thought I would kick but never really tried. That was an expensive bad habit, a lot easier for a rich playgirl than someone trying to learn to be lower middle class. All I felt was pressure, mounting pressure. How did Daddy handle the *real* stress of being under the federal microscope? Queens seemed so wrong, so preposterous, to me that I never unpacked. I could barely figure out how to buy subway fare. We put Gary in a public school near our apartment. I just assumed Vince would give in and accept Daddy's bottomless handouts. Meanwhile, how was I going to pay for my pills? That was the big question for me, the only thing that mattered.

By the time my weight went down to nearly ninety pounds, Vince had had enough. I was as crazy as I was skinny. None of my clothes fit. I looked like a mad bag lady. Vince moved out in June 1965, when Gary was off at the summer camp that Daddy had insisted on paying for. In September, I spent my first anniversary having dinner with Marvin at Spindletop, trying to hit him up for money. Before I remarried all he would give me was the $40 a week child support, down from the $100 he was supposed to pay but rarely did. I was so desperate I called Buddy begging for cash. He mailed me a five-dollar bill.

I did get a friend in Miami to send me care packages of pills from Florida, but I used them up and needed more. I stopped smoking to save money, stopped eating, though on pills that wasn't a hardship, as I had no appetite. I stopped buying clothes. I was so small I could wear Gary's. Unable to afford the bus, I'd ride Gary's bike, in his clothes, down to this pharmacy in Rego Park that gave me my drugs on credit. It was my equivalent of the last chance saloon.

I took money from everyone I could beg from, then stashed it inside the coats that I couldn't sell to used clothing stores. I tried to get money from Mommy, tried to get her to hock some of her jewels for me. But she ended up in the mental hospital at Creedmoor, with a breakdown that was precipitated when I took Gary away from her. She was stuck there for months, while I was falling apart myself. Daddy was always away now, in Europe and in Israel, investing his money from Las Vegas offshore, planning his retirement.

Havana proved to have been Meyer Lansky's last blaze of glory, his last chance at a monument to himself. Now he was fighting for his health and for his freedom. John Kennedy was dead, the only man left who could restrain his brother Bobby, who, along with J. Edgar Hoover, had kicked up their rampage of hatred against my father to a new high, even when Daddy was at a new low. Daddy's heart was too weak for me to risk breaking it by letting him see what a desperate addict I had become. Shielding him was the only shred of conscience I had left.

With nowhere else to turn, I turned to the Mafia. I called Vince's uncle, Sebastian "Buster" Aloi, a brutal but fair underboss in the powerful mob family of Joe Colombo. He liked playing King Solomon, doing the just thing. For some crazy reason, he liked me and thought that, if I ever got straightened up, I would make a great wife for Vince.

Accordingly, he decreed that Vince should come back to me and give me another chance. Vince had learned one thing in life, which was to obey his elders. So he came back to me, but as part of a mission.

The first order of business was to shut down the Rego Park pharmacy that was my chief enabler. Vince went in wearing a wire and found out that they were selling illegal prescription drugs not only to me but to lots of children. He took his information to the police, and the pharmacy was shuttered. In front of him, I ceremoniously threw my entire stash of drugs down the incinerator. I never took another diet pill. Then in 1966 Vince moved Gary, his own son, Davide, six months younger than Gary, and me down to Miami to get away from the toxins and temptations of New York, and to start a new life.

As happy as he was to have me near him in Florida, Daddy wanted to start a new life as well. Could life begin at sixty-three? He wanted to try. Besides, his beloved country wasn't giving him much of a choice. The Daddy in Miami in the sixties was a denatured version of the old lion of New York. Instead of power dinners at Dinty Moore's with Mayor O'Dwyer and Prime Minister Costello, he'd have lean corned beef sandwiches at the Rascal House with his buddy Hymie Siegel, a retired dress manufacturer about whom Teddy joked, "If I have to get a divorce, I'm naming him as correspondent."

Daddy's main exercise was no longer in gyms but on the palm-shaded pavements, walking Tiger, Teddy's Shih Tzu. When Tiger died, Teddy replaced him with another, named Bruiser. This one Daddy somehow grew to love, like Vince, whom he began calling "Vinnie Boy." Daddy got Vince a good job as a manager at the posh Eden Roc Hotel. Maybe somebody in the family would be the next Conrad Hilton after all. I discovered a passion for breeding Italian greyhounds.

Miami got too hot for Daddy. In 1970, he came home from a trip to Mexico, having been tailed the entire time by the FBI, who suspected that he was going to some international crime lord conclave in Acapulco. But Daddy was only there to lie in a winter sun that was warmer than the surprisingly chilly one that year in Florida.

However, at Miami airport, agents confiscated a bottle of Donnatal, an antispasmodic Daddy had taken for his digestive troubles. His pharmacist had sold the medication to him without a new prescription. You couldn't have too many digestive drugs when you went to Mexico in those days. I knew all about friendly druggists. There was nothing sinister there, but the agents jumped at the chance to make a federal case over it.

"Lansky Jailed on Drug Counts" screamed one Miami headline. "Mob Boss in Drug Sting!" screamed another. Daddy's Miami lawyer, Joe Varon, posted Daddy's bail. When the case went to trial in June, the judge basically laughed it out of court, dismissing all charges. Still, another bad impression had been made in the press, accentuated by two damning major articles about him that had appeared in May. The first was in *Reader's Digest:* "The Shocking Success Story of Public Enemy Number One." The other was in the *Atlantic Monthly:* "The Little Big Man Who Laughs at the Law." The Nixon administration had made Daddy's being brought to justice one of its highest priorities. Nixon knew it would be one of the great publicity coups.

Before the 1960 presidential election, Daddy had told me that Joseph Kennedy wasn't the only person who had sought his support. He had also had a visit from Donald Nixon, Richard Nixon's brother, seeking to get Daddy on the Republican bandwagon. Having chosen to stand with his old Prohibition mate, Daddy now faced the wrath of a vindictive Nixon, who blamed him for keeping him out of office and for the long eight years he had to wander in the political wilderness, seething for redemption.

Nixon had another axe to grind. Biding his time until he could run again, Nixon was a big Wall Street lawyer and had gotten a taste of what New York money could buy. He learned through his best friend, Key Biscayne magnate Bebe Rebozo, that Daddy might be turning the Bahamas into the next Cuba, the new gaming paradise. Nixon wanted to get in on the ground floor and watch his stock in Meyer Lansky Resorts, or whatever the enterprise would be called, explode.

Already famous, Nixon wanted to be rich, Kennedy rich, and he believed it took connections to a Meyer Lansky to get to that level. Because Daddy didn't trust any politician, particularly Tricky Dick, he wouldn't take his money. I'm not sure how much skin Daddy had in the new Bahamas game, but like the rest of the world, Nixon saw Daddy as the mastermind behind all things gaming and blamed Daddy accordingly for one more slight to his hair-trigger ego.

Now, having such a vengeful enemy in the White House pushed Daddy out of America. Taking a cue from one of his oldest friends, Uncle Doc Stacher, who dealt with a heavy IRS pursuit by moving to Israel, Daddy, with Bruiser and Teddy in tow, flew off to Tel Aviv in July, never expecting to return. For a girl who grew up with Christmas trees and barely knew a bar mitzvah from an Irish bar, I couldn't believe that my father was going to live in Israel, of all places. Rio was one famous place that master criminals used to escape to in those days because Brazil had no extradition treaty with America. But Israel?

Why not Israel? Aside for his admiration for Colonel Mickey Marcus, Daddy never talked Jewish politics or Jewish identity. For all his superficial ethnic neutrality and his remarkable ability to get along with, and even make peace among, all the Italians and Irish in gangland, Daddy was in his own way a Super Jew. His financial and military support was a cornerstone of this new state. His own grandparents, who had fled to Palestine from the Russian pogroms, were buried there. He had called out Estes Kefauver for his anti-Semitism. Israel was a logical safe harbor for Meyer Lansky. Israel had something called the Law of Return, which granted automatic citizenship to any Jew who wanted to emigrate to Israel. Doc Stacher had used it to seek asylum in Israel, and now Daddy would as well.

Not so fast! That's what Israel said once Richard Nixon began strong-arming Prime Minister Golda Meir. Nixon wasn't about to let Lansky pull another fast one on him. What Israel needed now, and always needed, were more weapons. Daddy had discovered in 1948 that weapons were the way into the heart of Israel. In 1970, the weapons that Israel wanted were fighter planes, and Nixon held that trump card in his presidential hand. Want our jets? Give us Lansky!

Daddy arrived with his wife and his dog in the Holy Land in July 1970. He spent the next two years and an endless fortune in legal fees trying to assert what seemed like his God-given right to live in the land where his oppressed Jewish forebears were interred. An amendment to the Law of Return stated that Israel could exclude a Jew "with a criminal past likely to endanger public welfare." Daddy had that one minor gambling conviction in Saratoga, but he would be hard-pressed to deny that his past was full of criminals. His whole life was one criminal past. On the other hand, Doc Stacher's past was far worse, and they let him in.

What Doc Stacher did not have was Richard Nixon leaning on Golda Meir. Having grown up in Milwaukee on the eve of Prohibition, Meir had an American's knee-jerk revulsion to the notions "Mafia" and "gangsters." Meyer Lansky sounded bad enough. She did not want Israel to be flooded with his associates and an army of Italian wiseguys at the Wailing Wall. She was concerned about the image of her country and about the future goodwill of America's president, which would have turned to ill will had she said "welcome" to Daddy.

I visited Israel once with Gary while Daddy was there, in the summer of 1971. Vince stayed home. Because I had had no Jewish upbringing, much of Israel was lost on me. On the surface, the country seemed like Florida, hot and full of Jews, but with mountains and history. Jerusalem was ancient, but Tel Aviv was quite similar to Miami, a very twentieth-century white deco city on the beach.

Despite all the efforts of this master string puller, nothing Daddy could do would soothe the hard hoodlum-fearing heart of Israel's supreme court, which declared him *non grata* in what he thought was his own country. Still, not about to go back to America and, if Nixon had his way, spend the rest of his life behind bars, Daddy made a deal to go to Paraguay, which was notorious for welcoming fleeing Nazi war criminals. After he left Israel, tailed by American agents, he spent close to two days on jets, zigzagging around the world, looking for refuge. I think of the Rolling Stones' song *Gimme Shelter.*

Daddy's odyssey took him from Tel Aviv to Zurich to Rio to Buenos Aires and finally to Asunción, Paraguay, where he had reputedly bribed the corrupt Stroessner dictatorship with millions of dollars to take him in. But the country that had offered its hospitality to the likes of Joseph Mengele and Martin Bormann out of nowhere got religion and rejected Daddy at the airport as an "undesirable." With a suitcase of money, and accompanied by only one Israeli advance man/ bodyguard, Daddy made last-ditch tries in Lima and Panama City before giving up the ghost. Where was George Wood to fix things when he needed him?

Daddy's heart was doing flips. His stomach spasms were excruciating. It was amazing he survived the airborne ordeal at all. In the fusillade of a thousand news cameras, he arrived at Miami airport where an ambulance was waiting to take him straight to the hospital. It was preferable to a squad car to jail, though this was a homecoming Daddy never expected to have. Miami's Mt. Sinai Hospital was as close to Mt. Sinai and the promised land as Daddy was going to get in this lifetime. That promised land was, like Nixon's America, the land of broken promises.

Remarkably enough, Meyer Lansky, and not Richard Nixon, was the last man standing. While Nixon imploded in Watergate, Daddy was able to defeat, one by one, the barrage of criminal actions the Nixonians launched at him, mostly variations on the theme of contempt of court and tax evasion. One of the government's biggest cases went up in smoke after the key witness, a Boston hoodlum named Vincent "Fat Vinnie" Teresa testified that he was a bag man for Daddy. He described his job collecting the gambling debts of American tourists in Lansky-controlled London casinos, like the Colony, which had George Raft as its front man.

Teresa claimed that he had flown from London to Miami to deliver the undeclared loot to Daddy in person. The problem was that on the days that Teresa specified, Daddy was in a Boston hospital, under the care of the august Dr. Seymour Gray. Dr. Gray testified on Daddy's behalf. Guess who the jury believed, Fat Vinnie or Dr. Gray? I had never seen Daddy happier than he was the day he walked out of that courtroom in July 1973, free and vindicated. He was seventy-one. He looked great, with hardly a gray hair, notwithstanding the endless harassments of Richard Nixon.

Daddy would live another decade. The only jail he would ever see was the prison of his own ill health. His next ordeal, in 1976, was heart bypass surgery, which was much riskier then than it is now, especially at his age. Again, Daddy was a cat with more than nine lives. After his long recovery, we began planning a big seventy-fifth birthday celebration for July 4, 1977. Paul, who was now divorced and working as a high-level American military adviser, often in the Far East, decided to join the festivities. After years of not speaking to me, he had seen I was on the straight and narrow path at long last. He forgave me for all my trespasses, and that meant everything to me. But the celebration we planned for Daddy got derailed when we had our immediate family's first murder.

Teddy had a son from her first marriage, Richard Schwartz, whom Daddy had set up in the restaurant business in Miami. Richard, then forty-eight, was Buddy's age. They were not friends. Buddy resented him as a "family crasher." Daddy did everything he could for Richard, loyally dining at his restaurant, The Inside, once a week, often with his famous friends. Big names, even if they were crime names, were good for business. Teddy personally baked The Inside's cheesecakes. I'm not sure if it was symbolic, but Daddy usually sat outside at The Inside.

One night at The Forge, a Miami steak house that was once Al Capone's favorite speakeasy, Richard got into a fight with a young golf pro named Craig Teriaca over a ten-dollar bill someone had left at the bar. Richard, who always carried a gun, shot and killed the man point blank. He killed the wrong man. Teriaca's father was a big local book-maker and a made man in the Mafia. The Miami press blew the matter up into a Jews-versus-Italians gang war. Footing the legal costs of Rich-ard's criminal defense, Daddy found his name was all over the front pages again: "Meyer Lansky's Killer Son." Richard was forever using the L-word, dropping Daddy's name, creating the illusion of blood ties. Blood was the word. While awaiting trial, Richard was getting into his big Cadillac when someone with a sawed-off shotgun blasted a huge hole through the driver's side window, killing Richard instantly. No wit-nesses came forward. Another Lansky-related murder was never solved.

Buddy was getting sadder and sadder. He'd gotten divorced, losing Annette and his one chance of normalcy. He was living and working the switchboard in the Hawaiian Isle Motel, which belonged to Daddy's developer friends, the Bloom brothers. Lapsing back into gambling, he had cashed in an insurance policy worth tens of thou-sands, bet it and lost it. Not only loan sharks, but the sharks of the IRS, who had a unique sense of smell for Lansky blood, had come after him. Overwhelmed, and deeply ashamed of letting Daddy down once again, Buddy took an overdose of sleeping pills. He managed to survive. He had those Lansky cat lives as well.

Everyone's luck has to run out at some point. Daddy's did. In the spring of 1980 he began coughing up blood. He flew to Minnesota, to the Mayo Clinic. He came back and told us he was fine. He was lying. After a lifetime of Benson and Hedges, he had lung cancer. He had several operations, but the cancer was more tenacious than Richard Nixon. In 1981 his beloved Bruiser died and was buried besides Ted-dy's beloved Tiger in Miami's Pet Heaven cemetery. Bruiser became a hot paparazzi item on his walks with Daddy, and the press used him as a symbol of how the mighty had fallen.

Bruiser's death seemed to sap Daddy of his will to go on. One night at dinner with Vince and me in the fall of 1982, he mentioned, casually in passing, "I only have a few more months." It was as if he were talking about the weather. There was no fear, no self-pity. Just the facts of life and death. Always game for a fight, Daddy began outpatient radiation treatments in Miami. They made things worse, preventing him from swallowing. The last food I remember him enjoying was a box of pears from Harry & David's Fruit of the Month Club. He loved their sweetness.

Then it got worse. In late 1982 Daddy went back into Mt. Sinai Hospital for the last time. I went every day. I had a hard time handling how tiny, frail, and weak my great hero had become. Daddy could barely speak. I tried to move him in the bed, trying to make him as comfortable as a man could be all trussed up with tubes and wires, a dying puppet dancing to the dirge of the doctors. His feet were like ice. I put two pairs of wool socks on them to keep him warm. He conducted no nostalgia sessions on his life. He just stared at me with longing in his eyes. I hated sharing his last days with Teddy. Maybe he did as well. Once when Teddy started to go out for a break, saying, "Will you be all right without me?" Daddy snapped back and out of his fog, "As long as my beautiful daughter is here. Go!"

Daddy's colleague Benny Sigelbaum was at Mt. Sinai at the same time. He told us how he could hear Daddy's blood-curdling screams of pain down the corridor. I couldn't imagine it. Daddy was the quietest, most controlled man who ever lived. Nothing could make him scream. Whatever they were doing had to be beyond torture. I wanted it to end. Finally it did. On January 15, 1983, Daddy's last words to me were the simplest. "I love you."

At the funeral home I viewed Daddy in his casket. Teddy had dressed him. Terribly. The impeccable dresser had a stain on his tie. I also saw that she had not put on shoes and socks. His feet were as ice cold as they had been in the hospital. "Who's gonna look?" she said. I couldn't stand that. The bravest man in the world could not go out with cold feet. Vince went home to get a new tie, a new suit, the best shoes and socks in Daddy's vast collection. Daddy always wanted to look his best. Now Vince and I saw to that.

The burial was at Mt. Nebo Cemetery in Miami. There were prob- ably ten times as many journalists and FBI agents at the burial than the forty or so mourners. Paul had flown in from Japan to see Daddy, but had gone home just before he died. Jewish burials are so fast, there was no time for Daddy's pride and joy to come back and pay further last respects. The group of friends numbered a few of Daddy's fellow "organized crime" suspects, Nig Rosen from Philadelphia, Niggy and Ida Devine from Las Vegas, the sunshine boys, the ones with the tans. Benny Sigelbaum got out of his Mt. Sinai sickbed to say goodbye.

But the "big guys" who were still alive, like Daddy's dearest pal, Jimmy Blue Eyes, followed tradition and did not show, even though Uncle Jimmy was right there in Miami. Charley Luciano was long gone, having died of a heart attack at the Naples airport in 1962. Frank Costello died in 1973, also of a heart attack, at the Majestic. Daddy didn't go to either of their funerals. Daddy probably would have skipped Uncle Jimmy's last rites if he had the chance. Call it the denial of death.

Mommy died in New York, a year later. We brought her body down to Mt. Nebo, and buried her just one hundred yards or so from the man she loved and whom she could never get over. Buddy died in 1989. He was buried right next to Daddy. When Teddy passed away in 1996, she ended up in the Sigelbaum plot. She had an overwhelming phobia about being buried, and this was the only available spot for an above-ground mausoleum. Only after Teddy died did we install Dad- dy's rose-colored marble headstone, which read simply "LANSKY."

The big question was the one the family never answered. Where was the money? *Forbes* had estimated that Daddy was worth three hundred million dollars. How could it have possibly disappeared? There was very little money in the will, barely enough to keep Buddy going as long as he did. Vince had gotten a new job through Daddy, in the restaurant supplies business. Daddy loved those restaurants, and the restaurants loved him. Vince was doing fine. His whole thing was never, ever to ask Daddy for money.

Daddy had told us that if we ever needed anything, just go see Uncle Jack. With all the Nixon lawsuits threatening to take everything he had, Daddy had transferred that everything to his low-profile younger brother, who, while not the financial wizard Daddy was, had learned quite a bit from the master about moving money around. Where he moved it to, we didn't know. Switzerland? The Bahamas? Buried in some mountains like in *The Treasure of the Sierra Madre?* In the hands of some mystery uncle? It could have been anywhere. But it had to be somewhere. I pushed for it, for Gary, for D.J., whose medical maintenance was enormously expensive. Daddy wanted to care for him the way he cared for Buddy. So I dragged Vince to do the unmentionable: Ask Uncle Jack where the treasure was.

Uncle Jack went crazy at the mere question of Daddy's wealth. "I'm broke!" he screamed. "Broke! I have now idea what you're talking about. Don't do this to me. I have enough trouble with Teddy. She's here every day *hocking* me for money."

As we left Uncle Jack to his self-proclaimed poverty and misery, Vince turned to me and said, in mock-wiseguy style, "We have only two choices. Kill him, or kidnap him and torture him until he tells us where the money is. What do you want to do?"

I laughed. It felt good to laugh, after the months and months of tears. "Screw the money," I said. "We have each other." Jake Lansky may not have been crying wolf. Without his brother to guide his life, he died that September 1983. His will left his family vastly better off than Daddy's, but didn't come close to solving the three hundred million dollar mystery. Vince, the former private eye, didn't even want to try. Vince didn't care about money, and, in the end, which has turned out to be wonderfully happy, neither did I.

INDEX